Local Socialism?

Local Socialism?

Labour Councils and New Left Alternatives

Edited by
Martin Boddy
and
Colin Fudge

MACMILLAN

First published 1984 by
Higher and Further Education Division
MACMILLAN PUBLISHERS LTD
London and Basingstoke
Companies and representatives
throughout the world

Typeset in Hong Kong
Printed in Hong Kong

British Library Cataloguing in Publication Data
Local socialism?
1. Local government—England
I. Boddy, Martin   II. Fudge, Colin
352.042   JS3111
ISBN 0–333–35185–1
ISBN 0–333–35187–8 pbk

Contents

Preface

In a very real way this book represents a collective effort. As in a sense the facilitators it might, however, be appropriate to explain how or why we think we came to involve the others in the project. The idea was generated from our work at the School for Advanced Urban Studies in Bristol and our involvement with the labour movement and local politics. Working at SAUS presents the uncomfortably productive need to straddle the worlds of practice and the academic arena. Through a continuous stream of seminars and workshops and through practice-oriented and policy-related research, much of it for local authorities, government departments and other public-sector bodies, we are involved daily with local government officers and members, civil servants, trades unionists, other political activists and people working in the voluntary sector, their experiences and concerns. On the other hand, we engage with the more detached, intellectual world through academic teaching and seminars, research, our own writing and an attempt to digest at least a small part of what others produce. The two arenas are often worlds apart. They are, however, we believe, frequently at their most powerful when brought together.

More specifically, the book developed as a result of two seminars at SAUS. The first 'The Local State: Theory and Practice', happened in December 1980 and the second, 'Local Politics and the State', in September 1982. Keith Bassett, Patrick Dunleavy, Sue Goss and Peter Saunders all contributed to one or other of these seminars. The idea that emerged was to bring together theoretical developments focusing on the nature of local government and local political processes with an account and assessment of the radical initiatives and alternatives emerging in a number of localities in the early 1980s. In part it reflected also a desire to explore the possibilities of what seemed, amidst the ravages of Thatcherism and the bankruptcy of Labour's post-war legacy, to be one area that offered a glimmer of hope for the development of radical alternatives, a desire to understand more clearly the possibilities and limitations.

Of the individual chapters, those by Peter Saunders and Patrick Dunleavy draw on their work initiated in the late 1970s on the nature of local politics and the limits of local government. Keith Bassett's chapter, which provides a historical context for more recent moves by Labour councils in terms of the legacy of Labour's attitudes to local government, started life at the 1980 seminar. Women's issues, race, economic and employment policy and decentralisation soon emerged in the 1980s as the main areas in which new initiatives were being pursued and the overarching significance of battles over finance became apparent. As the book took shape we were able with the forebearance of some contributors and some rapid writing by others to cover these key areas – further topics, in particular policing, might well have been included. David Blunkett and Ken Livingstone speak for themselves.

Given the nature of this enterprise we have incurred a host of debts, personal and intellectual, along the way. We would like to thank friends, colleagues and comrades in the labour movement and at SAUS for the ideas, insights and comments which have stimulated and sustained us, and which we have tried to reflect in our work. Thanks are owed to the multiplicity of members, officers and friends in the many local authorities who have contributed wittingly or unwittingly to, in particular, our own chapters. Finally, special thanks are owed for the work of the range of people at SAUS and elsewhere involved in the production process.

MARTIN BODDY

December 1983 COLIN FUDGE

Notes on Contributors

Keith Bassett is a lecturer in geography at Bristol University and has been a Labour Party councillor representing the St Paul's area of Bristol since 1979. He is the author, with John Short, of *Housing and Residential Structure* (1980).

Martin Boddy works at the School for Advanced Urban Studies, Bristol University. He is a co-opted member of the Labour Party NEC Housing and Financial Institutions Sub-Committees and has written *The Building Societies* (1979).

Patrick Dunleavy is a lecturer in government at the London School of Economics and Political Science and is a Labour member of Buckinghamshire County Council. He is the author of *Urban Political Analysis* (1980) and *The Politics of Mass Housing in Britain 1945–1975* (1981).

Colin Fudge works at the School for Advanced Urban Studies, Bristol University. In 1984 he became Director of Planning Services, State of Victoria, Australia, on secondment from SAUS. With Sue Barrett he edited *Policy and Action* (1980) and he is editor, with Robin Hambleton, of the Macmillan 'Public Policy and Politics' series.

Sue Goss is currently carrying out research for a Ph.D. at Sussex University and is focusing on local politics in Southwark from 1922 to 1982. She is a Labour Party member of Southwark Borough Council, chairs the Women's Committee and lives full time in Southwark.

Herman Ouseley is Principal Race Relations Advisor for the Greater London Council, leading the Ethnic Minorities Unit set up after Labour took control in 1981. He was previously Race Relations Advisor for Lambeth Borough Council and wrote *The System* (1981), a study of positive action in Lambeth Council. He writes in a personal capacity and the views expressed are not necessarily those of his employer.

Peter Saunders is a lecturer in sociology at Sussex University. He is the author of *Urban Politics: A Sociological Interpretation* (1979) and *Social Theory and the Urban Question* (1981).

Profiles of David Blunkett and Ken Livingstone are included in Chapter 10.

List of Tables and Figures

Tables

Figures

1 Labour Councils and New Left Alternatives

MARTIN BODDY and COLIN FUDGE

Conservative rule in Westminster, with the Thatcher Government intent on rolling back the state, cutting public expenditure and freeing market forces has meant a state of permanent crisis for local government. It is a crisis felt most keenly by progressive Labour councils, intent on maintaining and developing the collective provision of services at the local level. It represents also, however, a more general challenge to local democracy and to the established position of local government in the country's political system. Out of the crisis, we can start to see a radical restructuring of the relationship between national government and local councils and between political power at the national and local levels.

Already in the 1980s we have seen the Greater London Council's cheap fares policy outlawed by a House of Lords judgement, and a new Transport Act to limit subsidies to public transport in urban areas; Norwich City Council forced by the courts to comply with the 1980 Housing Act and sell off council houses; and Lothian Regional Council impelled to capitulate to the Secretary of State's demands for expenditure cuts, in the face of the imminent appointment of commissioners to take over from the elected council.[1] More fundamentally, we have seen financial cut-backs and controls. Government grant to local authorities has been cut, shifting the cost of services increasingly on to local communities. The Local Government, Planning and Land Act 1980 introduced a system of financial control in England and Wales, with centrally determined targets and penalties designed to contain the spending of individual local councils. Meanwhile in Scotland, under different legislation, the government already had complete control of rate levels and

1

expenditure. Following re-election in June 1983, the government then went ahead with its plans to take control of local authority expenditure and rate levels in England and Wales, with an initial selective scheme directed at high-spending Labour councils.[2] Plans were also announced to take control of London Transport away from the GLC, and subsequently to abolish the six metropolitan county councils and the GLC itself. Electorally secure, the government set out to challenge both the principles of collective provision and the basis for political power and opposition afforded by local government.

Faced with this onslaught of cuts and controls, local councils, together with unions and groups outside the town hall, have struggled to defend the level and quality of service provision, and local authority employment. In many areas substantial rate rises have been necessary simply to compensate for withdrawal of grant by central government, shifting the burden of service provision more on to the local area. Some councils, particularly the larger, Labour-controlled urban administrations have been able to maintain services and employment largely intact. More commonly, however, the picture has been one of real and often substantial cuts in services and capital investment and a progressive run-down in employment.

At the same time, some more progressive Labour councils have been striving to develop new policy initiatives, relating in particular to employment, women, race, and the decentralisation of town-hall bureaucracy and administration. New committees have been established, strategy groups set up with politically committed and experienced officers, money has been put into these new areas and departments have been reorganised. These moves reflect a concern to develop a more positive defence against cuts in expenditure, to mobilise support behind the principles of collective provision and to build new political alliances. It reflects also, the Left's concern to explore the socialist potential of local government and local political space.

This book focusses on the attempts of more radical, Labour councils to maintain and defend the collective provision of services in the face of cuts, controls and pressures to privatise public provision; to develop new initiatives and alternatives; to mobilise popular support and build alliances behind progressive policies; and to explore and develop the role of local government in a viable socialist alternative. In Chapters 2 and 3, Peter Saunders and Patrick Dunleavy examine the nature of local politics and the limits of local government. They provide a conceptual framework which helps to make sense of current developments, and to establish the possibilities for political action at the local level. Keith Bassett looks at the legacy of Labour's approach to local government, in order to evaluate more recent developments in local Labour politics and the Party's attempts to redefine the role of local government. Chapters 5 to 8 then concentrated in more detail on four of the key areas on which new initiatives have focussed. Sue Goss looks at Women's Committees, Herman Ouseley at race initiatives, Martin Boddy at local economic and employment strategies and Colin Fudge at decentralisation. Examples are drawn from a range of local authorities, in order to discuss the potential of these new moves and set out some of the issues and dilemmas they raise. Chapter 9 then looks at the all-pervasive issue of financial cuts and controls, including the latest proposals for rate limits, examining the government's apparent rationale for these measures and setting out their impact and implications. Finally, Chapter 10 presents interviews with David Blunkett and Ken Livingstone, leaders of two of the most progressive Labour councils, in which they discuss the possibilities for defending collective provision, developing new initiatives and mobilising popular support behind socialist alternatives.

New directions

Initially, as with earlier anti-cuts campaigns, local government was involved in essentially defensive struggles against the Thatcher Government's strategy of cuts, controls and privatisation. In material, political and ideological terms, the government has set out to roll back the historic gains of the labour movement, substituting a reactionary, individualist 'common sense' in place of the social democratic consensus.[3] One by one, the major principles of the post-war political consensus have been contested – full employment, the welfare state and the 'caring' society, equality of opportunity, neo-Keynesian economic management and corporatist incomes policies – to be replaced by a new order, the ideology of the 'new Right'. Built around slogans of freedom, individualism and the role of market forces, it is rooted in the reactionary social values of self-interest, patriarchy and imperialism:

> The strength of Thatcherism is its ability to ventriloquise the genuine anxieties of working-class experience. The declining economy and reduced living standards are explained by the expensive burden of public services, as the economics of the state are reduced to the accoutancy of the kitchen in a compelling and credible simplicity. Frustrations with unresponsive and undemocratic welfare services are equated with the overweening bureaucracy of socialism.[4]

In the absence of credible alternatives, this reactionary 'common sense' has won elections and shifted the political terrain emphatically to the Right, benefitting capital and leaving the labour movement and the Left in disarray.

As Freeman reminds us, however, 'When the Titanic – with which Labourism has much in common – went down there was a widespread and natural tendency to blame the iceberg.'[5] Thatcherism may well have been the labour movement's iceberg. Its creative reconstruction cannot, however, be built on a critique of the Right, or on purely defensive struggles. Above all, this calls for recognition of the flaws and fundamental shortcomings of the Left and the labour movement, recognition of how we got where we are, and the lessons to be learnt.

In part this has involved recognising the implications of Labour's electoral disaster in 1983 and, more fundamentally, the long-term decline of Labour's share of votes cast. This fell from 49 per cent in 1951 to 43 per cent in the February 1974 election, then collapsed to 28 per cent in 1983. As Hobsbawm observed, 'the forward march of Labour and the labour movement ... appears to have come to a halt in this country about twenty-five to thirty years ago', the single major reason being that 'the manual working class, core of traditional socialist labour parties, is today contracting.'[6]

The arithmetic of defeat in June 1983 emphatically illustrates Hobsbawm's claim, leaving Labour with only two clear geographical bases, the declining regional, industrial heartlands and the inner cities. But as Doreen Massey points out, 'they are very different politically: the old Labourism dominates the regions ... new alliances are growing in some cities'.[7] Clearly there is a need for

TABLE 1.1 How Britain voted (figures in percentages)

	All (100%)			Men (48%)			Women (52%)			TU members (25%)		
	Oct '74	1979	1983	Oct '74	1979	1983	Oct '74	1979	1983	Oct '74	1979	1983
CON	37	45	44	32	43	44	39	47	46	23	33	31
LAB	40	38	28	43	40	31	38	35	26	55	51	39
LIB/SDP	19	14	26	18	13	25	20	15	27	16	13	29

	Upper/middle class ABC1 (41%)			Skilled working class C2 (30%)			Semi/unskilled working class DE (29%)		
	Oct '74	1979	1983	Oct '74	1979	1983	Oct '74	1979	1983
CON	56	59	55	26	41	40	22	34	33
LAB	19	24	16	49	41	32	57	49	41
LIB/SDP	21	15	28	20	15	26	16	13	24

	Age: 18–24 (13%)			25–34 (21%)			35–54 (32%)			55+ (34%)		
	Oct '74	1979	1983	Oct '74	1979	1983	Oct '74	1979	1983	Oct '74	1979	1983
CON	24	42	42	33	43	40	34	46	44	42	47	47
LAB	42	15	33	38	38	29	42	35	26	40	38	27
LIB/SDP	27	12	22	24	15	29	20	16	27	14	13	24

Source: P. Kellner, 'How Britain Voted', *New Statesman*, 17 June 1983, p. 7, drawn from MORI poll.

FIGURE 1.1   The Labour constituencies* June 1983

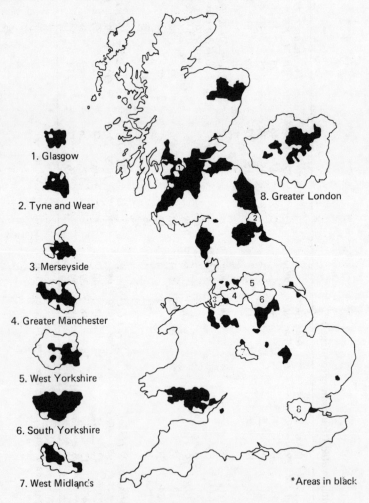

1. Glasgow

2. Tyne and Wear

3. Merseyside

4. Greater Manchester

5. West Yorkshire

6. South Yorkshire

7. West Midlands

8. Greater London

*Areas in black

Source: D. Massey, 'The Contours of Victory ... the Dimensions of Defeat',
           Marxism Today, July 1983, p. 16.

programmes which foster a common electoral interest between
this traditional support and the emerging new urban alliances.
Hobsbawm himself points to the success of new alliances made in
the neo-socialist parties of Spain, France and Greece, showing that

'a wide and heterogenous range of discontented voters can be brought together'.[8] In the case of Britain, many urban local authorities remain Labour strongholds. Indeed, Labour has consolidated and extended its strength in local elections since 1979. Given Labour's collapse at a parliamentary level and the failure of traditional Labour support at a national scale, local authorities have taken on a particular importance as a base from which to challenge Thatcherism.

More fundamentally, the Left's reappraisal has involved recognising the bankruptcy of Labour's post-war legacy, and disillusion with the tradition of centralised state socialism both within the Labour Party and beyond it. It reflects the attempt to come to terms with and go beyond a legacy of Morrisonian nationalisation, massive alienating public bureaucracies, and the paternalism and inadequacies of the welfare state. Thatcherism has derived much of its strength from precisely this legacy, which has fed the popular image of socialism as a caricature of a centralised soviet-style state. And if Thatcher drove home the attack, it is clear that the battle lines had been already sketched in by Labour's initial moves to cut back and control public expenditure in the 1970s.

As the Labour Left established its strength in a number of local authorities, there emerged therefore a commitment to go beyond purely defensive struggles. Local government offered the opportunity to develop new initiatives and explore new ways forward. This, however, has been based on a much broader political grouping, which Gyford among others has termed the 'new urban Left'.[9] This embraces socialist councillors, party and community activists and radicalised elements of local government professions particularly social work, planning and, to a lesser extent, housing, as well as the growing number of 'political' appointments to strategy groups within the town halls. The origins of this grouping with its complex overlapping membership, alliances and divisions are diverse. They include the community action campaigns starting in the 1960s, the Community Development Projects and other local action groups, campaigns against cuts and closures, the development of the women's movement and campaigns on abortion and equal rights, the radicalisation of elements of the public sector unions plus union initiatives on alternative products, the student politics of 1968 and after, black organisations, CND and environmentalists.

The relationship of different elements of the new urban Left to the formal politics of the Labour Party and local council has varied, and shifted through time. They have, however, been an increasingly important influence in changing the Labour Party, particulary at the local level and on local councils. Many individuals have moved more into the formal political arena as councillors, party activists or committed officers. Active members of other left parties, and those who might previously have been attracted to them, have increasingly been drawn into the Labour Party. As the promise of 1968 faded, many came to see it as the only viable, albeit unsatisfactory arena for formal radical politics. In many localities therefore, the Labour Party at the local level has become increasingly radicalised, generating significant shifts and divisions within local Labour parties and ruling groups on councils. This has produced struggles between Left and Right for control of local parties and groups, over accountability of councillors and Labour groups to the local party and over policy formulation and manifestos. Local disputes have thus paralleled wider debates within the Party nationally around democracy, re-selection, the manifesto, union block votes and the leadership. The early 1980s, then, saw the Labour Party in many localities more closely tied to the new urban Left. The Left made important gains in the elections of 1980 and 1981 both when Labour won control of a number of councils, notably the GLC and West Midlands County Council, and by displacing the Labour Right, particularly in a number of London Boroughs and in Sheffield.

An important influence on the emerging practice and analysis of the new urban Left has been the intellectual input of work which has started to make sense of local politics and local government in relation to capital, the capitalist state and notions of class and power. John Benington's *Local Government Becomes Big Business,*[10] followed by Cynthia Cockburn's *The Local State*[11] were major contributions to the Left's analysis, regardless or perhaps because of subsequent criticism which has taken the debate on. Subsequent analysis, to which Peter Saunders and Patrick Dunleavy contribute in Chapters 2 and 3, has helped to clarify the specific form of local politics and political interests, the limits on local government and local political action and the complex and multi-faceted nature of the state. Their analyses point to both opportunities and problems which the Left's cruder analyses of class and the monolithic capitalist state failed to capture.

Finally, going beyond the response of more radical Labour authorities and the new urban Left, the Thatcher Government's measures, in particular the financial controls, have provoked a much broader defence of local government and local democracy. All three main local authority associations in England and Wales, despite being Conservative controlled, opposed the introduction of the new grant system and controls in the 1980 Act during most of its passage through Parliament, with support from back bench Tory MPs. Opposition to proposals for rates limits in 1983 also included the Conservative-controlled Association of District Councils and Association of County Councils, as well as the Association of Metropolitan Authorities, by then under Labour control.

As this indicates, there is a broad basis of support for the principles of local democracy and the role of local government, which goes beyond purely party lines. Local government in Britain has never in any sense been independent. It has operated in the legislative and financial context structured by Parliament. The local electoral mandate and local taxation have, however, given it a degree of independence seen in an informal sense as some sort of constitutional status. The broader case for preserving a relatively autonomous, local political level within the British political system has thus been argued on 'constitutional' grounds, and in terms of the intrinsic values of local democracy. This, it is argued, makes for more responsive, accessible and accountable service delivery and a government responsive to local needs and political interests. This in turn has been legitimated and reinforced by the increasing concern of mainstream political science and public policy studies with issues of central local relations, public finance, management and administration, and policy implementation which has developed the 'localist' or constitutional case for local democracy.[12] We can distinguish, therefore, between a 'local socialist', or 'collectivist' perspective on local government and a broader 'localist' or 'constitutional' perspective. The ultimate aims may have little in common. However, the broadly based localist opposition to the Thatcher government has been and remains of major importance, and is possibly essential, to the continued viability of local socialist objectives both in a defensive sense and in maintaining autonomy and space within which to pursue new initiatives.

New roles and relationships

In practice, developing effective defence, exploring new initiatives and building support and new alliances involves a major restructuring of relationships both within local government and beyond. A major change is required in the way local councils, activists and groups outside the town hall and 'ordinary' people relate and interact. In a general sense, the new initiatives are a response to the shortcomings of democracy and the way interests are represented in the formal political arena. This is seen as structured in a centralised, bureaucratic and professionalised fashion –distorted representation rather than a more participatory democracy. Women's committees, race relations committees and to some extent new-style employment committees have been created, to bring forward previously suppressed interests into the formal political arena. Politically-committed officers have been appointed to work on initiatives relating in particular to women, blacks employment and the police to link policy development at officer level more directly to issues in these areas and to the political aims of elected members. Members themselves are increasingly tending to work on a virtually full-time basis with much greater involvement in policy development. Decentralisation and the co-option on to council committees of non-elected members, and greater commitment to a more consultative style of policy debate via open meetings and forums, have opened up new forms of communication between the town hall and groups individuals and activists outside. There has, in principle at least, been a shift towards a more participatory democratic mode of working with a view to building new alliances and mobilising popular support. This is not of course without its dangers and dilemmas.

Inside local government

One approach has been to set up new formal structures within the local authority. This brings the danger that new initiatives on women, race and employment in particular will be marginalised from the established mainstream of local authority activity. New committees focus on particular issues which cut across traditional departmental responsibilities. Strategy units and 'political' officers working closely with councillors, are committed to breaking away from the traditional culture and routines of the town hall and to building new relations with outside groups and the community. The risk is that new initiatives will therefore fail to draw on and to shift existing structures and practices. This will be reinforced by the strength of officer professionalism, monopoly of 'expertise' and attachment to formal and hierarchical structures, and by a willingness to ghettoise and 'deal' with issues by setting up special arrangements, rather than by taking them on in mainstream activity. With decentralisation, the normal structures and practices of service departments are being challenged directly. The risk, however, is that it will be incorporated as an essentially administrative, managerial reform. It may be adopted for obvious services such as housing, but rejected as a general principle governing relationships to groups and people beyond the town hall. The issues being raised do, however, cut across traditional service boundaries. They are unlikely to be addressed seriously without new structures being set up. It is important that habitual links and working relations are established, which integrate new initiatives and structures into local authorities' everyday work practices.

This is particularly important because initiatives on race, women and employment need to be as much concerned with practices inside local government as with the policies and relationships of local government to the outside world. Indeed, the two are linked. As Sue Goss and Herman Ouseley emphasise in Chapters 5 and 6, there is still a long way to go to eliminate ingrained sexism and racism within local government, to effectively challenge the dominance of 'white patriarchy' and professionalism in employment and personnel practices, modes of policy-making and decision-taking and the everyday life of the organisation. And there are, as Chapter 7 suggests, major shortcomings in authorities' own employment practices, including the most radical authorities pursuing initiatives in this area. This is not to say that local authorities are necessarily worse than other bodies as organisations and employers. They are, however, major employers – often the largest in their locality – with the potential to effect changes within their organisational boundaries, which will in turn be reflected in the development of policies and practices in relation to the outside world.

The role of town-hall unions is a crucial factor in securing these changes within local government and defending and developing collective service provision. They are also potentially an important component in consolidating an electoral base at the local level. A key issue here is the extent to which defence of jobs, wages and benefits can be linked to the maintenance and development of services. The defence and development of local authority employment will depend on building popular support for the principles of collective provision. This entails the development of initiatives which build alliances and make collective provision relevant to people's lives, which build links from the producers of servicers to the consumers, and which establish a positive image of collective community provision in the popular and political consciousness.

This aim implies that any conflict between the interests of producers in higher wages, and of consumers in the costs of services must be overcome. It will also require significant changes in union structures and practices. Racism and sexism have to be combatted. And a major shift is required in the political consciousness of the trades unions, the issues they take up and the interests they represent. They must make new initiatives, structures and practices within local government relevant to their membership at large. As David Blunkett observes in Chapter 10, retrenchment is an understandable reaction in the face of cuts, privatisation and threatened redundancy rather than positive attempts to develop services. Further cuts enforced by rate limits, paralleled by cuts in the health service and elsewhere, will only reinforce this. Inevitably, however, the unions will be in the front line. How they react and the extent to which they establish links with other interests in the defence of jobs and services will, as Peter Saunders' analysis in Chapter 2 suggests, be crucial.

Building alliances and mobilising support

Beyond the town hall, any attempt simply to build alliances with women's groups, black organisations, tenants' organisations or union campaigns around existing policies, issues and structures has little hope of success. As Sue Goss argues in Chapter 5, alliances have to be negotiated in a positive way, taking account of the material interests of different groups. This implies a redefinition of priorities, issues and debates within the Labour Party and the displacement of demands traditionally put forward on behalf of 'the working class'.

This then poses the crucial question discussed in particular by Peter Saunders in Chapter 2: to what extent can local political struggles form the basis for enduring political alliances, given that they are not essentially class struggles (i.e. struggles between capital and labour), are they inherently shifting and fragmentary? For the attempt to build such alliances and constitute a stable coalition of interests rests on an assumption that the alternative to strictly defined class-based politics – the decaying basis for the Labour Party's traditional support – is not unstable and issue based. It assumes that material interests, political identification, voting behaviour and political action are more enduring than a pessimistic interpretation of Saunders' analysis would imply.

There may in fact be grounds for such a view. First, as Sue Goss argues, sexism and racism are enduring structures irreducible to class relations. Second, those who are particularly reliant on local authority goods and services (consumption classes in Saunders' terminology) have, potentially at least, a continuing interest in their maintenance and development, even though this group may be shrinking in size. Third, local authority employees and the public sector unions share this interest in the maintenance and expansion of services, which ensure continuing employment opportunities. There are possibilities here for a positive alliance of interests although not, as already noted, without complications. Finally, Labour Party activists, the new urban Left and new sources of middle-class Labour support identified by Massey, though divorced in many ways culturally and materially from the traditional working class, may nevertheless be closely identified with it politically. It is this sort of grouping of interests, allied electorally at least to enduring elements of the traditional working class which, as Ken Livingstone argues in Chapter 10, hold the potential for a new coalition of interests.

This raises a number of more specific issues. One is the extent to which power is actually devolved through establishing links with groups outside the council, co-options, political appointments and decentralisation. These may simply represent a more elaborate form of consultation and legitimation. It might, however, be argued that devolution of power and decision making, particularly where this involves spending rate-payers' money, conflicts with a model of democratically-elected councillors bound by manifesto commitments and local party policy. This reflects the more basic dilemmas for local councils, activists and the Party trying to build support for and develop specifically socialist initiatives and ways forward, while seeking active inputs and popular involvement from the grass roots. Their aim after all is to foster some form of socialist alternative, rather than political pluralism in the locality *per se*.

A specific danger is the tendency of groups and interests with which links are established to become incorporated and debilitated, their political energy sapped through involvement in the routines of the formal political processes of the overwhelmingly white, male, professionalised local government machine. Those actively involved as representatives, delegates, co-optees or councillors may become increasingly divorced from their groups and interests. Financial support and grant aid from the local authority to sustain autonomous groups and foster alliances with women's organisations, black groups, community organisations or cooperatives for example, can bring particular dangers of incorporation, dependency and control. Initiatives fostered and supported financially by local councils may also be insulated from basic structures of economic power, sexism and racism, and therefore fail to challenge them. Local authorities are reluctant to forego their customary vetting and monitoring in the name of accountability, and it would be equally wrong to advocate indiscriminate distribution of ratepayers' money. What is needed is a different approach to risk-taking and administration.

A further problem is the extent to which the groups and interests with which links are forged are integrated with 'ordinary people'. By linking up with existing groups and particular 'activists' – themselves possibly a part of the new urban Left – the potential split between 'activists' and 'ordinary people', and between the council or the Party and the community, will be exacerbated. Possibilities for building popular support will thus be denied. Sue Goss identifies this as a danger for women's committees, in Chapter 5. It is a more general problem in relation to the new urban Left and middle-class activists, who claim to represent the demands of the working class and ordinary people. For in terms of class, lifestyle and personal and sexual politics they are often very distant from them. This is not to deny the importance of activists in whatever arena. Nor is it to argue for a crude populist appeal to the prejudices of the masses in the belief that popular consciousness is somehow unchanging, although the strength of the media and other forms of socialisation should not be underestimated. The dangers of marginality and of elitism are clear, however. The key issue comes down to precisely who is involved through the new structures, who is involved in giving advice, in consultation and decision-making, where issues come from and how agendas are set.

Crucial also is the identification of relevant issues, beyond the immediate agendas of the new Left. Sexual politics and co-ops may be central to the new Left but are less relevant as rallying points for mass support, or as keys to unlock popular political consciousness for socialist advance. Coupled with media hysteria they can foster alienation rather than alliances. Attention to maintaining, improving and developing existing service provision and in particular, people's experience of local government may well be at least as important as new initiatives. This means looking at the forms and mechanisms of service delivery and at the relations they generate between producers and consumers, workers and managers, officers and elected members. It means, above all, facing up to the shortcomings of public service delivery be it housing repairs, social services, public transport or, more generally, the public experience of local government as bureaucracy. It means shifting the debate from questions of money and rate levels to the services people receive. And there is considerable evidence that people do make the link between rates and services, suggesting that such a shift is far from impossible. A survey for the Layfield Committee in 1975 found significantly more people (28 per cent) prepared to see an increase in the rates to improve services than would prefer a rates cut and reduced spending on services (19 per cent).[13] Similarly, a Gallup poll in 1982 found 70 per cent of people opposed to any service reductions and 38 per cent prepared to see maintenance or extension of services even if it meant some increase in the rates.[14] With the prospect of further rounds of expenditure cuts and evidence already of deteriorating standards, in particular in education, opposition from consumers is likely to become an increasingly significant factor.

The current challenge

The emphasis then, in the immediate future, is likely to be once more on defence. The government's plans to limit local authority rates and expenditure, to take over London Transport and to abolish the metropolitan counties and the GLC represent a major challenge to collective provision, local democracy and the role of local government in the country's political system.

Rate limits, discussed in more detail in Chapter 9, effectively remove from individual councils the power to set their own rate and expenditure levels. This represents a major centralisation of power and control. These controls seriously undermine the right of local communities to determine the extent of service provision, spending and the necessary rate levels. Central government is in effect usurping the traditional accountability of local government to the ratepayers, accountability not only in a narrowly financial sense but also in terms of amounts and forms of service provision. In terms of the earlier discussion, there is thus a clear case against rate limits on two levels. From a localist or 'constitutional' perspective, it clearly represents a severe challenge to local democracy and the principles of accountable, accessible and responsive government. From a more radical perspective, equally clearly, it challenges the freedom of local councils to maintain and develop levels and forms of service provision on a collective, community basis.

The introduction of rate limits, while it would leave some scope for the continued development of new initiatives, will inevitably bring real cuts in spending deterioration in the level and quality of services and redundancies among town-hall employees. Nor, as suggested in Chapter 9 is there any real hope of the government's plans being frustrated, although the extent of opposition remains to be seen. Preoccupation with these immediate issues, plus a tightening of the financial screw, is likely to sap enthusiasm and political energy for the development of new, more positive initiatives, particularly those such as decentralisation, which involve considerable expenditure and upheaval of departmental structures and jobs. The danger is again of retrenchment and demoralisation rather than a positive commitment to exploring alternative ways forward.

Transfer of control of London Transport from the GLC to a non-elected London Regional Transport authority will clearly reduce democratic accountability and influence. It will see the end of the GLC's cheap-fares policy which had achieved some success and wide public support. Privatisation of profitable elements will doubtless be encouraged while less directly profitable but socially desirable elements of the system are likely to be run down. In a wider sense removing public transport, a major function around which popular support had to some extent been mobilised, paves the way for the overall abolition of the GLC.

Abolition of the GLC and the metropolitan county councils (MCCs) was spelt out in the third of the Government's anti-local White Papers, in October 1983. Reorganisation is planned to take effect from April 1986. In the metropolitan areas, public transport and the fire service will be run by joint boards made up of elected members nominated by the district councils, as will local authority membership of police authorities. In London, the fire service and inner London education will be run by joint boards, while control of the police will remain with the Home Secretary. Joint boards will reflect the party balance on each nominating authority, each will have a separate rate and for the first three years their rate and manpower levels will be controlled by the Secretary of State. A range of other functions including structure plans, highways and traffic and waste disposal will pass to the districts and boroughs. In the transitional year from May 1985, when GLC and MCC elections would have been held, to April 1986, when the new system is planned to start, the councils will be constituted from members nominated from the borough and district councils such that the party balance of the lower tier authorities is reflected.

The Government case is that reorganisation will 'remove a source of conflict and tension between tiers of government . . . save money . . . provide a system which is simpler for the public to understand'. The case as presented in the White Paper is, however, woefully inadequate. The new system will require close co-operation between London Boroughs and district councils which would seem to be more the 'recipe for conflict and uncertainty' which the Government is seeking to remove, than existing arrangements. Crucially, the White Paper offers no analysis or estimates of the costs likely to be saved or incurred by reorganisation simply noting that 'It is not possible to put a figure on the savings arising from abolition, or transitional costs.' Insofar as cost 'savings' are achieved these are likely to result from real cuts in the standard of services rather than the streamlining of bureacracy which had so much electoral appeal. The danger indeed is of massive and costly disruption of local government to create a complex, fragmentary replacement for current structures which is less cost effective. Finally, the replacement of seven elected authorities by non-elected transitional councils followed a year later by a plethora of joint boards under the control of the Secretary of State and each levying their own rates, with other functions fragmented among districts and boroughs, is hardly likely to promote public understanding.

In a more general sense the proposals represent a further assault on democratic accountability and control. The transitional arrangements would install on the GLC and MCCs a group of people who had previously been elected as district and borough councillors. Furthermore, in London in a travesty of electoral democracy this would have the effect of changing control of the GLC by central government edict, without an election and without Londoners themselves having the chance to pass judgement on the GLC's record. The subsequent replacement of directly elected councils by joint boards clearly reduces immediate accountability. The ministerial control of finance and manpower will in any case reduce joint boards to mere outposts of central government.

There are undoubtedly shortcomings in the existing structures of local government. There has been some confusion of roles and functions between tiers and the overdevelopment of bureaucractic structures. The Labour Party itself has in the past argued the case for single-tier local government outside London. The Government has, however, failed completely to provide any real analysis of the issues and alternatives or support for the White Paper proposals. They have all the appearances of a cynical and ill-thought-out political exercise. Clearly they are a further threat to democratically accountable and effective local government and promise further cuts in the level and standards of collective service provision. Going beyond this, from a more radical perspective, abolition will eliminate a powerful arena from within which Labour councils have in the recent past been able to explore and develop new initiatives. As later chapters describe, West Midlands County Council and the GLC in particular have been pushing ahead in the economic development and employment fields; the GLC has provided a base for initiatives relating to women, blacks and policing; and fares policies have been politically important and high-profile public issues in Greater London, South Yorkshire and elsewhere. The immediate challenge of rate limits and abolition is thus crucially important to the future of new left alternatives. However, the extent to which that challenge can be met will depend crucially on the extent to which broader-based opposition can be mobilised around localist or constitutional issues and the requirements of effective public service delivery, which goes well beyond the reaction of those authorities in the front line.

Aims and issues

The emergence of new initiatives and alliances, and the exploration of alternative socialist models and ways forward, have been as much a response to the electoral decline of the traditional Labour Party and disatisfaction with Labour's post-war legacy – with its stale visions of a centralised, state socialism – as a reaction to the assaults of Thatcherism. The major objectives have been:

- to defend levels and standards of collective service provision and local authority employment against cuts, controls and privatisation and to resist increasing control over local expenditure and rate levels;
- to develop and explore what socialist initiatives and alternatives might look like in practice;
- To illustrate and build awareness of the alternatives by providing working models, as a means of bridging the credibility gap between vision and reality and to change popular political consciousness;
- to mobilise popular support and to build alliances as the basis for rebuilding an electoral majority, and to establish a coalition of interests behind the development of an alternative, socialist model.

These initiatives, then, represent to an extent an attempt to explore the local road to socialism, to develop a socialism based not on some form of radical town-hall politics, but on a broad alliance of interests at the local level which can command popular support. They have operated in part at the level of defence and opposition, but have been attempting to move on from this to explore and develop socialist alternatives. The implication is not that socialism can in any sense be built from a local government base in isolation, or indeed from the local level alone. The aim is rather to explore the potential contribution of local government and local political space to the development of a viable socialist alternative which is relevant and credible to people in their everyday lives. This leaves a number of key questions to be confronted:

- To what extent does local government represent an appropriate or effective base from which to contest and challenge politically the government's strategies, to rebuild electoral support behind a progressive coalition of interests and from which to move forward to develop some form of radical alternative?
- With the prospect of rate limits and abolition, is defence of service provision and local government employment possible; what is it that is being defended; and will there be any political space left at the local level in which to develop and explore alternatives?
- Can an enduring and politically effective alliance of interests be successfully established around local government provision and employment; in particular, can effective links be established between producers and consumers; is there a real prospect of mobilising widespread popular support and changing political consciousness around local government and collective provision?
- To the extent that initiatives do move beyond purely defensive struggles, how far are they in some sense 'socialist'; what socialist principles are being pursued, and is there any coherent picture of a socialist alternative towards which these initiatives are directed; what is the future role of local government and local democracy in this?
- Is it possible to move beyond marginal and localised defensive struggles and new initiatives, in the absence of Labour or centre-left control at parliamentary level; as and when this is achieved, will it be possible to build on and generalise these initiatives, and to resist a reassertion of the sort of centralised strategy we have seen in the past?

These are just some of the questions which radical Labour authorities and the new urban Left have to answer in practice.

Notes and References

1. For an extended analysis, see M. Boddy, 'Central-Local Government Relation: Theory and Practice', *Political Geography Quarterly*, 2.2, April 1983, 119–138.
2. *Rates,* Cmnd 9008 (HMSO, 1983); *Public Transport in London,* Cmnd. 9004 (HMSO, 1983); *Streamlining the Cities*, Cmnd. 9063 (HMSO, 1983).
3. S. Hall and M. Jacques, *The Politics of Thatcherism* (Lawrence & Wishart, 1983).
4. P. Golding, 'Rethinking Common Sense about Social Policy', in D. Bull and P. Wilding (eds), *Thatcherism and the Poor,* Child Poverty Action Group, Poverty Pamphlet 59, April 1983, pp. 10–11.
5. A. Freeman, 'Rebuilding the Labour Party', *International,* 8.4, 1983, p. 4.
6. E. Hobsbawm, 'The Forward March of Labour Halted?', in M. Jacques and F. Mulhern (eds), *The Forward March of Labour Halted?* (Verso, 1981).
7. D. Massey, 'The Contours of Victory . . . the Dimensions of Defeat', *Marxism Today,* July 1983.
8. Hobsbawm, 'The Forward March of Labour Halted?'.
9. J. Gyford, 'The New Urban Left: a Local Road to Socialism?', *New Society* 21 April 1983, 91–3. Our account of the new urban Left benefits from Gyford's perceptive analysis.
10. J. Benington, *Local Government Becomes Big Business* (Community Development Project Information and Intelligence Unit, 1976).
11. C. Cockburn *The Local State* (Pluto, 1977).
12. See for example J. D. Stewart, G. Jones, R. Greenwood and J. Raine, *In Defence of Local Government* (Institute of Local Government Studies, University of Birmingham, 1981); T. Burgess and T. Travers, *Ten Billion Pounds* (Grant McIntyre, 1980).
13. Detailed in C. Game, 'Social Services and Street Lights Still Top the Polls', *Local Government Studies* 9.1, 1983, pp. 1–7.
14. Ibid.

2 Rethinking Local Politics

PETER SAUNDERS

Introduction

In Britain, as in all other developed industrial nations, the scale and scope of state activity has expanded dramatically during this century. Before the First World War, total state expenditure represented one-eighth of the country's Gross National Product; today it accounts for over half. As the state has assumed an increasing degree of responsibility for an increasing range of provisions, so its organisation has become ever more complex. The specific focus of this chapter is on just one aspect of this complex organisation – the relation between central government and elected local authorities. It is important to remember, however, that the modern state apparatus consists of much more than simply elected agencies of government. Nobody in Britain elects the civil service mandarins in Whitehall, the military chiefs, the High Court judges, the Chief Constables, the heads of the nationalised industries, or the chairmen of the bewildering array of boards, commissions and authorities which are today responsible for developing and implementing many aspects of economic and social policy; yet all of these people occupy crucially powerful positions within the state system.

This fragmentation of the state apparatus into different 'branches', some elected, some not, means that conflict and tension within the state is always possible. The possibility of such conflict is, furthermore, exacerbated by internal differentiation within each branch. Even in the most rigid and hierarchical of state bureaucracies, those occupying lower-level positions invariably retain some degree of autonomy and discretion in their relations with those at the top, for in no organisation can the formal leadership hope to lay down and monitor all aspects of policy and its implementation.

Conflicts within the state may therefore occur along two dimensions; horizontally, between different branches of the state apparatus, and vertically, between different levels within each branch. This alone should be enough to alert us to the fact that the state in Britain is not some unitary monolith which can be controlled and manipulated by any single group (for example, the Cabinet) or by any single and cohesive interest (for example, the capitalist class). The sheer organisational complexity entailed in the division of functions and responsibilities between and within the different branches of the state, makes it increasingly unlikely that any single coherent strategy culminating in specific desired out-comes can successfully by imposed by any one group.[1] Theories of *the* state, which attempt to explain the various operations of the different branches and levels of the state system in terms of a single general theory, should thus be treated with some caution and scepticism, for it seems more plausible to suggest that different aspects of state policy-making and administration will need to be explained in terms of different kinds of factors.

This argument is particularly pertinent when applied to the analysis of different levels of government, for here the organi-sational tensions and conflicts, which are found in all branches of the state, are reinforced by the fact that both central and local government are elected and are thus to some degree subject to various popular pressures from outside the state system as well as to diverse influences from within it. This is not to endorse some naive interpretation of the British political process as 'government by the people', but it is to recognise that in the liberal–democratic states, elected agencies of government are to some extent in-fluenced by the weight of popular pressure and opinion. Analysis of the relation between central and local government may therefore begin by focusing on the internal organisational sources of conflict, but will need to go on from this to consider the different pressures which are brought to bear on the different levels of government from outside.

The four dimensions of central–local government relations

The framework for analysing central–local government relations, which I set out in this section is derived from earlier work by Alan

Cawson and myself in which we have attempted to develop a
'dualistic' theoretical approach to the analysis of contemporary
British politics.[2] What is entailed in such an approach is the
argument that two different political theories, which have often
been seen as incompatible, are both necessary if we are to make
sense of two different types of political process which have
developed side by side in the modern British state. These two types
of political process can be distinguished on four main dimensions –
the organisational division between different levels of government,
the functional division between different areas of state intervention, the political division between different modes of interest
mediation, and the ideological division between different principles
of political and social organisation.[3]

The organisational dimension

Much of the conventional political science literature on central–
local government relations has focused exclusively on the question
of how government organisations at these two levels relate to each
other. As Rhodes[4] suggests, argument has tended to revolve around
the rather unhelpful dichotomy between 'agency' models, in which
local government is seen as little more than an extension of the
centre, and 'partnership' models, in which some degree of local
autonomy is recognised and the relation with the centre is seen in
terms of cooperation between equal partners. Rhodes himself
attempts to transcend the somewhat sterile parameters of this
debate by drawing on sociological theories of organisations which
focus explicitly on the question of power.

The foundation of this approach lies in the recognition that
organisations form part of a wider environment which includes
other organisations. To achieve their objectives, dominant groups
within a particular organisation have to mobilise the power
resources which are available to them – resources such as their
constitutional or legal powers, sources of finance, claims to
legitimacy and control over information or expertise. Applied to
the analysis of central–local government relations, this means that
local authorities are neither the agents of the centre nor partners
with the centre, but are rather loci of power which is mobilised in
relation to the power exerted by the central authority. There is, in

other words, an organisational power struggle between central and local government in which each side draws upon its particular power resources in pursuit of its particular objectives. This power struggle may sometimes be waged openly, as in various examples in recent years of local authorites explicitly defying central government circulars and legislation, but is more often carried on through negotiation, bargaining and compromise within what Dunleavy has termed the 'national local government system'[5] of professional associations, political parties, quangos and so on. As Rhodes points out, these processes of negotiation and bargaining are governed by implicit 'rules of the game' which are understood by both sides, and the stakes are generally limited by a 'mobilisation of bias' which limits the scope of the agenda under consideration. The struggle, in other words, takes place on familiar territory and is carried out on the basis of familiar ground rules. It is an attempt by each side to defend and extend the degree of its autonomy and control in relation to the other.

But what are these people struggling about? What are they bargaining over? What is at issue? Such organisational interests can only be the starting point for our analysis, for to render recent conflicts between different levels of government intelligible, we need to go on to situate them in a broader economic, political and ideological context. Other interests are being mediated through such organisational conflicts. To identify what these interests are, it is necessary to consider the different funtional responsibilities of central and local government in Britain today.

The functional dimension

The British state is engaged in the provision of a wide range of services which extend from defence of the realm to cleaning the streets. Recognising that any system of classification in social science will to some extent be arbitrary, it is nevertheless useful to group these services into three main categories.[6] One set of services, which we shall not discuss in any detail in the present context, is aimed primarily at the maintenance of order at home and abroad. This includes the provision by the state of an internal policing system, military organisation, a judicial and penal system, means of propaganda and so on. A second is aimed at maintenance of production of goods and services in the economy by supporting the profitability of private sector firms. This includes the provision by the state of raw materials such as coal, steel, gas and electricity which are required by private sector producers, provision of physical infrastructure such as roads, railways and ports which service the private sector, and direct financial support in the form of loans, equity shareholdings, grants, tax concessions and so on designed to bolster profit margins in various firms or industries. Finally, a third set of services is aimed primarily at supporting the consumption needs of various groups in the population who, for various reasons, cannot fulfill all their requirements through market purchases. This category of services includes direct income support such as pensions, social security benefits and family allowances, and provision in kind of education, health care, housing and so on.

It has to be admitted at the outset that this system of classification is not mutually exclusive, in that most state provisions perform more than one of these functions. Military spending, for example, has the indirect effect of sustaining the profitability of private sector arms producers, just as provision of state housing creates demand for private builders and the National Health Service has proved a lucrative market for drugs manufacturers. The point of the classification, however, is to identify the primary objective of different kinds of state intervention.

The distinction between production-oriented and consumption-oriented state provision is crucial to the analysis of central–local government relations in Britain, for the functional specificity of local government lies in its responsibilities in respect of social consumption. Again we need to enter a note of caution at this point, for elements of all three categories of state provision can be found at both of these levels of government. While defence and law and order, for example, are primarily central government functions, local authorities do retain some degree of power through local police committees and their responsibilities for organising civil defence. Similarly, production-oriented provisions have increasingly become concentrated in central government and its regional outposts (for example, the regional offices of the Department of Industry or the Manpower Services Commission), but local authorities still retain a small though dwindling degree of responsibility for supplying infrastructure such as roads, and they have been able to exploit some limited powers enabling them to support local industries by means of municipal enterprise boards and other similar schemes. The fact remains, however, that the principal sphere of local government responsibility in Britain today lies in control over certain key areas of consumption provision.

It is this responsibility for consumption services which has in recent years brought many local authorities into conflict with central government. For thirty years after the war, state expenditure on consumption items (social security, personal social services, education, health and housing) rose from 16 per cent of GNP in 1951 to 29 per cent in 1975. Expenditure on production items (infrastructure and industrial policy) also rose during this period, though less quickly, from 11 per cent to 15 per cent of GNP. This increased level of spending, which until the 1970s was financed mainly through increased taxation and reduced military budgets, was reflected in a massive increase in the share of public expenditure accounted for by local authorities, where much of the consumption provision was located. By the mid–1970s, local government was raising in rates less than one-tenth of total government revenue, but was spending on services one-third of total government expenditure.[7]

This increased spending on both consumption and production provision was financed through the early years of the 1970s by increased government borrowing until eventually, in 1976, central government attempted to resolve the ensuing 'fiscal crisis' by halting and if possible reversing the trend. This decision, which followed a severe sterling crisis and the intervention of the International Monetary Fund, reflected a recognition that expanding social provision was exacerbating the dramatic decline in profitability of private sector producers in that it was directing resources away from industrial investment. There was, in other words, a conflict between production and consumption priorities, and given the distribution of functions between the different levels of government, this became manifest in attempts by central government to increase controls over local authority expenditure on consumption items.

Seen in this way, the increased tension in recent years between central and local government is not simply a function of an organisational power struggle, but is a product of the deeper tension between production and consumption priorities within the state. The first priority of central government is and always has been to maintain private sector profitability, whereas that of local authorities has been to provide for the consumption requirements of various groups in the local population. The attempts by both Labour and Conservative governments since the mid–1970s to subordinate local to central government has thus been part and parcel of the attempt to subordinate social to economic priorities in order to restore profitability to private sector investment. The Department of the Environment's concern to control local councils is, to put it another way, a reflection of the Treasury's concern to control the money supply.

The political dimension

This struggle between the differing priorities of central and local authorities has been made all the more intense by the relative openness of the latter to popular pressures and aspirations. Elections, pressure group activity, lobbying, petitions and all the other paraphernalia of the democratic process occur, of course, at both central and local levels of government. However, over a period of years, power at the centre has tended to shift away from the elected agencies of government into a relatively exclusive 'corporate' sector consisting of bodies whose membership is not directly elected but is appointed from representatives of particular producer interests such as the Confederation of British Industry, professional associations and trades unions. This process, which Middlemas has termed the development of a 'corporate bias',[8] reflects the desire of central government to insulate itself from the diverse pressures of competing interests and to direct its economic policy in the light of expressed needs and demands of particular private sector interests. These interests have thus achieved direct access to government, both formally (through agencies such as the National Economic Planning Council, the Manpower Services Commission and the many other quasi-governmental and non-governmental organisations) and informally (through links between, for example, the Treasury, the Bank of England and City-based financial institutions) with the result that the political process has become bifurcated between democractic and corporate sectors.[9] As we shall see later, the development of a corporate bias can also be traced in recent years at the local level. However, the scale and organisation of local government is such that it has remained more accessible to a much wider range of interests, involving competition between different 'consumption sectors'.[10]

The bifurcation between a democratic or 'pluralist' sector of politics and a more closed and exclusive 'corporatist' sector is thus reflected to a large extent in the division between local and central government. This is the source of a third area of tension and conflict between the two levels, as strategies which evolve in the corporatist sector are constantly threatened by responsiveness to non-incorporated political pressures exerted within the more open pluralist sector. It is this tension which has given rise to the alleged 'ungovernability' of Britain. The complaint in this literature is precisely that the pursuit by government of formally rational economic strategies is persistently undermined by the need to take account of unrealistic popular aspirations expressed through the democratic process. The rising level of tension and conflict between central and local authorities in recent years is thus in part a reflection of the relative openness of local government to a range of popular interests which do not find a voice within the corporatist sector at national level.

The ideological dimension

Ever since the British state first began to tax property to pay for social provision aimed at the relief of poverty, there has been a recurring tension in British political culture between the principles of market organisation and the rights of private property on the one hand, and those of collectivism and the rights of citizenship on the other. These two core components of political ideology are, of course, polarised to a large extent in different levels of government. Increasingly, central government addresses itself to, and is evaluated in terms of, criteria of economic efficiency and prosperity (the control of inflation, the balance of payments, the strength of the pound, the rate of economic growth, and so on), while local government has become associated with provision for need and a concern with the quality of life, and its performance tends to be evaluated accordingly (for example, on the length of the housing waiting list, the quality of public transport, protection of the environment, and so on). As Cockburn suggests: 'We have been taught to think of local government as a kind of humane official charity, a service that looks after us from the cradle to the grave, protects us from the misfortunes of life, hardships such as poverty and homelessness.'[11]

The tension between rights of property (that is, the right to exclude others from access to resources) and rights of citizenship (that is, the right not to be excluded from such access) thus constitutes a fourth aspect of the relation between central and local government in Britain. To the extent that the ideology of citizenship comes under attack, as happened from 1979 onwards under the Thatcher government, this ideological dimension is likely to figure prominently in conflicts between the two levels of government.

The four dimensions

We have seen that, underlying the manifest organisational problem of reconciling pressures to centralised control with pressures for local self-determination, there are three other sets of tensions at work in the relation between central and local government in Britain. The argument is summarised in Table 2.1.

State intervention in relation to the process of production is typically concentrated at central government level, where policies are developed through a process of corporatist interest mediation

TABLE 2.1 The dual state thesis

Dimension	Class politics	Sector politics	Tension
Organisational	Central	Local	Centralised direction versus local self-determination
Functional	Production	Consumption	Economic versus social priorities
Political	Corporate	Competitive	Rational planning versus democratic accountability
Ideological	Profit	Need	Private property rights versus citizenship rights

and are addressed to the principle of private property and the need to maintain profitability. The interests which are mobilised at this level are primarily those which are formed on the basis of the social organisation of production in society – that is, the organised class interests of industrial and finance capital, the professions and organised labour.

State intervention in relation to the process of consumption, on the other hand, is achieved to a large extent at local government level, where policies are developed through a process of competitive political struggle between a plurality of shifting interests and alliances, which address themselves in various ways to the principles of social rights and the importance of meeting social needs. The interests mobilised at this level are sometimes organised on a class basis (for example, small businesses campaigning for rate reductions or public sector unions pressing for higher wages or improved working conditions), but are more typically formed on the basis of specific consumption sectors which often cross-cut lines of class cleavage – housing issues, for example, tend to be fought not on the basis of class membership but on tenure divisions which cut across social classes.

Adoption of this framework of analysis entails two crucial theoretical implications. The first is that we cannot apply the same general theory to both levels of government, since different processes can be seen to be operating at each level. The second is that class analysis is generally inappropriate if we wish to understand local struggles around issues of consumption. Both points must lead us to question recent Marxist analyses of the so-called 'local state'. For in the work of writers such as Duncan and Goodwin[12] and Cockburn[13], we find the questionable assumption that a class theory of politics is applicable to the explanation of local conflicts and struggles.

It is, of course, the case that working-class people are often involved in local campaigns over issues of consumption service provision. Indeed, in certain cases – such as action by council house tenants – such campaigns draw almost entirely on working-class people. This does not, however, constitute such actions as *class* struggles since the social base which they mobilise is defined, not in terms of people's relations to the social organisation of production, but in terms of their relations to the social organisation of consumption. Class is not the be all and end all of politics and people's class interests, determined through their location in the social division of labour, do not exhaust the range of their material interests. On some issues – incomes policies, unemployment, trades union reform and so on – they will act as members of a particular class, but on others they will act according to their sectoral interests as determined by their particular mode of consuming the service in question. At the local level, where government activity is addressed primarily to provision of consumption, most political mobilisation will occur around such sectoral as opposed to class cleavages.

To summarise: the specific character of local political processes suggests that we should reject analyses which rest either on a reduction of local government to central state, or on a reduction of local political struggles to class categories. Because they involve different functions, different modes of interest mediation and different ideological priorities, local political processes must be analysed by means of theories and categories which are distinct from those which are applicable to processes at national level. This is the rationale for developing a dualistic theory of British politics.

Strategies from above

It remains to trace the implications of my argument for an analysis of recent developments in the relation between central and local government. This relation has come to be seen as a 'problem' by central government and by many local authorities, although it goes without saying that the 'problem' assumes a different form according to which standpoint we adopt.[14] In both cases, however, the 'problem' and the strategies which have been evolved to deal with it can be analysed with reference to the four dimensions identified above.

The organisational problem

Seen from the centre, the organisational aspect of the problem of central–local relations is how to secure local obedience to central directives in the face of resistance from local authorities which have often claimed a mandate for opposing central government policies. The solution has been sought in a variety of strategies involving restructuring and organisational innovation.

The major restructuring was achieved through the 1974 reform of the local government system in England and Wales which created a two-tier system comprising a reduced number of larger authorities. Dearlove has suggested that this reorganisation, which reduced the number of local councils from over 1500 to just 548, was designed to weaken the hold of working-class militants over small local council strongholds such as the Clay Cross Urban District Council in Derbyshire whose twelve members resisted implementation of the Conservative Government's 1972 Housing Finance Act.[15] As things have turned out, however, some of the largest of the new authorities have fallen into the hands of the Left in recent years, with the result that further restructuring involving aboliton of the metropolitan countries and the GLC is now proposed.

Organisational innovations in local government have gone hand in hand with the restructuring of local government. One such innovation has been the move to corporate management techniques in local authorities resulting in a reduction in the influence of elected councillors. Another has been the growth of a regional, non-elected level of government which has progressively taken over many of the functions previously under the control of elected local councils. I discuss the significance of these two changes below with reference to the political problem, but here it is worth emphasising that central government's attack on local autonomy has included several different measures which have all resulted in a decline in councillor power and responsibility.

The economic problem

As the economic crisis deepened during the 1970s and the gap between public expenditure and state revenues widened, so the level of local government spending came to be identified as a major problem. The economic aspect of the problem of central–local relations as seen from the centre is how to control and reduce local authority expenditure on social consumption provisions.

Central government has attempted to reduce this level of spending in a number of ways. It has enforced increases in user charges in respect of school meals, higher education fees, health service charges, council house rents and public transport fares, and where this policy has been resisted by local councils, it has enlisted the support of the High Court and the Law Lords to enforce its decisions. It has sought to transfer key aspects of social provision to the private sector by offering council houses for sale at discounts of up to 50 per cent, expanding the assisted places scheme in private schools, encouraging the growth of private health insurance and pension schemes and the 'privatisation' of municipal services such as refuse collection and the school meals service. It has attempted to reduce the burden of local authority rates on small businesses and to erode local authority planning controls over the use and development of inner city land by establishing enterprise zones in selected inner urban areas. And, most significantly of all, it has successfully contained local government social expenditure.

The new Block Grant system, discussed in Chapter 9, is the lynchpin of central government's strategy. This has not been without its problems. Many councils have failed to reduce their spending to the level fixed by the government. Furthermore, the tightening of central controls has been opposed by the government's own supporters, both on the back benches in Parliament and in Conservative-controlled local councils. Local spending has, nevertheless been contained, the 1980 Act has been tightened up and rate limits are now being brought in. But this has not been easy, for the economic problem of controlling consumption expenditure has become mixed up with the organisational issue of local self-determination. One of the major difficulties encountered in central government's moves against the local authorities has been the way in which action on one dimension tends to spill over into others, thereby provoking widespread opposition from many different and unlikely quarters. Labour authorities worried about the decline in services have, on a number of occasions, joined forces with Conservative authorities worried about the erosion of local autonomy, and when such alliances have been forged, central government has tended to retreat.

The political problem

The political problem confronted by central government in its relations with local authorities is how to pursue its long-term economic strategy in the face of popular demands and expectations expressed through local councils. The broad strategy for dealing with this problem lies in removing key policy-making powers from the democratic sector so as to insulate them from popular pressures and render them more amenable to central direction. In this way, the organisational restructuring designed in part to reduce the risk of radical take-overs of local councils, and the increased economic controls designed to regulate local consumption expenditure, have been reinforced by a shift away from democratic modes of interest mediation towards 'corporatist' modes in which only particular kinds of interests achieve formal representation. This has been achieved first, by the introduction of corporate management within local authorities, second, by the expansion of the non-elected regional level of state administration, and third, by the introduction of new forms of local administration side by side with existing local authorities.

A number of commentators have shown how the move to corporate management in local authorities since the 1974 reorganisation has reduced the influence of elected members, removed key areas of policy-making from the contentious arena of public debate, and facilitated the development of close links between public authorities and private sector interests at local level. Benington, for example, argues on the basis of research in Coventry that: 'Problem are translated into technical terms ... The effect is to depoliticise issues ... Unlike the traditional local authority officer, the new corporate manager can move easily between local government, central government, the public corporations and even private industry and commerce.'[16] Similarly, research in Kent by Flynn has shown how local authority planners have met regularly with local private sector interests in order to plan for industry's future housing, transport and labour requirements.[17]

Such corporate strategies at local level are mirrored in the growth of regional administration. The reasons behind the development from the 1960s onwards of bodies such as regional Water Authorities, Health Authorities, Economic Planning Boards and so on vary, but the effect has been to remove key aspects of policy making and implementation from the electoral arena, thereby closing them off to popular demands while opening them up to the influence of central government, professional 'experts' and private sector interests. Academic work on this crucial area of state activity is still in its infancy in Britain, and there is a pressing need for serious research on how these bodies actually make their decisions.[18] What is clear, however, is that the scope for democratic control is very limited, for none of these bodies is directly elected, many do not even include local authority nominees in their membership, and of those that do (principally the Health Authorities), the local authority members are in a minority and enjoy little real influence.

The third aspect of the corporatist strategy has involved the establishment by central government of new, non-elected authorities at the local level which have taken over responsibility for planning from elected councils. The Urban Development Corporations in London and on Merseyside are modelled loosely on the New Town Corporations and, like them, have assumed responsibility for functions previously discharged by local authorities. In the view of Duncan and Goodwin, this change has facilitated unhindered commercial redevelopment in working-class areas where the land may otherwise have been put to more social uses: 'Urban Development Corporations ... represent even more of a major change in local–central relations ... The general aim seems to be commercial development without local authority involvement or indeed without pressure from any sort of local politics.'[19] This, of course, is precisely the logic of the corporatist strategy.

The ideological problem

The ideological problem for central government has in many ways underpinned the other three, for it refers to the issue of how to justify a marked shift away from social rights in favour of private property and the support of private sector profitability. For the 'new Right' of the Conservative Party, which gained power under Margaret Thatcher's leadership in the general election of 1979: 'The translation of a want or need into a right is one of the most widespread and dangerous of modern heresies.'[20] The problem has been how to convince the rest of us that this is the case, for the erosion of social consumption provisions at local level depends upon winning substantial public support for the government's so-called 'social market strategy'.

Since 1976, both Labour and Conservative governments have

pursued monetary targets involving cuts in local authority spending on social services, but only the latter has done so as a matter of principle. Support for this principle has been mobilised through a populist anti-state ideology: 'Thatcherism has successfully identified itself with the *popular* struggle against a bureaucratically centralist form of the capitalist state.'[21] Put into practice, this has involved the privatisation of the welfare sector by enforcing a market discipline in existing areas of state provision and then by transferring as much as possible to private ownership. The principle of social need as the criterion of access to services has in this way consciously and deliberately been eroded in favour of the principle of market eligibility. The implications for central–local relations have been that local government has increasingly come to symbolise and defend the principle of social rights: 'Insofar as councils provide services to meet needs not met by market forces, local government is inherently progressive. The Tory attack is part of the attempt to shift any economic activity away from meeting needs, and instead devote it all to maximising profits.'[22]

The ideological success of Thatcherism in the early years of the 1980s was mixed – a survey in 1982 found that only 22 per cent of those questioned favoured cutting local services in order to reduce rates,[23] and yet privatisation has by no means proved widely unpopular and policies such as the sale of council housing have met with considerable working-class support. We shall consider the reasons for this in the next section of this chapter.

Strategies from above: a qualified success

Summarising this section, we have seen that central government has, in recent years, acted on all four dimensions of its relation with local authorities in order to shift the balance of power in its favour. The organisational problem has been how to enforce central uniformity of policies in the face of open challenges to central authority, and the answer here has been sought in restructuring the institutions of local government and its internal mode of operation. The economic problem has been how to enforce reductions in local social consumption expenditure, and the solution here has been sought in revisions to the method of funding local spending in order to reduce local discretion. The political problem has been how to outflank local democracy, and the answer here has been sought in the development of local and regional corporatist strategies designed to insulate key functions from popular influence and control. Finally, the ideological problem has been how to break down popular expectations regarding social rights which were established and extended during the post-war years of Keynesian consensus politics, and the answer here has been sought in the mobilisation of anti-state sentiment and the extension of the private ownership solution to those who can afford it.

Each of these problems is interrelated, and the degree of success achieved in any one has depended to a large extent on progress made in the other three. Sometimes, this interpenetration of problems has led to difficulties, as action on one dimension has triggered off opposition on others. The problems, in other words, have fused and on occasions widespread opposition has resulted. Generally, however, this danger of fusion has been averted and the overall strategy has been pursued with considerable success. Certainly, the difficulties encountered have been relatively minor as compared with those confronted by local authorities and local activists who have attempted to resist central government on each of the four dimensions.

Strategies from below

For many years, left activists in Britain have largely ignored local government as an arena of political struggle. More recently, as described in Chapter 1, this has changed, with the advances of 'community politics' during the 1960s and the growing battles between central and local government from the 1970s onwards, and since 1979 the Left has increasingly come to identify local government as a significant arena in which to organise resistance to the Conservative government, to develop and try out new socialist initiatives and to wage a propaganda battle for the hearts and minds of the working class. In all of this, however, it has met with problems which have undermined effective organisation at the local level. Again, these problems can be considered in terms of the four dimensions of local–central relations identified in the framework set out above.

The organisational problem

The organisational problem as experienced from below is how to fight central government policies through local authorities which are subordinate to central departments. As Keith Bassett shows in Chapter 4, a number of strategies have been tried or canvassed including the maintenance of services by increasing rates, delaying tactics, resignation to seek a fresh mandate, majority opposition, mobilisation of public sector unions, and outright confrontation involving a refusal to make cuts, increase rates or declare redundancies.

As Bassett shows, however, none of these options is very encouraging, and the organisational problems confronting radical local authorities appear daunting. Furthermore, it has proved difficult to organise effective joint action involving many different councils, and local authorities have in consequence been 'picked off' one by one (Lothian, Norwich, the GLC) as they have attempted to resist central government legislation.

The economic problem

The economic problem faced by local authorities is two-fold. First, there is the problem of how to respond to the Thatcher government's attack on a welfare state when many people on the Left have long been critical of it themselves. Defence of the status quo is hardly a radical posture, and the problem has been how to fight cuts in social consumption while at the same time sustaining a critique of such provisions: 'The immediate reaction of the Left is to fight the cuts, to defend the state. This is very contradictory . . . because it implies the state is "our" state.'[24] To the extent that the welfare system is bureaucratic, hierarchical and unresponsive to user demands, Labour councils have found themselves in the uncomfortable position of managing and defending, often at the expense of high rates, a set of institutions which many people experience as alienating.

The seond aspect of the problem is that local councils have precious little control over economic policy. It is true, as shown in Chapter 7 that some councils have placed considerable emphasis on developing local economic and employment policies. These are inevitably limited, however, given the tight legal and financial constraints on local economic interventions, and their impact has been slight due to the dependence of most local economies on national and international factors. It is also true that local authority planning powers may have some effect on local economies, but here too, their significance is restricted, for local authority planning is generally limited to considerations of land use and is more negative than positive. In short, local councils at district and county level exercise little effective control over private sector investment and employment.

The economic problem as seen from below thus lies in the fact that radical local authorities find themselves defending a system of social consumption provision which they wish to change, and that they have to discharge these consumption functions in isolation from effective control over the crucial levers of economic management. As the recession cuts ever deeper and more factories close, throwing more local people out of work, so local authorities are obliged to respond as best they can by propping up the occasional precarious business and by administering an inadequate system of welfare first-aid to the casualties.

The political problem

In Chapter 4 Keith Bassett suggests that it is necessary to forge local alliances among different groups of consumers of council services, if a concerted attack on central government policy is to be mounted from the local level. The political problem confronted by radical local authorities and local activists lies precisely in how to develop such alliances, for different groups are affected by local social provisions in different ways and are often relatively unconcerned with issues which do not directly affect them. There is, in other words, a basic and fundamental problem of political fragmentation between different 'consumption sectors' – parents concerned about school closures, commuters and shoppers angered by a deteriorating public transport service, council tenants hit by rent rises, and so on. The question is whether there is an 'social base' which can be mobilised to unite these fragments.

It has often been suggested that one such social base is class. In his theory of 'urban social movements', for example, Castells argued that crises in the provision of social consumption could have the effect of bringing together various groups under a class-based socialist movement which would submerge their differences wihin a broad anti-capitalist strategy.[25] The assumption behind this sort of argument is that divisions between different consumption sectors are in some way superficial or artificial as compare with more 'basic' class relations, and that people's complaints and grievances as consumers of state services can therefore be treated as a manifestation of deeper and more fundamental conflicts in society. As a group of British socialists put it:

Many of the effects of capitalism hit us in specific ways that we experience in common with others in similar specific situations. Problems do present themselves to parents of children differently from the way they present themselves to teachers of those same children. Cyclists do experience the roads in a different way to car users. The way into a socialist consciousness is often through such experiences. *The challenge is how to transcend these categories, to see and respond to the more fundamental causes of our problems* without losing the sense of immediacy and reality that alone can drive people to act.[26]

What this argument ignores, however, is that people's material interests as consumers are no less 'fundamental' than their interests as workers or employers and cannot simply be 'transcended'. This is a crucial point, for as Sue Goss notes in her chapter, struggles over the state do not always boil down to class struggles, and many members of the working class today no longer depend on state provision for key aspects of their consumption requirements. Why should we expect working-class home-owners to mobilise over council house rent rises, or trades unionists who are covered by private health insurance to take action in defence of standards in National Health hospitals? Political struggles in the sphere of consumption are constituted not on the basis of class, but according to divisions of interest which arise out of the social organisation of consumption itself and which cut across lines of class cleavage according to whether or not the group in question depends upon state provision.[27]

Consumption sectors, moreover, cut across gender divisions just as they cut across class divisions – men as well as women depend upon public transport, live in council houses, rely on meals-on-wheels, require their children to be educated, and so on. The truth is that consumption sectors are irreducible to any other basis, and that people's interests as consumers of a particular service are not disguised class interests or distorted gender interests but are simply what they appear to be – consumption interests.

It follows from this that local politics as they relate to issues of consumption are inherently pluralistic and fragmented, for different people have different interests in different things, and these differences cannot be transcended through an appeal to a common social base.

The only possible source of cohesion amid all this fragmentation lies in the peculiar role of the public sector unions, for they occupy a strategic position since they straddle both the division between production and consumption and that between the national and the local. In one respect, their interests as national, class-based organisations do relate to the interests of the various local consumption sectors, for their concern to defend public sector jobs is broadly consistent with the concern of council tenants to have their houses repaired, of parents to keep local schools open and well-staffed, and so on. Yet even here there are problems. Demands for higher wages by public sector employees conflict with consumers' interests in reducing their rates and taxes. Industrial action by public sector workers – such as the so-called 'dirty jobs' strikes in 1978–9 or the health workers and water workers strikes in 1982 and 1983 – have proved highly unpopular among those who depend upon the very services which such action disrupts. And attempts to develop a common strategy among the producers and consumers of services, as in the 'Can't pay, won't pay' campaign in London over increased public transport fares, have generally collapsed without success. The problems of building coherent local alliances have therefore proved virtually insurmountable.

The ideological problem

The ideological problem of central–local relations as seen from below is how to defend and assert the principles of collectivism in the face of the new individualism unleashed by the Thatcher government from 1979 onwards. Most of the social provisions made by local authorities are either free, or are allocated according to criteria of needs rather than market power. This means that local government services represent an important alternative and challenge to the capitalist commodity form: 'Local government . . . is one mechanism through which it is possible to assert values based on social needs as a counter to values based on profit or on the interests of the corporate state.'[28]

It would be an exaggeration to see local government as an oasis of socialism within a desert of capitalist social relations, but it would equally be a mistake to underestimate the importance of local government in recent and contemporary ideological struggles. Cheap bus fares in South Yorkshire, a responsive system of council house management in Walsall and support for worker cooperatives in the West Midlands may not add up to a socialist transformation, but they are visible manifestations of an alternative philosophy put into practice, and as such they threaten to undermine the assertions of political leaders who claim that there is no option but to follow the logic of the market.

The problem for radical local authorities comes, however, when these alternative values come into conflict with popular aspirations. The obvious example of this concerns the attempts by Labour-controlled councils to hinder and obstruct council tenants seeking to purchase their homes. In cases like this, local authorities' commitment to collectivism flies in the face of the individualistic goals pursued by many working-class people. Two points should be made about this.

The first is that the popularity of private or individualistic modes of consumption provision cannot be explained away as the product of some dominant ruling-class ideology. Such private modes of consumption are now financially viable for increasing numbers of people, and their popularity reflects the widespread desire to escape from dependency upon the state and to extend personal control over one's life through, for example, a 'home of one's own'. In this context, defence of collectivistic values by local councils is only likely to generate support among the increasingly marginalised sections of the population who cannot afford private provision, and on those issues such as education where private sector provision remains at present beyond the reach of most people.

The second point, which follows directly from this, is that the defence and assertion of collectivistic values at the local level is becoming increasingly problematic as it comes into conflict with popular demands for individualistic and private modes of provision. For Labour local authorities, collective provision is almost an article of faith while individualism is deeply distrusted.[29] It is assumed that because socialism stands opposed to private ownership of the means of production it must also be opposed to private ownership of the means of consumption, and because most local authority responsibilities are limited to consumption provision, this has resulted in support for policies (such as bans on council house sales) which oppose popular aspirations for private ownership. This has in turn undoubtedly strengthened popular support for the new Right with its radical commitment to 'getting the state off people's backs'.

Strategies from below: fragmentation and incoherence

On all four dimensions of central–local relations, local councils have in recent years attempted yet failed to resist central government. Their organisational problem has been how to avoid implementing policies which in most cases are backed by force of law, and although many different tactics have been tried or advocated, few, if any, have succeeded and local authority resistance has been overcome time and again. Their economic problem has been how to gain some leverage over the local economic situation, and although attempts to solve this problem have resulted in important initiatives such as municipal enteprise boards and cooperative development agencies, the effective impact of council strategies has remained very limited. Their political problem has been how to mobilise alliances among consumers of council services, and here it has proved impossible to overcome the inherent fragmentation between consumption sectors which relate neither to a class nor a gender basis. Finally, their ideological problem – one that few radical authorities have faced up to – has been how to defend and assert principles of collectivism in respect of consumption, when popular aspirations tend increasingly towards individualised private ownership solutions.

Failure to resolve, or in some cases even confront, these problems has resulted in a fragmented and incoherent response to central government by local authorities. Although central government has itself encountered problems in its attempts to overrule, by-pass or remove power from local councils, it is clear that the initiatives on each of the dimensions considered in the above discussion lie firmly with the centre.

Concluding comment

Throughout this chapter, I have emphasised that local government in Britain cannot be seen simply as an inconsequential appendage of a monolithic capitalist state. Local political processes have their own specific character. It follows from this that there is scope for positive political action at the local level, but that the limitations of such action must be recognised. Local politics are essentially consumption politics and local campaigns around issues of consumption cannot easily be integrated into a nationally organised class-based movement centred on the politics of production. Put another way, the battle at the local level is distinct from that at national level, and the attempt to fight national issues through local government reflects a failure to understand this distinction.

The politics of consumption at the local level should be understood and evaluated on their own terms. Once we accept that local struggles over the provision of day nurseries, the prevention of school closures or the improvement of council housing repair services have their own specificity and cannot be treated as part of a much grander class struggle for socialism, then much can be achieved.

Notes and References

1. As Max Weber noted, there is a fundamental tension between the formal rationality of the organisation of the modern state and the recurrent possibility of substantive irrationality of outcomes, in the sense that the objectives set by leaders are rarely fulfilled. More recently, this issue has been taken up in Marxist political analyses which have identified a 'rationality crisis' in the modern liberal–democratic state. The argument here is basically that the interventionist state lacks the capacity to respond in a coherent and directive manner to problems of mounting complexity and severity. See particularly J. Habermas, *Legitimation Crisis* (Heinemann, 1976)

and C. Offe, 'The Theory of the Capitalist State and the Problem of Policy-formation', in L. Lindberg, R. Alford, C. Crouch and C. Offe (eds), *Stress and Contradiction in Modern Capitalism* (Lexington Books, 1975).

2. A. Cawson and P. Saunders, 'Corporatism, Competitive Politics and Class Struggle', in R. King (ed.), *Capital and Politics* (Routledge and Kegan Paul, 1983). See also: A. Cawson, *Corporatism and Welfare* (Heinemann, 1982); P. Saunders, *Social Theory and the Urban Question* (Hutchinson, 1981), Ch. 8.

3. It is important to emphasise that these distinctions are ideal types; it hardly needs to be said that empirical reality is considerably less tidy. Nevertheless, such ideal typical modes of conceptualisation can help in clarifying some important aspects of the real world.

4. R. Rhodes, 'Some Myths in Central–Local Relations', *Town Planning Review,* 51, 1980, pp. 270–85. See also: R. Rhodes, 'Analysing Inter-governmental Relations', *European Journal of Political Research,* 8, 1980, pp. 289–322.

5. P. Dunleavy, *Urban Political Analysis* (Macmillan, 1980).

6. This three-fold classification closely follows that developed in J. O'Connor, *The Fiscal Crisis of the State* (St. Martin's Press, 1972). There is, however, a crucial difference in that O'Connor sees all three aspects of state expenditure (which he terms 'social expenses', 'social investment' and 'social consumption') as serving the functional needs of capital. As will become clear, I reject such a view, for although consumption provisions may in some instances be said to aid capital by reproducing labour-power and legitimating the capitalist system, this is by no means always the case, and it is more helpful to see the principal beneficiaries of such provisions as those who actually consume them.

7. The figures are from I. Gough, *The Political Economy of the Welfare State* (Macmillan, 1979). See also Chapter 9, this volume.

8. K. Middlemas, *Politics in Industrial Society* (André Deutsch, 1979).

9. B. Jessop, 'Capitalism and Democracy: the Best Possible Political Shell?' in G. Littlejohn, B. Smart, J. Wakeford and N. Yuval-Davis (eds), *Power and the State* (Croom Helm, 1973).

10. P. Dunleavy, 'The Urban Bases of Political Alignment', *British Journal of Political Science,* 9, 1979, pp. 409–43.

11. C. Cockburn, *The Local State* (Pluto, 1977), p. 41.

12. S. Duncan and M. Goodwin, 'The Local State: Functionalism, Autonomy and Class Relations in Cockburn and Saunders', *Political Geography Quarterly,* 1, 1982, p. 92. See also: S. Duncan and M. Goodwin, 'The Local State and Restructuring Social Relations: Theory and Practice', *International Journal of Urban and Regional Research,* 6, 1982, pp. 157–86.

13. Ibid., p. 2.

14. It is a weakness of some recent work in this field that it has identified the 'problem' solely from the perspective of central government. This appears to be the case, for example, in the Social Science Research Council's initiative on central–local relations which set out the

problem as one of 'ungovernability' and policy implementation – see Jones' introduction to G. Jones (ed.), *New Approaches to the Study of Central–Local Government Relationships* (Gower, 1980). From the point of view of many local authorities, the problem is not how to get policies implemented but how to prevent it.

15. J. Dearlove, *The Reorganisation of British Local Government* (Cambridge University Press, 1979).

16. J. Benington, *Local Government Becomes Big Business* (Community Development Project Information and Intelligence Unit, 1976), pp. 19 and 23.

17. R. Flynn, 'Managing consensus: the Infrastructure of Policy-making in Planning', in M. Harloe (ed.), *New Perspectives in Urban Change and Conflict* (Heinemann, 1982).

18. A useful guide to the various regional authorities operating in Britain is B. Hodgwood and M. Keating (eds), *Regional Government in England* (Clarendon Press, 1982). Much of this material is descriptive – as Keating himself suggests in his conclusion, 'What is lacking ... is a well developed theory of the state and the division of power within it and a theory of intermediate administration between the centre and locality' (p. 235). The sort of attention paid in recent years to the question of the 'local state' needs, therefore, to be paid to the 'regional state' as well. A study of regional administration forms part of current research on central–local relations by Simon Duncan, Mark Goodwin and myself, based at the University of Sussex, and a Sussex *Urban and Regional Studies Working Paper* on the 'regional state' should be published late in 1983.

19. Duncan and Goodwin, 'The Local State and Restructuring Social Relations', p. 177.

20. E. Powell, *Still to Decide* (Elliott Right Way Books, 1972), p. 12.

21. S. Hall, 'Thatcherism: a New Stage?' *Marxism Today,* February 1980, p. 27.

22. Labour Coordinating Committee, *Can Local Government Survive?* (LCC, no date), p. 3.

23. See *New Society,* 4 March 1982, pp. 345–6.

24. London–Edinburgh Weekend Return Group, *In and Against the State* (Pluto, 1980), p. 53.

25. See, for example, M. Castells, 'Advanced Capitalism, Collective Consumption and Urban Contradictions', in L. Lindberg *et al.* (eds), *Stress and Contradiction in Modern Capitalism*; reprinted in his *City, Class and Power* (Macmillan, 1978).

26. London–Edinburgh Weekend Return Group, *In and Against the State,* p. 49 (emphasis added).

27. I have developed this argument in much more detail in 'beyond Housing Classes: the Sociological Significance of Private Property Rights in Means of Consumption', *International Journal of Urban and Regional Research*, forthcoming.

28. Labour Coordinating Committee, *Can Local Government Survive?* p. 30.

29. As Russel Keat has noted, 'For many socialists, capitalism is to be

condemned not only as a system based on the exploitation of one class
by another ... but also for the individualistic character of its social
relationships'; 'Individualism and Community in Socialist Thought',
in J. Mepham and D. Ruben (eds), *Issues in Marxist Philosophy,
Volume 4: Social and Political Philosophy* (Harvester, 1981), p. 127.
It seems clear, however, that socialism must be reconciled with
individualism, for the demand for common ownership of the means
of production cannot extend to common ownership of all forms of
property. The problem of establishing the limits to collectivism is one
which is particularly acute at the local level where collective provision
is oriented more towards personal consumption than to corporate
production.

3 The Limits to Local Government

PATRICK DUNLEAVY

The unprecedented assault on local government powers pursued by the Conservative Government of 1979–83 has once more projected questions about the role of local authorities within the state apparatus to the forefront of attention. Perhaps as important has been the attempt by Labour local authorities to combat the artificial recession which lies at the heart of monetarist strategy by protecting the social wage and promoting economic development. The interplay between these efforts and Whitehall's counter-moves demonstrates yet again the need for some sound theory of the potential of and limits to such local political action. This involves explaining why local governments end up with the powers they have in market societies, what causal processes determine the distribution of functions between central and local/regional governments, and how the interests of working people may best be advanced given these constraints.

Tackling these interrelated questions involves looking first at the general context of the limits of local government. Cross-national and historical evidence is important here as a means of situating the contemporary UK experience against that of other market societies and that of other periods. Second, I look at a range of liberal and orthodox Marxist explanations of why central and local governments have come to have different functions. Third, I examine critically in more detail the 'dual state thesis' set out by Peter Saunders in the previous chapter and elaborated in various forms elsewhere.[1] In conclusion, I argue that it is vital to be able to explain both the overall role which local government plays as a form of fragmentation in the advanced industrial state, and the

49

substantive character of the functions which local government performs.

Setting the context

If we are to understand the limits on local government within liberal democratic capitalist societies, it is important not to fall into the trap of generalising from current British experience alone. Unfortunately, collecting systematic information about a large number of countries is difficult, so that the scope for comparison is rather restricted. One area where it is feasible is the pattern of government spending across central and local government. Table 3.1 shows the declining proportion of government spending undertaken by central government in the UK during the post-war period compared with similar trends in other liberal democracies, and contrasted with the high concentration of expenditure in central departments characteristic of less developed countries and non-democractic Western regimes. The UK is one of twelve liberal democracies

TABLE 3.1 The share of government current spending taken by central government*

| | Central government share (%) | | |
	1973	1960	1950
United Kingdom	56	65	73
Decentralising liberal democracies	41	51	55
All liberal democracies	49	56	59
Less developed countries and non-democratic regimes	75	77	–

*Countries included (plus 1973 central government share per cent) are:
Decentralising liberal democracies – United Kingdom (56), Australia (56), Belgium (49), Finland (47), France (46), Canada (42), Italy (40), USA (38), Austria (37), Sweden (32), Holland (28), West Germany (21).
All liberal democracies – as above, plus Israel (82), New Zealand (82), Ireland (76), Norway (74).
Less developed countries and non-democratic regimes – Jamaica (100), Mauritius (97), Peru (96), Thailand (95), Zambia (94), Libya (91), Rhodesia (91), Venezuela (87), Botswana (85), Argentina (85), Malaysia (81), Burma (78), Pakistan (76), Portugal (70), Greece (66), South Africa (65), Bolivia (65), Nigeria (63), Chile (41).
Central government share after transfers between levels of government.
Source: C. D. Foster, R. Jackman and M. Perlman, *Local Government Finance in a Unitary State* (Allen and Unwin, 1980), pp. 102–26, recomputed.

where there has been a consistent tendency for the central share of government spending to fall (at least up to the mid–1970s). In this group the UK has remained obstinately one of the most unitary states. There are a further six liberal democracies which either show no trend, or where central spending remains high because of heavy military expenditures, the agricultural nature of the economy, or the small size of the state which makes viable local government hard to sustain.

The shift of expenditures out of the central state charted in Table 3.1 probably reflects the increasing importance of socialised consumption in advanced industrialised societies, and the key role of local or regional governments as an implementation tier within Western 'welfare states'. The end of consumption spending growth and the onset of generalised fiscal strains in the mid–1970s, together with the escalating world-wide employment crisis of the early 1980s, has almost certainly halted or partially reversed this spending shift.

Data about expenditure patterns, of course, are limited because they say nothing directly about *control* over policy, about where decisions are made about the objectives or levels of funding. There are relatively few developed policy studies on a cross-national basis to fill this gap. Some studies point up continuities in functional allocations for direct service provision across countries.[2] But equally interesting is the extent to which local authorities are uniformly excluded from apparently key policy areas – for example, in the field of urban planning. This policy area has been frozen into an increasingly anachronistic mould, defined in the 1930s by the 'town and country planning' movement in Britain, a mould which focusses attention almost exclusively on trying to regulate the quality or amenity of consumption processes by controlling land uses – while increasingly critical determinants of living conditions are shaped by separate institutions pursuing contradictory priorities.

A second key consideration in setting the context of contemporary British experience is to situate it in a historical perspective. Table 3.2 shows how the pattern of local government expenditure across different services has changed in the last century since modern, directly elected councils were established. Two changes stand out. On the one hand overall local government spending has grown massively in real terms. On the other hand, the

TABLE 3.2   **Rank orderings of local government services by spending levels: England, Wales and Scotland, combined current and capital accounts, at 1975 prices**

Major services*	£m	%	Minor services (£m)†	
1884 (England & Wales only)				
Highways & lighting	127	16	Parks	4
Poor relief/workhouses	111	14	Housing	3
Education & libraries	63	8	Hospitals	2
Police & fire	55	7		
Gas	42	5		
Water	32	4		
Harbours	29	4		
Sewers	29	4		
1900				
Highways & lighting	262	13	Refuse	30
Education & libraries	239	12	Hospitals	30
Poor relief/workhouses	189	9	Parks	20
Gas	131	7	Housing	15
Water	121	6		
Police & fire	98	5		
Harbours	80	4		
Sewers	73	4		
Electricity	73	4		
Transport	61	3		
1914				
Education & libraries	604	21	Hospitals	47
Highways & lighting	359	12	Refuse	45
Poor relief/workhouses	218	8	Parks	36
Transport	194	7	Housing	23
Water	189	7		
Gas	183	6		
Harbours	165	6		
Police & fire	138	5		
Electricity	123	4		
Sewers	116	4		
1928				
Housing	940	19	Hospitals	133
Education & libraries	830	16	Sewers	127
Highways & lighting	616	12	Refuse	69
Electricity	350	7	Parks	57

53

TABLE 3.2   Contd.

Major services*	£m	%	Minor services (£m)†	
Poor relief/workhouses	350	7		
Transport	274	5		
Police & fire	220	4		
Water	216	4		
Gas	210	4		
Harbours	182	4		
1938				
Education & libraries	1,143	18	Sewers	189
Housing	1,012	16	Harbours	165
Electricity	698	11	Parks	103
Highways & lighting	676	10	Refuse	89
Workhouses	369	6		
Hospitals	309	5		
Transport	304	5		
Police & fire	291	4		
Gas	225	3		
1947				
Education & libraries	901	18	Harbours	104
Housing	816	17	Refuse	80
Electricity	556	11	Sewers	77
Highways & lighting	310	6	Parks	49
Health	271	6		
Transport	213	4		
Police & fire	192	4		
Welfare	179	4		
Gas	173	4		
Water	165	3		
1954				
Housing	2,056	32	Health	167
Education & libraries	1,804	28	Sewers	161
Highways & lighting	399	6	Welfare	158
Police & fire	354	5	Harbours	148
Water	276	4	Refuse	120
Transport	273	4	Parks	78
1964				
Education & libraries	3,318	32	Transport	282

TABLE 3.2   Contd.

Major services*	£m	%	Minor services (£m)†	
Housing	2,702	26	Health	281
Highways & lighting	729	7	Welfare	262
Police & fire	600	6	Harbours	173
Water	347	3	Refuse	161
Sewers	319	3	Parks	121
1975				
Education & libraries	5,685	31	Refuse	291
Housing	5,260	29	Parks	263
Police & fire	964	5	Transport	97
Highways & lighting	932	5	Harbours	62
Personal social services	910	5		

*Major services: all those accounting for 3 per cent or more of total local government spending.
†Minor services: services accounting for under 3 per cent of total local government spending.
Source: As Table 3.1.

number of areas where local authorities are engaged in providing services or making investments has dramatically reduced, especially since the 1940s. The growth of spending was concentrated more and more into two key areas, education (which grew originally in the Edwardian period to be the premier service and regained this position after further spectacular spending increases in the 1950s and 1960s), and public housing (which started in 1918, fluctuated in importance between the wars and boomed again after 1945). The top two local services accounted for barely a quarter of all local expenditures in 1900, around 35 per cent between the wars, over half the total in the mid–1950s, and 60 per cent by the mid–1970s.

The initial turning point in this process of local government focussing attention on fewer and fewer services˙ was clearly the 1920s when the first loss of local functions occurred. Really massive losses of Local service control however only occurred as a result of the 1945–51 Labour Government's industry nationalisations, which removed council's role in gas and electricity supply to quasi-governmental agencies (QGAs) organised as public corporations, and the creation of the National Health Service (NHS), which vested control of basic health care in a complex structure of appointed single-function health authorities. Ancillary health services were later removed from council responsibilities in the 1974 NHS reorganisation, and almost at the same time water and sewage functions were vested in a new set of regional agencies, again quasi-governmental bodies. Only the emergence and growth of a consolidated notion of the personal social services in the 1960s, and the attempt to transfer some client groups from NHS to council care in the 1970s, in any way offset this post-war trend for local government to lose functions to public corporations or other single function QGAs. Even the continued inclusion of police functions in local government spending figures disguises the extent to which control of police forces has passed from committees of individual local authorities (albeit with a third of their members being appointed JPs), to enlarged police authorities, spanning several county areas, and to all intents and purposes indistinguishable from regional QGAs in their character and mode of operation.

So far I have emphasised two dimensions of the limits on local government: the presence of gaps in local authority policy concerns which seem to negate many of the formal powers they do possess, and the losses of control and responsibilities which have occurred, particularly in the post-war period, with the growth of quasi-governmental agencies. But even in the areas which remain formally under the local government mantle, it is important to note that problems of *control* over policy may still be crucial. The evidence generated by long-run policy studies in British local government suggests overwhelmingly that local areas are decreasingly significant forums for policy determination.[3] Local authorities have seen effective influence over their policies seep away from them, not just to central government or QGAs, but also to the nationally organised and structured organs of local government and its constituent professions, to national parties, the mass media and the trades unions, and very importantly to corporate business and capital interests. Of course, there remains some scope for local political decision between options, some area of discretion within which genuinely localist forces can operate in response to élite or polular opinions, some area of modification necessary if overall solutions generated in the local government system or outside it are to be made to fit the differentiated positions of different localities. But policy studies of all but the most short-range of issues suggest strongly that the options considered and the agenda within which they are set are increasingly defined non-locally.

These observations are essentially a cautionary aside, however. To pursue them in any detail would require an investigation of the whole character and operations of local political institutions. In practice, I focus in the rest of the chapter on the more limited and manageable task of explaining why local government has lost functions, and what functional pressures underlie the distribution of responsibilities between local government and central departments or quasi-governmental agencies.

Existing explanations of functional allocation in the state

There are four existing accounts of the distribution of policy responsibilities between tiers of government: a conventional public administration view, which distinguishes 'intrinsically local' from 'intrinsically national' functions of government; a complex intergovernmental relations model, closely associated with neo-pluralist arguments about the modern need for interactive policy systems; a public choice model which explains functional allocations between tiers of government in terms of the behaviour of economically 'rational' actors concerned to maximise overall social welfare; and a Marxist account put forward in the 'local state' literature.

Public administration

Exponents of traditional public administration usually confine themselves to simply describing allocations between tiers of government as the result of historically specific processes of administrative decision and change. But just as this literature has 'principles' for distributing tasks between one government department and another, so it in practice relies on a number of latent or implicit claims about the rationale for local functions being as they are.

This explanation starts from the simple proposition that because we can observe some continuities in the treatment of particular services or responsibilities across countries, we can deduce something about their respective characteristics. Thus in virtually all

Western democracies small-scale environmental services, local planning, small-scale community facilities and primary education are locally administered, leading to the view that these functions are 'essentially local'. By contrast, the organisation of defence forces, economic management, major taxation policy and inter-urban transportation are almost uniformly the prerogatives of central government, and hence are presented as 'inherently national' in scope. The problem is that very few functions can be unequivocally classified in this simple way, leaving the vast bulk of 'welfare state' activities in an uneasy no-man's land of activities, organised within local government in some countries but outside it in others. The contrasts between similar countries in their treatment of services are far too stark for comfort; for example, in Britain, education is the quintessentially local service, absorbing over half of all council spending, yet in France, education is tightly organised by a central ministry, teachers are civil servants, and the curriculum is standardised across all areas of the country.

Conventional accounts rarely confront such problems, preferring a comfortable ethnocentrism for the most part, which vaguely relates particular patterns of administration to 'national character' or traditions. However, some authors do take comparisons across countries more seriously.[4] They analyse variations in service allocations in terms of the particular combinations of benefits and costs for given forms of organisation in different contexts. General principles include the avoidance of duplication; balancing the need for diversity and initiative-taking against counter-demands for control, accountability or uniformity of service levels; situating administration in optimally-sized units which can exploit economies of scale without being over-managed; fostering citizen participation and improving area-level co-ordination of services via decentralisation; avoiding overloading central departments; and preserving an administrative system susceptible to control by the politically and constitutionally predominant levels of government. The overall claim here acknowledges that these principles (considered in the abstract) cannot produce determinate or generalisable conclusions about how most government functions should be distributed between tiers of government. But they nonetheless provide a framework which, once filled out with a minimum of country-specific data on political culture and administrative history, can help to explain continuities and variations in systems of functional allocation. Unfortunately the evidence cited in support of these claims has remained unsystematic. It remains a collection of 'apt illustrations' or plausible interpretations of some prominent cases of divergent allocations across countries, rather than a comprehensively tested set of propositions. Public administration writing seems to provide a format and a standard set of incompatible propositions which can be selectively cited to 'explain' diametrically opposed solutions to service-allocation questions.

Inter-governmental relations

The inter-governmental relations model avoids this problem by declining to offer any account of why particular patterns of functional allocation are adopted in different circumstances, concentrating instead on explaining overall tendencies towards governmental fragmentation and decentralisation. This view explicitly acknowledges that multiple patterns of service responsibilities may be functionally equivalent, achieving the same desired effect in a wide variety of ways. The character of individual solutions is hence relatively unimportant; instead explanation should concentrate on the over-arching continuities in government organisation which underlie the surface differences between cases. Chief of these is the fact that government growth has overwhelmingly been accommodated in the post-war period not by creating a central Leviathan, but by progressively articulating an ever more complex network of interacting agencies unified by relations of interdependency and control.

There are two functional processes underlying the general adoption of this deconcentrated and decentralised pattern of state organisation. First, the neo-pluralist theory which underlies the inter-governmental relations model claims that modern government confronts severe and immediately limiting technological problems. Rational decision-making and the 'policy sciences' are in practice applicable to only a limited range of small-scale issues; they cannot even begin to address problems of aggregating separate policy decisions into societal-level policies. Comprehensive planning systems fail even at a technical level, lapsing either into quais-market strategies for co-ordinating the public sector, or becoming prone to distortions and co-ordination failures on a large scale.[5]

Second, to some extent balancing the technological pessimism outlined above is a recognition that as policy decisions in advanced industrial societies become increasingly complex, so the need to deploy expertise efficiently within the public sector increases. And if synoptic planning remains an impossible ideal, the importance of forecasting and the potential for disaggregated or 'partisan' planning by individual decision units has greatly increased. Traditional political arrangements, emphasising direct control by representative political institutions over a bureaucracy otherwise prone to advance its own interests, have simply become less appropriate as a general mode of arranging the relationship between expert and lay opinion. Instead Western states have shifted towards progressively more professionalised policy systems in which particular occupational groups are accorded above-average discretionary influence over policy development or implementation, in return for operating strong internal controls tying group members to a code of ethics, doctrines of social responsibility or a commitment to the objective pursuit of knowledge. Governmental fragmentation remains important in such systems, however, as a means of building in controls and forcing different professional groups to balance out different aspects of public interest concerns. It enables decisions to be 'factorised', or broken down into component parts, each of which can be entrusted to a separate agency.[6] This can be achieved by creating single-issue quasi-governmental agencies (QGAs), or by spatially decentralising responsibility within a larger, system of such agencies (for example, the NHS), or by locating professional groups in organisational contexts which reinforce internal public interest controls from external sources. Key mechanisms here are making professionally-controlled agencies operate in a market context, or locating professionals within local governments. The inter-governmental relations model stresses that local authority relations with professionals they employ will not be the straight-forward political control over an impartial bureaucracy suggested by traditional theories of representative government. Because professions are nationally organised and orientated they will be resistant to excessive local control, tending to fragment local administration into areas of professional domination.

Central–local relations are distinctive because of the higher profile political conflicts liable where governments drawing electoral legitimacy from different sources (and changing political complexion in different time-scales) are forced to bring their policies into some degree of congruence. The inter-governmental relations model stresses that power–dependency relationships are always two-way, no matter how apparently dominant one tier of government may seem.[7] Also distinctive is the powerful articulation of national-level interest groups representing the interests of local authorities, and the extent to which loose professional or policy 'communities', constituted at an ideological level and sustained by personal interactions, may both influence national policy-making and simultaneously set the parameters of local decisions.

Clearly, the inter-governmental relations model is much more sophisticated than conventional public administration explanations. Its theme of the functional equivalence of different patterns of organisational deconcentration, of different modes of factorising the decision process and then forcing policy to emerge out of the interactions of the new administrative network, seems to offer an attractive rationale of cross-national variations in the treatment of particular government activities which are for conventional accounts bafflingly problematic. But explaining cross-national variations is bought at a high price – namely an inability to say anything about variations across policy areas, even across broad categories of issues. Because the organisational and technological logic detected at work in the fragmentation of the extended state is quite general – one might say, socially 'neutral' – it simply cannot be plugged into evidence about substantive social conflicts. It operates from an 'end of ideology' perspective and explicitly asserts the convergence of interests in the modern industrial state between capital, organised labour and government.[8] We are left then with a formal framework of explanation, apparently powerful in its ability to systematise contemporary trends, but loaded to such an extent that it cannot address the highly differentiated patterns of inter-governmental relations from one issue area to another. These variations have more to do with the social interests involved in different issues than with the universalised organisational or technological imperatives which the theory seeks to explain.

Public choice

The public choice approach starts by assuming that citizens are rational actors concerned to maximise the ratio of benefits received from local government for taxes paid. Local authorities are assumed to be run by entrepreneurial managers, interested primarily in maximising the tax base of their localities. Peterson[9] views local authorities as fiscal clubs in competition for high income residents (and also high value, non-polluting industry or commerce in most areas) as the basis upon which to develop his public choice model of how functions will be allocated between central and local governments. Again, the starting point of the theory is to assume a blank canvas and to ask what sort of functional allocations would be agreed by rational actors starting from scratch.

The model assumes three types of services which local authorities might supply to citizens: *allocational services* are those which improve facilities for the community generally, providing benefits widely to all residents, and are financed out of general taxation (for example environmental services). *Redistributive services* are those where the local authority raises taxes from one group of citizens in order to provide benefits for a separate, usually poorer, group (for example, social insurance programmes, public health care and public housing). Finally, *developmental services* are those which encourage economic growth and attract new industry or residents which add to the community's tax base while making a smaller increment to demands for local public services (for example, tourist developments, transport investment or economic infrastructure). This typology is not necessarily exhaustive; for example, Peterson does not allocate education expenditures between categories.

The characteristics of these service types dictate a varying pattern of influences on local expenditures. Redistributive policies are most developed in wealthy local authorities which have most elbow room to raise extra finance without increasing tax rates above those of their neighbours and hence losing dissatisfied high income taxpayers. Developmental policies by contrast are influenced most by the demand for such services from potential new residents or industry, and by how expensive such provision is. Even fairly impoverished local authorities may sustain high levels of developmental spending as a means of improving their position. Finally, allocational policies respond most directly to the demands of existing residents in a local authority area, but are also sensitive to fiscal capacity, since a wealthy council can provide a given level of services at a lower tax rate than its neighbours.

This pattern of influences suggests that, as the level of overall government intervention increases, three functional allocations emerge. First redistributive services are increasingly funded by central government. This is because the process of competition between localities is such that if local government retains redistributive functions a very regressive effect becomes apparent in service provision – that is, redistributive spending is highest in local authorities with large fiscal capacities and low social needs, but lowest in poorer localities where the need for such services is actually greater. To avoid such irrational outcomes, and because competition between localities in this area does not maximise social welfare or local government efficiency, these services will be centralised. Second, allocational services are still funded primarily from local sources, because here competition between local governments is useful in maintaining efficiency of service provision, and in sorting people out spatially into the locality where their individual return in terms of benefits received for taxes paid is maximised. Social welfare is maximised because people with similar preferences are grouped in the locality with a tax/service profile closest to their optimum. Third, developmental functions will tend to be split up between the two tiers of government, responding to the feasibility of 'internalising' most or all of the planned benefits within local areas. Where the benefits can be spatially confined (as with local infrastructure or tourism) services are provided locally, but where benefits leak out of the area (for example, attempts to stimulate the local economy) local authorities will neglect services because the costs would still have to be borne locally, while the benefits cannot be contained. Central government will hence have to take on such functions if they are to be provided at all. There will typically be a good deal of mixed central/local initiative-taking for developmental services lying between these twin poles.

Public choice accounts clearly tackle questions of functional allocation quite directly, and in some areas successfully. Their explanation of the centralisation of redistributive functions is almost the only available one which tackles variations in the 'SHEW' services successfully. Similarly explaining the physical development orientation of local authority developmental functions in terms of a concentration on interventions with low levels of spatial leakage, seems to provide some powerful insights. But this apparent applicability of public choice models is bought at a high price, namely the misrepresentation of political processes in terms of a depoliticised logic of welfare maximisation, where social conflicts are hidden beneath pervasive assumptions of rationality.

Local state theory

The local state literature has not developed an explicit account of functional allocations within the capitalist state, although implicit within most Marxist writings on local government and central–local relations are two divergent perspectives relevant to this question. [10] The dominant Marxist view of local government stresses its potential utility as a defence of working-class interests against central government attacks, fiscal retrenchment, and attempts to reintroduce 'market disciplines' into areas of social life previously dominated by 'welfarism'. On this view local government in its modern form originated in the early nineteenth century as a crucial way of managing relations between different fractions and sections of capital during the early phases of industrialisation. Different business requirements for the reproduction of labour and local provision of means of production could be managed fairly easily under a local government system dominated by local entrepreneurs and corporations. But the progressive development of monopoly capital produced a withdrawal of business influence from participation in local affairs, while the liberalisation of the franchise and the growth of working-class movements and parties in Europe (and to some extent the Progressives' attack on city corruption in the USA) all tended to reduce the scope for external control of local authorities by businessmen. Indeed, the more local government became a focus for working-class action and socialist politics, the greater became the pressures from business on the central state to withdraw powers or by-pass local governments altogether. Even the

control of councils by intermediate social classes posed problems
by promoting consumption-oriented politics in potential opposition to industrial interests.

That local political institutions have survived at all in Western
Europe is seen as largely attributable to their legitimising functions
which prevent their outright abolition, and to the fairly slow emergence of left-wing local control as an unintended by-product of
liberal democratic development. As tighter fiscal constraints have
progressively been imposed to check local autonomy, and critical
issues have increasingly been displaced to other tiers of government
(especially non-elected regional administrations), so the main trend
of local government politics has been to develop as an 'implementation front' devoid of many genuine powers but serving to
legitimate state activity as a response to local 'needs'. Nonetheless
'the play within the structure of the state, needed to enable the co-
ordination of a divided dominant class, also affords opportunities
for working-class militancy to win concessions'.[11] Super-optimists
of the school, by focussing almost exclusively on the history of 'red
islands' in some European countries, are even prepared to claim
that local political institutions act as 'condensates' of 'local class
relations'[12] – conveniently omitting mention of the pervasive non-
involvement of the wider labour movement in local governments'
spheres of responsibility.

The second strand of the local state literature takes a diametrically opposite view of local government, pointing out that
working-class mobilisations into local politics at the end of the
nineteenth and beginning of the twentieth centuries were frequently
disruptive – designed to force issues such as social insurance,
pension provision and hospital care on to the central state's
agenda, by exposing the limits of local government as a forum
for progressive redistribution. On this view, working-class movements have been a major source of pressure for centralising state
responsibilities – because an acceptance of responsibility by national government is a prerequisite for successful reform pressures
to be applied by labour unions and left parties. A fragmented local
government system and the continued decentralisation of functions
to local authorities serves mainly to break up this process to the
benefit of dominant class interests. Local governments are, for
example, especially vulnerable to domestic spatial movements of
capital designed to impose a common 'market discipline' on them,

which dictates business-oriented tax and service policies. This pressure, of course, bears hardest on initially disadvantaged areas such as inner cities or depressed industrial regions with the greatest concentrations of working-class residents and the most vulnerable fiscal bases. Furthermore, there is ample cross-national evidence to suggest that local political institutions commonly attract involvement and participation differentially from intermediate social categories (in Marxist terms the petit bourgeoisie and controllers of labour) rather than workers, because control of local government can be used by such classes to enforce social exclusion practices and maintain their 'middle-class' identifications with capitalist interests. Hence local authorities are typically a focus for home-owner groups, local business and self-employed people, and defenders of minor privileges or status concessions accorded to intermediate class categories under capitalism. A spatial fragmentation of issues or policy problems serves to disguise their roots in social conflicts, locating them instead in a 'naturalistic' set of 'urban/environmental' considerations, and emphasising a community consciousness which serves primarily to obstruct the development of class-based social identities or awareness. The asymmetrical character of mobilisation into local politics plus the largely negative implementation powers of councils combine to make local political institutions powerful in their ability to frustrate the initiatives which might be taken at a national level by a left government, but weak and ineffective vehicles from which to try to build popular support for sweeping social change.

These conflicting views do not remotely add up to a theory of functional allocations in the capitalist state, but they do suggest something of the contradictory social implications of a local government system in liberal democracies, embodying as they do very different perspectives on the effect of this tier of government on different social classes' ability to formulate and mobilise around their interests. This theme can be usefully offset against the bogus neutralism of most liberal theories and their attempt to distance questions about functional allocations from questions about the conflicting social interests in advanced industrial states. The two strands of Marxist and radical accounts also feed directly into an assessment of the dual state thesis, an explicit attempt to formulate a theory of functional allocation in Western states to which we now turn.

The dual state thesis

Like some of the models already reviewed, the dual state thesis suggests that questions of functional allocation within the state apparatus are of critical significance in understanding contemporary political and social development in advanced capitalist societies. Exponents (such as Peter Saunders in this volume) claim that the model can both by-pass some of the central problems inherent in 'unitary theories' of the state, and remedy the 'conspicuous failure in the Marxist tradition to take account of [the local state's] specificity in terms of its operations'.[13] Underlying the model is a radicalised Weberian position mingled with some contemporary neo-Marxist themes. The thesis has four stages: a typology of state expenditures; a theory of how different modes of state action can be combined with available decision-making strategies within government; an argument that the allocation of functions between central, regional and local governments is a key mechanism for resolving the contradictory pressures on government in market societies; and a discussion of the broader implications of functional allocations for political mobilisation and ideological development.

State expenditure

The dual state thesis uses the typology developed by O'Connor[14] which distinguishes between three main categories of spending: *social expenses* (which are necessary provisions for social order but which do not contribute directly to economic growth or profit accumulation); *social investment* (which provides means of production for capital – such as a road system allowing goods to be distributed – and hence enhances profits directly); and *social consumption* (where government socialises labour costs otherwise borne by businesses, and hence contributes in a more mediated way towards raising profitability). This typology can be articulated into quite a complex set of categories, which offer a framework for 'fiscal sociology' to map out the interconnections between state budget-making and the interests of conflicting social classes and groupings (see Figure 3.1). These categorisations are, of course, premised on a kind of functionalism, although one appropriate to a

FIGURE 3.1 A typology of state expenditure

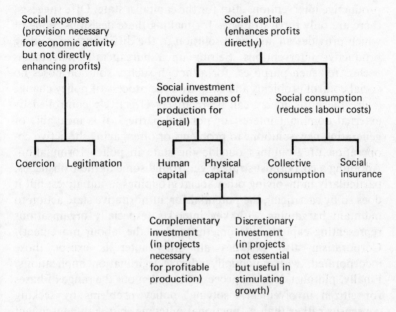

Source: After J. O'Connor, *The Fiscal Crisis of the State* (St. Martin's Press, 1973); C. Offe in Lindberg *et al.*, *Stress and Contradiction in Modern Capitalism* (Lexington, 1975); P. Saunders, *Social Theory and the Urban Question* (Hutchinson, 1981).

class-biased state acting to maintain a structure of domination in a society torn by deep conflicts of interest and ideology.

State action

Claus Offe[15] has analysed the fundamental problems for the state in market societies. State action may be 'allocative', where the government is primarily using resources over which it already has 'property rights' and is acting in an authoritative, self-guided way; or it may be 'productive', where the government is trying to create a change in broader social arrangements, and to make initiatives which rely on engaging the co-operation of external interests if they are to succeed. Advanced industrial states have moved beyond the essentially allocative role of the nineteenth century governments, so that they are extensively involved in trying to guide complex productive interventions. But for the capitalist state, Offe suggests, there are only three strategies for making these decisions, none of which provides an adequate solution to the difficulties of guiding productive interventions. Setting up a bureaucratic machine is useless for such purposes, for although such a solution poses no social control problems and simplifies the process of policy change (since the bureaucracy can be relatively effectively controlled by external dominant interest or political parties), it is incapable of generating new solutions to problems or of engaging the active co-operation of groupings outside the state in policy formulation. Adopting a corporatist strategy gets round some of these obstacles, particularly in involving other social groupings in initiatives; but it does so by sacrificing the potential for authoritative state action to maintain bargaining with key interests (especially organisations representing capital, but sometimes also the labour movement). Corporatism also excludes all other interests except those incorporated, with potentially adverse legitimation implications. Finally, pluralist decision processes broaden out the range of bases for citizen involvement, 'solving' policy problems by seeking consensus rather than a functional outcome, but with consequent severe risks that policy formulation may come to be controlled by non-dominant social classes and directed into channels inimical to capital interests.

Saunders[16] suggests that by combining the O'Connor typology of state spending with Offe's discussion of modes of state intervention and decision-making, these apparently serious problems can be avoided. Those kinds of allocative intervention which involve social investment can be satisfactorily run in a bureaucratic mode, since there is no need for the state to engage the co-operation of external groups or make initiatives, while the importance of these functions sets a premium on maintaining tight, centralised control over them. Productive interventions involving social investment spending are, in contrast, run in a corporatist way, with an emphasis on planning to disguise the very selective range of external interests involved, and with considerable efforts to make the relationship a closed and hierarchic negotiation process between the state and peak associations. Traditional ideologies of representative government and the impression of state neutrality and permeability to other interests can be maintained by using basically pluralist decision procedures for social consumption spending (and perhaps legitimation forms of social expenses), whether the interventions involved are allocative or productive in character. Because these expenditures are on the reproduction of labour-power rather than means of production directly relevant to business operations, they can be more safely entrusted to the vagaries of pluralist decision-making; even if control of these policies passes to non-dominant classes or left political parties, the scope for actions threatening the basic operations of the capitalist state is limited. Pluralist policy-setting can always be eroded, by selectively replacing it with bureaucratic or corporatist procedures when such threats arise around individual issues.

Levels of government

Central, regional and local government are important in establishing this complex set of arrangements on a stable institutional basis, which guarantees the fundamental interests of capital by locating social investment expenditures within sections of central government insulated from popular control (especially in quasi-governmental agencies), and in regional government (which Saunders and Cawson see in British terms as the most closed and corporatist tier of government). By contrast, social consumption spending is vested in local government, whose inferior con-stitutional position and fiscal dependency on the centre ensures that tightly circumscribed limits can be placed around the scope of pluralist decision-making. The pattern which results shows a fundamental dualism in state institutions (see Table 2.1, p. 30). Of course, dual state arrangements will not be without their own tensions requiring constant management, notably between cor-poratist planning and local electoral accountability, and between the secular trend towards centralisation in the contemporary state and the still powerful pressures in advanced capitalism to maintain some genuine decentralisation of political power.[17]

Social implications

The consequences of institutional dualism are extensive in two areas. First, the separation of social investment and social consumption responsibilities between distinct tiers of government helps to create and sustain a dualism in the forms of social and political mobilisation. The politics of corporatist central government are dominated by a class-based struggle between capital and labour, clearly expressed in the pyramid structure of interest groups in both trade associations and the labour movement. Characteristically, however, once orientated to processes at a national level, these major groupings may be almost uninvolved in the politics of local government issues or of social consumption – for example, labour unions in most Western countries only rarely get involved at the local level outside of economic and industrial policy concerns. As Saunders emphasises in Chapter 2, political conflicts over consumption issues are not just class conflicts. Different social interests are involved in different consumption issues, hence sustaining a typically pluralist, political process.

Second, the institutional separation of social investment and social consumption functions allows the state apparatus to maintain incompatible ideological themes in tension. The dominant ideology in production issues is market liberalism, stressing the primacy of the market, the vital role of private property and profit-making in wealth creation, and the overwhelming priority of economic management considerations. But the separation of social consumption functions into local government allows these sections of the state apparatus to legitimate the whole, by emphasising an ideology of equal citizenship and of concern for social needs and institutions (for example, individual self-development and opportunities, support for the family).

Compared with earlier accounts, the dual state thesis can successfully explain some of the key limits of local government. In particular, it tackles directly the conflicts of interest between social classes and groupings which underlie functional allocations within government, and provides a plausible rationale for the insulation of policy areas critical for business interests from control by local political institutions.

Some problems with the dual state thesis

The dual state thesis is clearly, however, still a partial model of why different levels of government have different functions, for three reasons: first, the associations between policy functions and tiers of government to which the thesis points can be interpreted in terms of different causal influences; second, ascribing social consumption functions to local government misrepresents the character of the 'consumption politics' which do indeed dominate local politics; and third, the thesis rests on an inadequate account of the decision-making modes open to the contemporary state apparatus.

Causes and effects

The flow of causation in the dual state thesis starts with a set of functional imperatives or pressures on the state apparatus (to pursue contradictory accumulation and legitimation objectives, to undertake productive interventions without losing social control). This leads to a dualism in institutional arrangements, which then creates or reinforces a broader dualism in political mobilisation and ideological orientations. But for this chain of influences to be established it is vital for the theory to demonstrate that it could conceivably be falsified, and in practice there are grounds for doubting this.

To start with, O'Connor's distinction between social expenses, investment and consumption is, as Saunders recognises, a set of 'ideal types'. This means 'that this system of classification is not mutually exclusive in that most state provisions perform more than one of these functions'.[18] Add to this the fact that O'Connor's typology has never been successfully applied in detail to any state budget since its production ten years ago, and it begins to be apparent that testing the dual state thesis is more difficult than it looks at first sight – the thesis predicts only 'tendencies' towards functional specialisation across institutional levels, and most spending will anyway be capable of multiple classification under the categories used. Education, for example, could be seen as a legitimation form of social expenses, or as social investment in human capital, or as a type of collective consumption.

So deciding if one type of spending should be classified as primarily social investment or social consumption, may come down to making judgements about whether it contributes directly to business profitability or only in a more indirect way by lowering the cost of reproducing labour. But such judgements will fluctuate sharply from one society and time period to another in respect of the same type of expenditures and conceivably, much of the classification will be indeterminate or in a state of flux.

In short, state expenditures may assume different functional characteristics, when they are administered by different kinds of agency, and when different kinds of political mobilisation occur around them. This undermines the causal sequence of the dual state model by suggesting that institutional allocations are logically and causally prior to the differentiation of state activities into social investment or consumption categories. What tier of government handles an issue, and the type of decision mode adopted, help to determine the character of state expenditures, rather than governments simply responding to a predetermined set of functional requirements or imperatives on the state apparatus. The dual state thesis thus tends to highlight a particular empirical patterning of governmental functions, but for the wrong reasons. I would suggest, in contrast that a broad-ranging social dualism, particularly the separation of home from workplace issues in ideological terms, helps to create two different ways in which people are mobilised into politics. This in turn fosters an institutional separation of functions, where both big business *and* the labour movement press for the centralisation of certain social investment and social consumption functions, leaving a residuum of collective consumption responsibilities for local government. This institutional pattern then progressively differentiates state spending into distinct functional categories.

Local government functions

The key concerns of local government in the dual state thesis relate to social consumption. However, because of the difficulty of applying the O'Connor categories, we cannot expect to see any watertight patterning, as indeed we do not (Table 3.3). In Britain at least, it is clear both that the contemporary functions of local authorities spread widely across the social expenses, social investment and social consumption categories, and that the patterns of lost local government functions shows a bunching in some public utility types of social investment, but also in important

TABLE 3.3 UK local government services (1982) classified by dual state categories

Category	Current LA functions	Former LA functions
(Social expenses) Coercion	police funding (indirectly controlled) fire regulation, safety	direct control
Legitimation	social work education* consumer protection conservation planning	private education subsidies (lost 1977–9)*
(Social investment) Human capital	education* environmental health	private education subsidies (lost 1977–9)* mainstream health services (lost 1947) ancillary health services (lost 1974)
Complementary physical investment	highway construction* road maintenance infrastructures trading services fire service public transport operating losses public transport operation (in cities)	gas and electricity supply (lost 1947) single authority water services (1962) remaining water functions (lost 1974) inter-urban road funding (lost 1934)*

TABLE 3.3 Cond't.

Category	Current LA functions	Former LA functions
Discretionary physical investment	council housing* housing improvements* highway construction* urban renewal structure planning local economic development	other public sector housing (lost since 1964) inter-urban road funding (lost 1934)*
'Collective consumption'	council housing* housing improvements* education* personal social services concessionary public transport cultural and recreational local planning	other public sector housing (since 1964)* mainstream health service (lost 1947)* ancillary health service (lost 1974)*
Social insurance	rent allowances and rebates rate rebates	unemployment assistance (lost 1946, and piecemeal from late 1920s)

*indicates a function present in more than one category.
Source: As Table 3.1.

TABLE 3.4 Local government spending by service category, 1884–1975: England, Wales and Scotland, combined current and capital accounts, at constant 1975 prices

Year	Social consumption*		Social investment†		Social expenses‡‡		Unallocated spending		Notes
	£m	%	£m	%	£m	%	£m	%	
1884	181	23	259	33	55	7	296	37	(England & Wales only)
1900	493	24	832	41	105	5	592	29	
1914	928	32	1,375	48	138	5	438	15	Public housing starts
1928	2,310	46	2,044	40	220	4	481	10	UAB set up
1938	2,937	45	2,633	40	291	4	695	11	
1947	2,216	45	1,677	34	192	4	800	16	NHS set up; gas, electricity nationalised
1954	4,262	66	1,375	21	354	5	502	10	
1964	6,685	65	2,011	20	600	6	1,037	10	
1974	11,892	62	2,848	15	1,008	5	3,345	17	Loss of health & water sewage functions
1975	12,118	67	1,497	8	964	5	3,588	20	

*Social consumption: education, libraries and museums, hospitals and health, poor relief and workhouses, welfare and personal social services, parks, housing (HRA and other).
†Social investment: water and sewage, refuse, highways and lighting, gas, electricity, transport, harbours.
‡Social expenses: police and fire protection.
Source: See Table 3.1.

types of social consumption provision (notably health care and social insurance). In other European countries there are important additional exceptions, such as the vesting of all key education responsibilities with central government in France, and the centralisation of social housing provision under joint central government/national housing association control in other countries. In addition, it is important to note that the fit between local government and social consumption in Britain (which is perhaps the closest of any country) is a very recent phenomenon (Table 3.4). In the period up to 1914, only just over a third of allocatable expenditure by local authorities could be classified as social consumption (on generous criteria). It was not until the 1950s that a clear predominance of social consumption spending was established even on this crude classification, and not until the mid–1970s that it became absolutely pre-eminent.

The most fundamental point here against the dual state thesis remains, however, its poor performance in explaining the allocation of social insurance functions between tiers of government compared with, say, the public choice model. In O'Connor's original typology such spending counts alongside collective consumption in the social consumption category. The dual state thesis conveniently fudges the issue by disregarding such functions, and by describing local government's role very much in terms of the narrower *collective* consumption category (which is limited to specific services supplied by the state apparatus). But since local government's role depends critically on the mix between transfer payments and public service provision which governments adopt, it would seem that a theory based more directly on an analysis of consumption issues and politics would have a better chance of explaining the character of local authority functions.[19]

Modes of decision-making

The decision-making options available to the state in market societies, and their association with particular levels of government, may be more complex than the dual state thesis assumes. In particular Offe's trichotomy of pluralist, bureaucratic and corporatist decision modes seems restrictive in leaving no readily identifiable location for policy systems dominated by the professions. Highly professionalised issue areas may be as different as the NHS or the civilian nuclear energy programme. Such policy systems do not fit easily into Offe's typology. Clearly professionalised systems are not simply bureaucracies, even when the personnel involved are mainly or solely state employees working in large agencies with line responsibilities. Professions have an obvious capacity to generate new initiatives, and they characteristically favour planning-orientated policies stressing rational analysis over simple bureaucratic routines. Efforts have been made by proponents of the dual state thesis to analyse professionalised policy systems as examples of a kind of corporatism. The conventional models of external interest group co-optation into the achievement of state objectives are here extended to include the professions working within the state apparatus, especially in local government.[20] But such attempts misrepresent the actual importance of the professions (both 'social' and 'technical') in originating substantive policy change through their internal processes of ideological development, rather than through the operations of their professional institutions in an interest group mould. The professions' role as interest groups has been important on a range of organisational issues – conditions of work and remunerations, composition of the government agencies running policy areas and so on. But it is in terms of originating, disseminating and implementing new ideas, technologies and innovations that professional influence has been greatest.[21] This distinctive influence requires separate analysis.[22] Hence we need to expand Offe's trichotomy to reintroduce a separate category for professionalised policy-making – a category which will be equivalent to 'technocracy' in many issue areas outside the control of the 'social' professions.

Introducing this new category raises questions immediately, however, about the associations which the dual state thesis makes between tiers of government and forms of decision-making. In particular, acknowledging the importance of professionalism in local government suggests that to see it as a differentially pluralist level of government is mistaken. Policy determination in local authorities does not respond in any simple way to local political inputs. Rather policy over large areas seems to be dominated for long periods of time by professionally promoted 'fashions' which are nationally produced and adopted with little variation from one local authority to another. Professionalism, in other words, undermines the effect of decentralisation in notionally increasing the scope for pluralism in local authorities.

Conclusion

This review suggests that any account of functional allocation in Western states needs to take into account five major trends in their recent development. First, there has been a clear tendency to centralise, corporatise, depoliticise and insulate from traditional representative institutions those areas of policy making which are of direct significance for business interests. There has apparently been a continuous structural pressure on central government to maintain tight social control over policy areas with major implications for capital accumulation and economic development. A sub-trend in this overall tendency has been towards centralising economic development activities with high levels of spatial leakage, but partly here to avoid the escalating fiscal pressure from business to which decentralised agencies might otherwise be exposed.

Second, there has been a clear trend for redistributive services to be centralised and in the process insulated from political mobilisations outside the state apparatus. This process not only strengthens tight control by the state apparatus of a policy area vital for social stabilisation, but also contributes to fiscal efficiency by ensuring that transfer payments are made at the 'optimal' tier of government. By aggregating redistributive payments (both progressive social insurance payments and regressive tax subsidies) into large-scale policy structures of considerable complexity, the central state takes on a limited bureaucratic burden. It also ensures that uniform standards of provision prevail which cannot be incrementally bid up between localities, and hence are immune to all but the most large-scale political pressures.

Third, there has been a consistent tendency in Western states towards increasing fragmentation of government. Organisational decentralisation at national or regional levels to quasi-governmental agencies and spatial decentralisation to local authorities or elected regional governments, are in many ways functionally equivalent strategies. Both permit increased organisational specialisation, some considerable factorisation of the decision process, and the creation of complex, interactive policy systems and structures of inter-organisational dependencies – all of which are of fundamental importance in allowing the state apparatus to manage (if not overcome) acute rationality constraints in policy-making. Governmental fragmentation also controls the incidence of 'overload' on central institutions of the extended state, and minimises the probability of serious policy distortions inherent in the new autonomy of many agencies from control by representative institutions. Decentralisation to sub-national governments is distinctive mainly in introducing a more explicitly political dimension into inter-governmental relations.

Fourth, the professionalisation of policy-making in Western governments has continued in parallel with the growth of organisational contexts favourable for increased occupational work autonomy. Single issue agencies in interacting networks, spatially decentralised systems of QGAs, and local authorities all provide appropriate settings where a high level of professionalisation of policy-making may be expected.[23] Although professionals in West European local authorities are formally under external political control, in practice the nationalisation of ideological change within their occupational communities (and their importance as conduits of private sector influence on to state policy) mean that localist influences normally have a secondary influence upon policy development.

Fifth, there has been a strong tendency in many countries to maintain or marginally increase the localisation of state services provision – even in the period since 1975. This counter vailing influence is most obviously manifest in political and ideological pressures against 'over-centralisation', and in the continued legitimation constraints which insulate local government systems against 'modernisations' or losses of powers in many countries. Where these political constraints are less developed (as in the UK) the functional pressures to maintain governmental fragmentation may still be sufficient to offset in part the drift towards centralisation.

Explaining state structures is never simple, for trends of development and conflicts of interest in the wider society are inescapably inscribed in the operations of government institutions. The picture set out here is a complex and multi-valent one. But it is towards exactly this kind of explanation that we must push if we

are to successfully analyse the limits of local government, and the
potential of political action at the local level, as discussed in the
chapters which follow.

Notes and References

1. A. Cawsan and P. Saunders, 'Corporatism, Competitive Politics and
    Class Struggle', in R. King (ed.), *Capital and Politics* (Routledge and
    Kegan Paul, 1983); A. Cawson, *Corporatism and Welfare* (Heine-
    mann, 1982); P. Saunders, *Social Theory and the Urban Question*
    (Hutchinson, 1981).
2. A. J. Heidenheimer, H. Heclo and C.T. Adams, *Comparative Public
    Policy* (Macmillan, 1983).
3. P. Dunleavy, 'Social and Political Theory and the Issues in Central–
    Local Relations', in G. Jones (ed.), *New Approaches to the Study of
    Central–Local Government Relationships* (Gower, 1980).
4. P. Self, *Administrative Theories and Politics* (Allen and Unwin,
    1977).
5. C. Lindblom, *Politics and Markets* (Basic Books, 1977); C. Lindblom
    and D. Cohen *Useable Knowledge* (Yale University Press, 1979).
6. P. Self, *Administrative Theories and Politics*.
7. R. Rhodes, *Control and Power in Central–Local Relations* (Gower,
    1981).
8. J. Galbraith, *The New Industrial State* (Penguin, 1969).
9. P. Peterson, 'A unitary model of local taxation and expenditure
    policies in the United States', *British Journal of Political Science*, 9,
    1979, pp. 287–314.
10. P. Dunleavy, *Urban Political Analysis*, (Macmillan, 1980).
11. C. Cockburn, *The Local State* (Pluto Press, 1977, p. 50.)
12. S. Duncan and M. Goodwin, 'The Local State and Restructuring
    Social Relations: Theory and Practice', *International Journal of
    Urban and Regional Research*, 6, 1982, pp. 157–86.
13. A. Cawson and P. Saunders, 'Corporatism, Competitive Politics and
    Class Struggle'.
14. J. O'Connor, *The Fiscal Crisis of the State*, (St. Martin's Press,
    1973).
15. C. Offe, 'The Theory of the Capitalist State and the Problem of
    Policy Formation', in L. Lindberg, R. Alford. C. Crouch and C.
    Offe (eds.), *Stress and Contradiction in Modern Capitalism*,
    (Lexington, 1975).
16. P. Saunders, *Social Theory and the Urban Question*, and A. Cawson
    and P. Saunders, 'Corporatism, Competitive Politics and Class
    Struggle'.
17. L. J. Sharpe, *Decentralist Trends in Western Democracies* (Sage,
    1980).

18. This book, ch. 2, p. 26.
19. P. Dunleavy, 'Socialised Consumption and Economic Development', *International Journal of Urban and Regional Research*, forthcoming (1984).
20. A. Cawson, *Corporatism and Welfare*.
21. P. Dunleavy, *The Politics of Mass Housing in Britain: A Study of Corporate Power and Professional Influence in the Welfare State*, (Clarendon Press, 1981).
22. P. Dunleavy, 'Professions and Policy Change: Notes Towards a Model of Ideological Corporatism', *Public Administration Bulletin*, August, 1981.
23. P. Dunleavy, 'Quasi-governmental sector professionalism: some implications for public policy-making in Britain', in A. Barker (ed.), *Quangos in Britain* (Macmillan, 1982).

4 Labour, Socialism and Local Democracy

KEITH BASSETT

Cuts and controls directed at local government since 1979 have clearly posed political problems for most councils. The problems posed for many Labour authorities have however been particularly acute. This chapter is concerned with the problems surrounding Labour's response to the recent restructuring of central–local relations. First, however, it locates these problems in a longer historical perspective by examining aspects of Labour's involvement in local government since the turn of the century. It then identifies some of the emerging trends in local Labour politics and discusses some of the problems associated with attempts in the Party to redefine the role of local government in socialist advance.

Labour and the local state: an historical perspective

Part of Labour's problem in developing a coherent response to the current restructuring of central–local relations lies in the Party's past involvement in centralisation policies which have led to the impoverishment of local democracy. The Party is thus not in a strong position to mobilise much support behind a radical and popular alternative to current policies. The reasons for this must be sought in the history of the Party's involvement in local government.

It has been argued that Britain's streamlined local government system has served to neutralise territorial politics more effectively than in any other state in Europe.[1] The end product has been a system that largely insulates the central administration and national parties from local politics. British local government has become geared to servicing and maintaining existing central policies rather than aggregating local preferences, formulating local demands and transmitting them to the centre. A primary function of local parties in this system is to act as electoral agents for national parties.

The outline of this system, Ashford has argued, can be discerned far back in the nineteenth century. The division between national and local politics was thus evident long before the rise of the Labour Party and was an integral part of the development of the British bourgeois state during the nineteenth century. Labour presented some challenge to this structure at the local level in the early part of this century, but the history of Labour's involvement in local government has predominantly taken the form of accommodating to this structure and then strengthening it.

There is no adequate history of Labour's involvement in local government. Most histories of the Party concentrate on central government, and histories of local government reform provide only intermittent references to changing views within the Party. There are also snapshot portraits of individual Labour authorities at various periods and recent theoretical work on the local state often uses evidence drawn from different historical periods to confirm broader hypotheses.[2] But there is no complete, theoretically informed, and adequate history. Such a history would have to relate changing views on local government to broader ideological shifts within the Party and relate these in turn to the Party's role in the development of bourgeois parliamentary democracy in the twentieth century. Duncan and Goodwin's survey goes some way towards this, although it focusses on particular salient events (Poplar, for example) and leaves long historical gaps.[3]

Historical roots and early developments

Although the Labour Party was established at the turn of the century primarily to contest national elections, its organisational activities were rapidly extended at the local level and by 1919 Labour controlled twelve metropolitan boroughs, Bradford and three Welsh counties.[4] Labour views on local government evolved out of diverse traditions as an integral part of the development – by the 1920s – of a distinct 'Labour Socialist ideology'.[5] Although both Fabians and the Independent Labour Party had been active in local government before 1900, it was the Fabian tradition that ultimately proved most influential in shaping the local dimension to this ideology.

The early Fabians had been particularly active in local government in London from 1896, and they placed high hopes on a progressive municipalisation of industries and services as a road to socialism.[6] These views were modified in the *New Heptarchy* Tracts, starting in 1905, and by the 1920s optimism in a municipal road to socialism was less evident. Nevertheless, the municipal dimension remained strong, and in the Webbs' *Constitution for a Socialist Commonwealth* it was still envisaged that the bulk of industry would ultimately be administered and controlled at the municipal level.[7]

The importance of a municipal dimension to socialist advance was formally recognised by the Labour Party in a resolution approved at the 1918 Conference along with the new, Fabian-inspired, Party Constitution. The resolution called for the strongest possible powers to enable local authorities to pursue socialist strategies at the local level. In practice, however, subsequent Labour Governments in the inter-war period did not give much priority to local government reform in spite of attempts by the Party to push through local authority 'enabling' bills whilst in opposition.

The orthodoxy that emerged by the later 1920s represented a diluted version of the Fabian municipal road to socialism, that stressed the efficiency rather than the participation aspects of decentralisation. This orthodoxy is perhaps best captured in the writings of Herbert Morrison who was an influential figure in local government, and wrote extensively on local government and socialism.[8] Morrison argued that by gaining control of local authorities, Labour could demonstrate its capacity to govern. To this end Labour-controlled authorities should be 'creative, progressive, public spirited' and display a business like administration in which municipal enterprise could be justified on grounds of efficiency. Local government could thus be made into 'an efficient machine for a high moral purpose'. Labour's local government machine must, however, act constitutionally. Morrison played a key role in sorting out the rules governing the relationships between Labour Groups and local Labour Parties, emphasising the independence of the former as befitted elected representatives of the people. He also opposed the kind of direct challenge to the central government thrown down by councils such as Poplar in the 1920s. In summary, Labour's local government machine should be representative, efficient, honest, dedicated to progressive incremental reform, but always strictly constitutional in behaviour, moving forward on the basis of widening support bred by its own obvious successes.

These values and assumptions were an integral part of the broader perspective on reform and the state implicit in mainstream Labour socialism. As MacIntyre has shown in his careful review of Labour thinking between the wars,[9] Labour socialism embraced a very uncritical view of the state as a potential agent of reform. The state was not viewed as intrinsically a class state. It was accepted that it had been used as an instrument of oppression on behalf of capital, through conspiratorial control by leading capitalists and financiers, but it could be wrested from capitalist control by constitutional means and used by a socialist majority on behalf of the community as a whole. Labour socialism did not envisage the smashing of the state and the construction of radically different state forms as a necessary part of socialist advance.

The development of Labour socialism as the dominant ideology of the Labour movement did not proceed unchallenged. There was opposition from the Labour Left, including the Independent Labour Party (ILP), and from Marxists both within and outside the Party. In the period before 1923 an alternative perspective was also offered by the Guild Socialists. These oppositional tendencies viewed local government and local–central relations in a more critical way, that either implied more radical political action at the local level or pointed towards a thorough-going reconstruction of central–local state relations.

Marxist and Labour Left elements, for example, were active in various militant localities such as Poplar and the 'Little Moscows' of the 1920s.[10] Councillors in those localities were prepared to use local government as an instrument for challenging the established social order and mobilising mass support for resistance to central government.

Poplar was, perhaps, the most famous of the militant localities.[11] The Council clashed repeatedly with the government after 1919 by paying higher wages to its workers and higher rates of unemployment relief to its poor, and by refusing to collect rate precepts for other authorities until a more equitable distribution of income had been introduced between rich and poor authorities. Thirty councillors went to gaol and various surcharges were imposed. However, Poplar was not alone in its militant tradition of open defiance. A number of authorities earned themselves the title of 'Little Moscow' and the Vale of Leven was also known as 'the Scottish Poplar'.[12]

However, if one examines these communities, certain characteristics stand out that could not be replicated everywhere. First, these were often occupational communities (overwhelmingly dependent on a single industry), and even where there were a diversity of industries they were overwhelmingly working-class communities. Second, they were areas experiencing very high rates of unemployment related to the collapse of their traditional industries. Third, their councils were overwhelmingly working class, with deep roots in the local community and the local trades unions. They were in a strong position to mobilise mass support behind their decisions. Fourth, their councils were strongly influenced from the Left through individual membership of organisations like the ILP, the Social Democratic Federation and the Communist Party. In some cases local control was based on an alliance between the Labour Party Left and the Communist Party.

Although local militancy achieved some limited success there were strong forces working against it. The willingness of local councils to break the law was viewed with disfavour by the mainstream Labour tradition. Morrison, for example, was critical of Poplar's extravagance in raising rates and its defiance of the law, because it undermined the image of Labour councils as sound alternatives to Tory ones. Some of the Little Moscows were wiped out by local government re-organisation in the 1930s. The traditional occupational communities were subject to decay and dissolution. The organisation of the Communist Party declined in many areas before the Second World War and the ILP became isolated and ineffectual in the 1930s. Nevertheless the resistance of the militant localities became part of popular consciousness and provided a point of reference to succeeding generations of local activists.

Finally, it is also worth noting the radical, anti-statist reform implication of the Guild Socialist tradition with its idea of a decentralised,self-governing social system.[13] Although theorists such as Cole placed much of their emphasis on the functional organisation of democracy through a system of guilds, their writings included strong arguments in favour of the decentralisation of power to small ward units which would be loosely co-ordinated through a system of local and regional communes. The main thrust of Guild Socialism was directed against the idea of a central state as a focus for bureaucratic activity. Guild Socialism did therefore encourage a more critical view of the state and the centralisation tendencies inherent in state socialism, but as a movement it was shortlived and exerted little influence from the mid–1920s.

There were thus different and often conflicting tendencies at work within the Party in its early years, which often found expression in different attitudes to local political action and the balance between central and local power in socialist advance. However, the emergence of a distinctive Labour Socialist ideology by the 1920s was associated with a progressive loss of interest in decentralised roads to socialism. The Party's retreat in 1929 from the Enabling Bill which it had supported in opposition marked, according to Sharpe, 'the final demise of the Labour Party's dabbling with the local road to socialism.'[14]

Finally, it is worth noting the relative insulation of the British debates from the broader and often acrimonious debates amongst continental socialists on the relation between local autonomy, democracy and socialist advance. The autonomy of local communes was one of the basic concerns of European socialist thought from the utopian socialism of the early nineteenth century through the work of Marx to the divergent perspectives of Lenin, Kautsky and Bernstein at the beginning of the twentieth century. Marx's writings, Anweiler suggests, reveal a basic tension in socialist support for expanding local autonomy.[15] In some writings, Marx called for communal self-government essentially as a way of challenging and bringing down bourgeois institutions through dual power. In the 'Address to the Communist League' in 1850 Marx distinguished this strategy from a simple advocacy of local self-government: 'the workers must strike ... for a clear cut centralisation of power in the hands of the state authority. They must not let themselves be led astray by democratic talk of communal liberties, self-government and the like.'[16] Yet later, in his

endorsement of the Paris Commune, Marx saw the establishment
of a pyramid of self-governing communes in a more positive way as
the very political structure for the economic liberation of the
proletariat. This basic tension in attitudes towards local self-
government underlay Menshevik and Bolshevik attitudes to the role
of local soviets, and surfaced more openly in the bitter arguments
amongst European socialists on the interpretation of the Commune
as a basis for a critique of the new Soviet state.[17] Bernstein's
criticisms of both Marx and Lenin led him to lay greater stress on
extending local government, as an indispensable preliminary to
the realisation of socialism through deepening working-class
experience of democracy.[19]

These tensions between centralism and decentralism, between
local autonomy as a tactical means of undermining the bourgeois
state and local autonomy as a training ground in socialist
democracy, were more weakly developed in the British debates.
The largely non-Marxist and even anti-theoretical basis of the
Labour Party insulated it from many aspects of the Continental
debate.

*Centralisation tendencies in Party ideology and the development of
the welfare state*

The progressive centralisation of the Party's focus and activities
from the 1920s on can be explained by a number of interlocking
factors. The ultimate defeat of Poplar and the 'Little Moscows'
and the blocking of advance at local levels by Conservative
majorities in Parliament in the 1930s were important factors, but
there were also deeper factors at work relating both to the
structural characteristics of the British state and the ideology of the
Party.

At a structural level, the Party operated within a government
setting that emphasised the power of Parliament over the local
authorities, lacked any intermediate levels between central and
local government, and provided no local government executive
structures as a basis for powerful local leaders to emerge. As has
been noted earlier, this distinctive form of local/central relations
had its origins far back in the nineteenth century. Labour did not
challenge this structure, and increasingly from 1926 onwards

became accommodated to it as part of an emerging social democratic compromise between capital and labour.

This accommodation was interlinked with certain ideological factors peculiar to the Party. Sharpe has identified three such factors.[19] Firstly, there were centralisation tendencies inherent in the trades unions with their concern for an orderly system of national wage bargaining. Insofar as the unions provided the foundation of the Party, their organisational pre-occupations shaped the Party's pyramidal and anti-localist form. Secondly, the Party's adoption of Keynesian policies for demand management led to an increasing emphasis on central macro-economic planning. Thirdly, the priority attached to combating inequality worked in favour of uniformity and the standardisation of services between areas, and worked against local autonomy and diversity. To these factors may be added a fourth. The uncritical, but dominant, Fabian view of the state offered little resistance to a shift in emphasis towards the central state as the most effective agent of reform. Although the early Fabians had sought a balance between local and central power and between participation and efficiency it was the centralising, efficiency-oriented, aspects of their complex formulae which proved easier to translate into policy.

The preoccupation with reform from the centre was as apparent on the Left as on the Right by the 1930s. Some of the publications of the Socialist League, for example, specifically dealt with the role of local authorities and local democracy under a future socialist government. It is significant that these blueprints assigned the major role in socialist advance to the central government and reduced local government to a relatively passive role, at least in a transition period. For example, in his paper in *Problems of a Socialist Government* published by the Socialist League in 1933, Atlee laid out the role of local government in the implementation of socialism.[20] Assuming that a socialist government had come to power at a time of national emergency, Atlee's initial concern in this transitional period was to ensure that recalcitrant local authorities could be brought into line with the national plan. This was to be done by establishing new regional authorities with appointed socialist commissioners who would work through a planning committee of experts to co-ordinate local authority programmes, particularly in housebuilding. A similar emphasis on controlling local government from the centre is found in G. R.

Mitchison's *The First Workers' Government*.[21] Both Atlee and
Mitchison certainly envisaged a greater devolution of power *after*
the emergency transitional period, but both also saw a key role
continuing to be played by the new and powerful regional tiers of
government.

The political and economic context of the sweeping 1945 victory
provided an ideal framework for these centralising tendencies to be
translated into practice, although not in the radical way conceived
by the Left. Central–local relations were transformed as part of the
construction of the welfare state which represented the 'post-war
settlement' between capital and labour. Although local government
lost some functions and gained others, the overall effect was
increased centralisation and the sacrifice of local autonomy to the
administrative needs of particular national services.[22] Now that it
had power, the Party was 'more interested in nationalisation than
municipalisation'[23] and local government, it was claimed, emerged
from the construction of the welfare state 'greatly weakened and
diminished in status'.[24] Although the need for some reform of
boundaries was recognised, the local authority associations could
not agree on what form they should take. Bevan, who had formal
responsibility for local government, had other priorities, and there
was no major discussion of local government at Party Conferences
for nearly a decade after the war. Decentralisation and local
democracy do not seem to have figured highly on the political
agenda of either the Left or the Right within the Party.

*'Technocratic-collectivism' and local government reform in the
1960s*

Although pressures for the reform of local government built up in
the 1950s, and tentative steps were taken by the Conservatives to re-
organise functions and territory, it was not until the 1960s that
major reforms were launched, and by a Labour government. These
reforms were shaped by a quite different economic and political
context to 1945 and reflected important shifts in Party ideology.
Local government reform had not been a theme in the 1964 election
and Crossman's decision in 1966 to start a major overhaul was
based upon short-term political considerations. However, the
restructuring of central/local relations on the scale that emerged

cannot be put down simply to impulsive gesture of one man. Crossman's decision precipitated reform in response to deeper pressures at work within the economy and the state.

Corrigan has attempted to relate these reforms to the beginnings of the economic crisis that deepened in the 1970s and 1980s, and in particular to the changing needs of monopoly capital.[25] Monopoly capital, he argues, played a leading role in capital restructuring in response to this crisis, but effective capital restructuring also necessitated the restructuring of the labour force, through greater labour mobility and a diminished attachment to area. For capital and labour restructuring to be carried out, Corrigan argues, 'it was necessary to have a set of state apparatuses that were themselves restructured; sets of relationships that could deal much more effectively with the large units of monopoly capital involved in the period.'[26] The needs of monopoly capital, therefore, underlay the reforms that produced larger units of local government better able to deal efficiently with bigger firms and plan larger labour-market areas. The introduction of 'corporate management' in this period also served the related needs of increasing the efficiency of local government decision-making and controlling public expenditure more tightly. 'The restructuring of the whole state machine occurred then to bring it into line with the structures and needs of monopoly capital and at the direct expense of areas of local democracy'.[27]

The bulk of the working class supported this restructuring, although for different reasons. The Labour Party launched the reforms in the name of rationality and efficiency and received support because 'the movement to larger units seemed to fit not only the needs of monopoly capital but also to build a stronger state in working-class interests.'[28] The fact that the reforms took place entirely within the constraints of capitalist social relations, however, effectively shifted the state structures more towards the interests of capital and further eroded the local terrain of class struggle.

The basic thrust of Corrigan's analysis, in linking forms of state restructuring and changing central–local relations to changes in capital accumulation and class conflict, is surely correct. However, his analysis is clearly a variant of the theory of 'state monopoly capitalism' and this theory is open to the criticisms that in its 'class-logic' variant it reduces the state to an instrument of monopoly capital, and in its 'capital-logic' form it reduces state policy to an automatic response to the changing technical needs of capital.[29] Corrigan's reference to class struggle and the articulation of working-class interests through Labour Party ideology partly counters this, but this aspect of the analysis remains underdeveloped. Yet the role of Labour's ideology in the construction of a consensus that appeared to reconcile both capitalist and working-class interests would appear to crucial. In this respect Warde's analysis of Labour's ideology in this period as 'technocratic-collectivism' seems particularly useful.[30]

Warde argues that the late 1960s saw the beginnings of the collapse of the post-war consensus with the onset of economic crisis and the re-emergence of class conflict. The collapse of the consensus undermined the dominant 'social reformist' ideology of the Party that had emerged by the 1950s. 'Technocratic-collectivism' developed in the period 1963–71, as a new ideology around which the Party could cohere. It was not just a form of pragmatic opportunism associated with the Wilson years, but a coherent perspective and an innovative response to the new social and economic conditions. Great emphasis was placed on the technical and scientific revolution as the motor of change for restructuring British capitalism (Wilson's 'white hot heat of the technological revolution'). Reconstructing the British state in the interests of rationality and efficiency was integral to this process. This emphasis on efficient administration by experts as the key to social progress represented a form of reconstructed Fabianism that contained none of the antipathy to the centralisation of state power apparent in social reformism. The 'rationalising' of local government into larger and more centrally-controlled units can be seen, therefore, as an integral component of this broader ideology. Through it the interests of capital and labour appeared to converge in the reconstruction of central–local relations. The tragedy for Labour was that the reconstruction worked in practice far more in the interests of capital.

In spite of this, technocratic-collectivism failed to reconstruct British capitalism, and the deepening of the economic crisis and the heightening of class tension from 1968 onwards undermined its viability as a strategy. The 1970s, therefore, saw attempts to construct a new ideological framework for the Party as the basis for a new relationship between capital and labour in the interests of restoring economic growth. Jessop and Warde have used the term 'tripartism' to describe this framework.[31] And its development had important implications for local government and local–central relations.

Tripartism and local government: 1972–79

Tripartism, Warde argues, represented a new collaborative solution to the crisis in the worsening conditions of the 1970s. It involved a transformation of technocratic-collectivism, recognising the collapse of consensus and the re-emergence of class division, and revolving around a 'corporatist' strategy based on an uneasy alliance between central government, the leading trades unions and leading sectors of big business. The 'social contract' was one product of this new collaborative style of politics.

This period also saw a turn-round in the growth of public expenditure as part of the programme for restoring private growth and investment.[32] As shown in Chapter 9 however, aggregate public expenditure figures conceal the fact that central government expenditure continued to rise while the cuts, and their attendant unpopularity, were displaced on to local government programmes. The re-organised local government structures, introduced earlier in the interests of efficiency, were now used to make cuts and exert more direct central control. It could be argued, however, that the extent of the cuts was constrained, at least initially, by the nature of the corporatist strategy adopted, in the sense that many local government services were clearly part of the 'social wage' and arguments over the social wage played at least some part in the bargaining over the social contract. In the event the worsening economic situation and pressure to reduce public expenditure even further undermined the strategy, and led to its collapse in 'the winter of discontent'. The defeat of the Labour Government in 1979 and the abandonment of tripartism, opened the way to much deeper cuts in local government expenditure and an unprecedented restructuring of central–local relations.

Labour and the local state in the 1970s

In conclusion, if the development of local government in Britain may be described as the 'neutralisation of territorial politics' then the Labour Party has certainly played a full part in the process. There has been no strong countervailing ideology to resist tendencies towards centralisation since the early years of the Party. Nevertheless, as I have tried to indicate, different phases in the development of Party ideology have not had the same consequences for local–central relations. The end results of these developments by the 1970s was a centralised local government system, heavily bureaucratised and professionalised, remote from a local public who often showed so little interest in electoral participation that were warnings of a breakdown in the system of representation. The implications for local Labour politics have been graphically portrayed in a number of studies of Labour authorities and Labour groups in the 1970s.[33] In the 1950s and 1960s it is possible to find evidence of cities being run by strong local leaders almost akin to 'city bosses'[34] but the development of corporate management structures in the 1970s tended to support the dominance of a leadership caucus of Party leader and committee chairmen. Green, for example, presents a picture of a closed and exclusionary system of one-party rule in Newcastle in which a Labour group, itself relatively insulated from Party influence, served largely as an uncritical forum for legitimising the decisions made by a small leadership clique. Cockburn presents a picture of Labour politics in Lambeth in which backbenchers were largely excluded from centres of decision-making by a high-level partnership between the leadership and senior officers. Lacking any clear ideological drive, such systems degenerated into mechanisms for containing crises and incorporating dissent. By the 1970s it could be argued, many Labour authorities were performing an essentially managerial role thinly dressed in the rhetoric of an impoverished form of municipal socialism.

The picture should not be overdrawn. There have always been differences between local Labour councils and parties in terms of radicalness and political style, reflecting local economic factors, local class structures and distinctive histories of past conflicts. Starting in the 1970s, a number of trends also began to emerge which started a re-examination of established orthodoxies. Firstly, deepening crises in many local economies, coupled with increasing demands on welfare services, imposed new pressures, and local authorities increasingly moved from being agents of an expanding welfare state to the role of inadequately financed managers of local crises. This development set up new strains and tensions in local political systems.

Secondly, many authorities were increasingly affected by internal divisions within the Labour Party associated with the increasing influence of the 'new urban Left'. A swing to the Left was often associated with an influx of new and younger councillors who viewed local government more in terms of a platform for alternative socialist policies and, if necessary, as a base for mobilising popular support for confrontation with central government, in the process challenging many of the traditional assumptions held by Labour groups. In some authorities changes in political composition followed from rapid shifts in local occupational and class structures.[35] However, 'the Left' was not an undifferentiated force within the Party. Its character varied in different localities. There were different balances of the traditional Tribunite left, the newer 'Bennite' left, and Militant in different localities, with important differences in class background, organisational structure and policy. These developments generated internal Party conflicts along lines that were partly political, partly generational, partly class based and partly a matter of political style.[36]

The rise of the Left was associated with increasing pressures to make Labour groups more internally democratic and more accountable to local Party organisations. Demands for more back bench involvement began to challenge patterns of leadership control based upon systems of corporate management, particularly where purely managerial solutions failed to deal adequately with local crises. The call for local council groups to be made more accountable to city-wide management committees, comprised of constituency and trades union delegates (a re-opening of the debates of the 1930s before the issuing of model standing orders for Labour groups) was the local dimension to the much wider debate within the Party on the accountability of the Parliamentary leadership to Conference and the crucial question of control of the Manifesto. Party organisations at the city level in many areas instituted annual party conferences, rolling manifestos and standing working groups to develop clearer policy objectives and exert more influence on the local manifesto and its implementation.[37] This resulted in greater involvement by grass roots activists and closer ties with trades councils and tenants organisations, but at the same time produced increasing conflict with Labour groups over boundaries of responsibility and accountability. These various tendencies, and their resultant conflicts, which emerged in the 1970s, have strengthened and deepened since the 1979 election.

The Conservative challenge and Labour's immediate response

The Conservative challenge

The acute political problems posed for the Labour Party by the Conservative challenge since 1979 can be more clearly appreciated by placing that challenge in the historical context outlined in the previous section. The attack on local government expenditure and autonomy has been part of a broader assault on the welfare state and has been supported by a powerful 'new Right' ideology. Hall, for example, has argued that this new ideology can best be described as 'authoritarian populism'.[38] Equipped with this ideology, Hall argues, the new Conservatism seeks to break out of the corporatist mould in which Labour's social democracy became trapped in the 1970s, and attempts to unite 'the people' against a corporatist alliance of big government, big unions and monopoly capital. In doing so it builds on the anti-statist and anti-collectivist feelings of many working people who have increasingly experienced the state as a remote form of bureaucratic repression rather than an agent of liberation working on their behalf. The 'neat elision by which the Labour Party equated gigantism and centralised planning with "socialism" '[39] has been cruelly exposed. The new Conservatism seeks to unite this new anti-statism with the traditional Conservative emphasis on responsibility and self-reliance and with popular, anti-liberal attitudes on law and order, education and race. The result is a new and powerful political and ideological base for right-wing policies. In respect of local government it underlies expenditure cuts, 'privatisation', and the 'rolling back of the state' to make way for an extension of market principles. Paradoxically it produces more centralisation but in a different form to previous periods. Central control of local authorities is justified in terms of 'setting people free' from local bureaucracies (through council house sales, for example) and protecting ratepayers from the high-spending fantasies of socialist-controlled town halls. It is part of a process where, through populist rhetoric, central government appeals direct to the local populace, by-passing the traditional mediatory structures of local elites and local bureaucracies. The result has been a qualitative shift in central–local relations which Labour has found difficult to counter. A call for a return to the situation of the 1970s does not constitute a popular and radical alternative.

The short-term response: defensive struggles

The reduction in local autonomy implicit in recent Conservative legislation has placed the whole question of opposition to central government on the local political agenda in a more acute form than at any time in the post-war period. Local Labour parties have become locked in arguments over what kind of resistance to central government would be legitimate and effective. Expanding on the organisation problems of local strategies, arguments have centred around a number of options.[40]

1. *Carry through the cuts while placing the blame for the rundown of services firmly on the Conservatives.* This may be justified in terms of bringing home to voters the folly of not electing a Labour government. It leaves Labour councils open to the criticism, however, that there is little point in having Labour control of councils if they are simply agents of central government.

2. *Protect key local services by raising the rates to offset cuts in central government grant.* This option simply passes on the costs of the cuts to ratepayers and only the poorest are shielded from reductions on real incomes by rent rebates. Apart from the electoral unpopularity of such a move including opposition from non-domestic ratepayers, the operation of the new block grant system, described in Chapter 9, has made this less feasible due to the increasing burden of extra spending thrown on to the ratepayer.

3. *Obstruct and delay implementation of new legislation within the law.* This may be possible in the short term in some policy areas, as was achieved for example with the sale of council houses. Capitulation to central government however seems inevitable in the long run, and it is hard to envisage building popular support around a strategy of bureacratic delay.

4. *Resign and strengthen the local mandate by seeking re-election*. The result might, however, be indecisive, the same problem of what to do would remain and political power would remain limited.

5. *Resign chairs but use 'majority opposition' to block cuts, redundancies and implementation of central government legislation*. This would lead sooner or later to financial chaos which might end up producing massive redundanices, direct control by central government with the appointment of commissioners and surcharging of councillors. It would require substantial community support in engineering such a crisis, which might be problematic. It would also depend on the willingness of the opposition to take up the reins in such circumstances.

6. *Directly challenge the government on a no cuts/no redundancies/no rate increases platform*. As with option 5, this would rapidly generate financial chaos, direct control from central government and surcharges. Again, it would require the mobilisation of popular support and neither this, nor option 5 would be open to any one council acting alone. Simultaneous action by most major Labour authorities with the active co-operation of public sector unions would be necessary. There is little experience of such action being successfully organised in the past and it is unlikely that the appointment of commissioners to take over 'spendthrift' councils would generate a wave of opposition among ordinary people at the local level.

The question of what is 'within the law' has been politically important. The Labour leadership has restricted its support to opposition within the law, though the 1983 Manifesto included proposals to extend these limits by abolishing the threat of surcharge and disqualification for action deemed *ultra vires*. Some of the actions proposed have however brought local Labour groups and parties up to and possibly beyond the limits of the law and the unwritten rules of parliamentary democracy. At what stage is it justifiable for local interests to unite to defy a democratically elected central government in the name of local democracy? Has the present government gone sufficiently far down the road towards economic suicide and the erosion of essential freedom to be deemed to have forfeited its mandate, thus justifying outright defiance? These are crucial issues for a Party believing in a democratic road to socialism. Moreover, they are the kinds of issues that most local councils have not had to confront since the days of Poplar in the 1920s. They proved divisive within the Party then and they have proved divisive now, with some local Labour groups split wide apart and left-wing rebels expelled.

Even if agreement could be reached on appropriate forms of action, major organisational problems would emerge reflective of the peculiar nature of urban-based political struggles. Saunders has argued in Chapter 2, for example, that local government in Britain is typically concerned with the provision of 'social consumption', and consumption issues typically evoke competitive struggles between different consumption sectors. Although Saunders' claim that local political struggles are therefore not typically class struggles is open to criticism, his analysis does draw attention to the acute problems surrounding the building of alliances between disparate interests at the local level.

The public sector unions are a key element in the building of such local alliances around the defence of local government services. In Chapter 2 in fact, Saunders suggests they could form the political cement to bind together different and competing interests. Certainly, local public service workers constitute a potentially powerful force as the result of a rapid growth in numbers and in terms of unionisation,[41] but important divisions exist within this occupational grouping that pose further organisational problems. Local state employment embraces both working-class positions and what might be termed either middle-class or 'contradictory' class positions,[42] which can be affected in quite different ways by the same public expenditure cuts. There is clearly, therefore, a long way to go in building up a coherent alliance of public sector workers, let alone linking up with the consumers of public services in effective urban coalitions.

It is also clear there is a need for local authorities to act together, to avoid individual initiatives resulting in authorities being isolated and picked off, as in the past. In this sense the coming together in July 1983 of those Labour authorities most at risk from selective government action, and the aim to initiate a broadly based 'Campaign for Local Democracy' was particularly important. It is not surprising, however, that faced with major political and organisational problems, most Labour councils have chosen to avoid the more extreme oppositional strategies, while those such as Lothian which have taken a more aggressive stance have found themselves isolated. However, the very fact that internal debates have taken place has been a powerful spur to rethinking the whole role of local government for the future. As a result, serious attention is now being paid within the Party, after a long period of neglect, to the connection between local government reform and socialist advance. This re-examination of traditional perspectives may have a much greater significance in the long run than the limited, defensive achievements of the immediate post–1979 years.

Socialism and local government: the longer-term perspective

Criticisms of traditional policies

Three lines of criticism of existing theories and practices seem to have underlain many of the proposals for longer-term reform.

1. *'Anti-statism' and the critique of the welfare state.* An important line of new thinking on local government reform has grown out of a wider critique of the welfare state. For example, critics have pointed to the inadequacy of traditional Fabian perspectives, which have led to the equating of socialism with the expansion of the welfare state.[43] An effective political strategy must, it has been argued, begin with a more critical understanding of the state, which recognises it as an expression of the class relations of capitalism, not an institution apart from those soical relations. This approach recognises that most people's experience of the state is contradictory, reflecting the contradictory nature of the state itself in responding to working-class pressure in ways that also serve capitalist interests. The state thus provides services that are socially needed, but it provides them in a way that fragments class consciousness, distorts the individual's awareness of the sources of social problems, and divides those in need into fragmented and competing client groups. It is accepted that the identification of Labour with this bureaucratic and often coercive apparatus has been a potent factor in the success of the new Right's appeal to bourgeois individualism. It is important, there-fore, that political struggles centering on the state must aim at a transformation of the social relations implicit in the state and not just concentrate on a defence of state services, or a simple extension of state provision. Given the importance of local government in the

structure of the welfare state, this line of argument has particular significance at the local level and underlies a number of 'anti-statist' reform proposals.

2. *Local democracy in socialist advance.* The above critique of the state has been linked to what might be termed the 'revaluation' of local democracy. The theme of expanding democratic control has become important in discussions on workers' control as part of the Alternative Economic Strategy. It has also played a significant part in the revival of interest in local government as an important component of a democratic system. Thus, on the left of the Party, the Labour Co-ordinating Committee has defended the system of democratic local government, as a way of making local services accountable to the local electorate and countering the centralisation of power in ministerial hands. Although the existing system is sharply criticised, it is claimed that 'local government is capable of being used for socialist advance' as part of the construction of a more decentralised form of socialism.[44]

This revaluation of local democracy has been paralleled in discussions in the non-Labour Party Left as well. Thus Corrigan's perspective on the local state has been part of a wider debate within the Communist Party on the relationship between Marxism and bourgeois parliamentary democracy.[45] Parliamentary democracy, it is argued, is bourgeois only in the sense that it has existed under conditions in which the bourgeoisie has been the hegemonic class. Socialism can be seen as, in a sense, the completion of capitalism through the liberation of democracy from its restraining framework of capitalist relations. Moreover, this transformation lies at the heart of the struggle for socialism. The extension of democracy is a precondition for socialist advance on other fronts, and is not something to be put off until after a revolutionary transition, or a kind of socialist icing on the post-revolutionary cake. The Left, it is argued, must therefore put much more emphasis on the possibilities for democratising state structures, and this applies with particular force at the local level. Thus Corrigan states: 'Politics around the local branches of the state and around the local area are intelligible to working people both as a target and in terms of have a real effect'... 'it is in the localities that any real participatory democratic close intrusion into the capitalist state will be made'.[46] This does not imply that the working class can simply colonise the state bit by bit, cumulatively transforming it through democratic control into a socialist state. Struggles to democratise the local state will rather provide a set of experiences to working people that could act as a springboard to socialism.

The increasing interest in the role of democracy has not been confined to the Left either within or outside the Labour Party. There have also been signs of a significant re-appraisal on the Right. Thus Luard[47] has argued against the corrupting influence of a bureaucratic and centralised state, and argued for a return to the original ideals of socialism which are equated with the aims of establishing small-scale, local cooperative communities. In practical terms, this means adopting policies which devolve greater power to a re-organised local government system with sufficient financial autonomy to permit local diversity and local experimentation in forms of communal organisation.

3. *Pre-figurative politics and Party reform.* Finally, the above strands have interacted with a third, which stresses the importance of reforming the whole organisation and style of local Labour politics. Some of the origins can be found in the idea of 'pre-figurative politics' developed in *Beyond the Fragments.*[48] The authors used the example of the women's movement to argue for a new non-hierarchical, participatory form of organisation standing outside of the traditional Party structure, bringing together loose federal alliances of fragmented opposition particularly at the local level. Criticism of traditional, male-dominated, hierarchical Party structures were coupled with the argument that the nature of the organisation and the nature of the struggles should itself 'prefigure' socialist forms of organisation, as an important means of developing socialist consciousness. The local state was seen very much as a focus for these political struggles.

Although the idea of 'loose federal alliances' does not seem to have resulted in significant political developments, the critique of traditional party structures and organisation has borne fruit in proposals for reform and re-orientation coming from currents within the Labour Party. A recent pamphlet by the Labour Co-ordinating Committee places great stress on building alliances with forces outside of the Party, and building an 'extra-Parliamentary' mass base to underpin Parliamentary advance.[49] The authors also criticise the traditional pyramidal structure of the Party with its hierarchies of delegates, oriented largely to electoral needs and the transmission of resolution to higher bodies. Such a structure, it is argued, is inadequate for the development of policy, the building of alliances and the involvement of a mass membership at the local level.

Proposals for reform

These criticisms have led to a range of proposals for reform, aiming to strengthen local democracy, open up the local state and restructure the style and organisation of local politics. These include proposals for decentralisation, local economic and employment initiatives and action relating to women and black people as discussed in later chapters. Other proposals have related to reform of local government's financial base, strengthening local government powers, and the role of central government in setting minimum standards. Finally there have been proposals for reform of Labour Party political structures and practices designed to provide more space at the lower level for policy discussion 'outside the resolution format and away from the pressure of routine Party business'[50] – local branches would operate more as centres for collective campaigning work, within a framework of greater accountability to local Party structures of elected Party groups on councils.

Such proposals, however, leave many problems to be resolved. In particular one can identify, first, the problems in economic and employment policy of integrating local initiatives with regional and national co-ordination and planning – the danger is that a future Labour government, elected possibly at a time of national economic crisis, would give immediate priority to centrally-initiated strategy. Second, in relation to decentralisation there are dilemmas in devolving real power and decision-making without (given scarcity) reinforcing or generating inequalities and injustices. Thirdly, it can be argued that effectiveness of service delivery has to be improved before any real interest in popular control will be generated – what Griffiths has termed 'bridging the credibility gap'.[51] Finally, the 'anti-statist' critique of the existing welfare state, which argues for a more participatory, decentralised welfare system with greater informal and voluntary sector involvement, has interesting and disturbing parallels with the Right's attacks on state bureaucracy and arguments for self-help and voluntary provision, which remain to be thought through.[52] What *is* clear, however, is that full implementation of the kinds of reforms discussed above would result in a dramatic restructuring of local–central government relations, open up new space for the development of radical municipal socialism, and fundamentally change the nature of Labour politics and government at the local level.

The next five years

To return closer to the realities of the moment, however, it is obvious that the election defeat of June 1983 was a crushing blow for Labour and came before the new initiatives and discussion of the issues they raised had proceeded very far. Theoretical discussion on the relationships between socialism and local government reform will probably continue, but Labour has lost any opportunity of introducing any fundamental reform of central–local relations. The immediate issue therefore is once again, what can a limited number of Labour authorities achieve under five more years of Thatcherism, and how can their actions contribute to a general Labour revival?

Some authorities will be under more immediate and direct threat – the Labour authorities singled out for selective action in retaliation for 'overspending', and the GLC and metropolitan counties, faced, on a slightly longer time-scale, with abolition. It will be a major challenge to Labour to resist these changes, given the evident unpopularity of large rate increases and the fact that some smaller authorities would be happy to gain powers and possibly finance as the result of the dismemberment of larger authorities.

Beyond immediate defensive strategies, the Left will undoubtedly place its hopes on the longer-term popularity of the kinds of innovative policies outlined earlier which are being pursued by authorities like Sheffield and the GLC, and future Parliamentary success. Clearly, the hope has gone in the short term, of linking local economic initiatives to an expansionary Alternative Economic Strategy at the national level. The aim of rebuilding a local industrial base and shortening the dole queue will have to take second place to a more limited strategy of using new forms of decentralised popular planning to present the elements of a socialist alternative, albeit in embryo form, and build a basis of popular support for more fundamental reforms in the future.

There is certainly no guarantee of the political success of such a strategy. Evidence of the electorate's response is admittedly limited, but gives grounds for cautious optimism at best. Labour Walsall's experiment in the decentralisation of council services and community mobilisation, much lauded in some left quarters, was followed by election defeat in 1982 (although the experiment survived the change in political control).[53] In the May 1983 local government elections, although the Labour vote appeared to hold up better in large rather than smaller cities, the regional effect was perhaps the most significant pattern. There was a 1 per cent swing to the Conservatives in the South, a 1 per cent swing to Labour in the Midlands and a 3 per cent swing to Labour in the North. It would require detailed analysis to establish the precise electoral effects of left-orientated councils within this regional pattern, although *The Economist* quickly came to the conclusion that 'extremists did as well as moderates everywhere'.[54] In the June General Election the regional pattern was even stronger, but Massey claims to detect some slight evidence of Labour's vote holding up in large cities where the elements of new urban alliances have been formed, and suggests that links between the new urban Left and the traditional Labourism of Labour's Northern heartland may provide a base for recovery.[55] One should not perhaps expect too much in electoral terms at this stage. The new urban strategies have so far drawn in only a thin layer of activists, community groups and trades unionists, and national and regional effects have overwhelmed local patterns.

Labour clearly has a major challenge in front of it, at the local as much as the national level. The scale of the challenge is now even greater than it was in the 1979–83 period. In the General Election, Labour lost heavily among skilled workers, owner occupiers and council house purchasers, and among those who live in the South. Arguably, to expand out of its shrunken urban and regional heartlands, Labour now needs local government policies that will not only meet the needs of poorer council tenants, local government workers, the unemployed and ethnic minorities (sectors of the electorate who continued to support Labour); it also needs policies that will appeal to owner occupiers, council tenants who want to become own occupiers and skilled workers in growing service and high technology industries. Labour cannot win power in many areas without support from these sectors. This is not for example an argument for a populist embrace of owner occupation and unrestrictive council house sales. It is however an argument for some fundamental thinking on what constitutes a program of reform that would be socialist *and* popular with broader sections of the community.

Notes and References

1. D. Ashford, *Policy and Politics in Britain* (Basil Blackwell, 1981); D. Ashford, *British Dogmatism and French Pragmatism* (Allen and Unwin, 1982).
2. S. S. Duncan and M. Goodwin, 'The Local State: Functionalism, Autonomy and Class Relations in Cockburn and Saunders', *Political Geography Quarterly*, vol. 1, no. 1 1982, pp. 66–77.
3. Ibid.
4. G. D. H. Cole, *A. History of the Labour Party from 1914* (Kegan Paul, 1948).
5. S. MacIntyre, *A Proletarian Science: Marxism in Britain* (Cambridge University Press, 1980).
6. A. M. McBriar, *Fabian Socialism and English Politics: 1884–1918* (Cambridge University Press, 1962): A. Sancton, 'British Socialist Theories of the Division of Power by Area', *Political Studies*, vol. XXIV, 1976, pp. 158–170.
7. S. Webb and B. Webb, *A Constitution for the Socialist Commonwealth of Great Britain* (Longman, 1920).
8. For a detailed analysis, see B. Donoughue and G. Jones, *Herbert Morrison: Portrait of a Politician* (Weidenfield and Nicolson, 1973).
9. S. MacIntyre, *A Proletarian Science*.
10. S. MacIntyre, *Little Moscows: Communism and Working-Class Militancy in Inter-War Britain* (Croom Helm, 1980).
11. N. Branson, *Poplarism, 1919–25* (Lawrence and Wishart, 1979).
12. S. MacIntyre, *Little Moscows*.
13. G. D. H. Cole, *Guild Socialism Re-stated* (Leonard Parson, 1920); A. L. Wright, *G. D. H. Cole and Socialist Democracy* (Clarendon Press, 1979).
14. I. J. Sharpe, 'The Labour Party and the Geography of Inequality: a Puzzle', in D. Kavanagh (ed.), *The Politics of the Labour Party* (Allen and Unwin, 1982), p. 154.
15 O. Anweiler, *The Soviets: The Russian Workers, Peasants and Soldiers Councils*, (Pantheon, 1974).
16. Quoted by Anweiler, *The Soviets*, p. 15.
17. K. Kautsky, *The Dictatorship of the Proletariat* (University of Michigan Press, 1964): M. Salvadani, *Karl Kautsky and the Socialist Revolution 1880–1938*, (New Left Books, 1976).
18. E. Bernstein, *Evolutionary Socialism* (Schocken Books, 1961).
19. I. J. Sharpe, 'The Labour Party and the Geography of Inequality: a Puzzle'.

20. C. Atlee, 'Local Government and the Socialist Plan', in C. Addison *et al., Problems of a Socialist Government* (Gollancz, 1933).
21. G. Mitchison, *The First Worker's Government* (Gollancz, 1934).
22. E. Dell, 'Labour and Local Government', *Political Quarterly*, vol. 31, 1960, pp. 333–347.
23. B. Keith-Lucas and P. Richards, *A History of Local Government in the Twentieth Century* (Allen and Unwin, 1978), p. 40.
24. W. A. Robson, 'Labour and Local government', *Political Quarterly*, vol. XXIV, no. 1, 1953, pp. 39–55.
25. P. Corrigan, 'The Local State: the Struggle for Democracy', *Marxism Today*, July 1979, pp. 203–9.
26. Ibid, p. 206.
27. Ibid, p. 207.
28. Ibid, p. 207.
29. B. Jessop, *The Capitalist State* (Martin Robertson, 1982), Ch. 2.
30. A. Warde, *Consensus and Beyond: the Development of Labour Party Strategy since the Second World War* (Manchester University Press, 1982).
31. Ibid; B. Jessop, 'Corporatism, Parliamentarism and Social Democracy,' in P. Schmitter and G. Lehmbruch (ed.), *Trends Towards Corporatist Intermediation* (Sage, 1979).
32. I. Gough, *The Political Economy of the Welfare State* (Macmillan, 1979).
33. See, for example, K. Newton, *Second City Politics* (Oxford University Press, 1976); C. Cockburn, *The Local State* (Pluto Press, 1977); P. Saunders, *Urban Politics* (Penguin, 1980); D. Green *Power and Party in an English City* (Allen and Unwin, 1981).
34. See case studies in G. W. Jones and A. Norton, *Political Leadership in Local Authorities* (University of Birmingham, Institute of Local Government Studies, 1978); H. Elcock, 'Tradition and Change in Labour Party Politics: The Decline and Fall of the City Boss', *Political Studies*, vol. XXIX, no. 3, 1981.
35. See, for example, A. Glassberg, *Representation and Urban Community* (Macmillan, 1981).
36. I. Gordon and P. Whiteley, 'Social Class and Political Attitudes: The Case of Labour Councillors', *Political Studies*, vol. XXVII, no. 1, pp. 99–113.
37. For example, see C. Fudge, 'Winning an Election and Gaining Control: the Formulation and Implementation of a "Local" Political Manifesto', S. Barrett and C. Fudge (eds), *Policy and Action* (Methuen 1981), pp. 133–142.
38. S. Hall, 'The Great Moving Right Show', *Marxism Today*, January 1979, pp. 14–20,; S. Hall, 'Popular–Democratic versus Authoritarian Populism: Two Ways of "Taking Democracy Seriously"', in A. Hunt (ed.) *Marxism and Democracy* (Lawrence and Wishart, 1980).
39. H. Rose and S. Rose, 'Moving Right Out of Welfare – and the Way Back', *Critical Social Policy*, vol. 2, no. 2, 1982, p. 13.
40. E. Preston, *The Local Counter Attack* (Independent Labour Party,

1980); P. Dunnipace and R. Jones, *No Cuts, No Rate or Rent Rises* (Socialist Challenge Pamphlet, not dated); Labour Co-ordinating Committee, *Can Local Government Survive?* (Labour Co-ordinating Committee, not dated); K. Bassett, 'Which Way for Labour Councils?', *Local Government Studies*, vol. 8, no. 1, 1982, pp. 8–12.

41. P. Dunleavy, *Urban Political Analysis* (Macmillan 1980), Ch. 3.
42. See D. Johnson and C. O'Donnel, 'The Accumulation Crisis and Service Professionals' and J. Gregg Robinson, 'A Class Analysis of State Workers', in Reader Editorial Collection, *Crisis in the Public Sector* (Monthly Review Press, not dated).
43. London–Edinburgh Weekend Return Group, *In and Against the State* (Pluto, 1980).
44. Labour Co-ordinating Committee, *Can Local Government Survive?*
45. See the various contributions to A. Hunt (ed.), *Marxism and Democracy* (Lawrence and Wishart, 1980).
46. P. Corrigan, 'The Local State: the Struggle for Democracy', p. 209.
47. E. Luard, *Socialism without the State* (Macmillan, 1979); E. Luard, *Socialism or the Grass Roots* (Fabian Tracts 468, 1980).
48. S. Rowbotham, L, Segal and H. Wainwright, *Beyond the Fragments* (Merlin Press, 1979).
49. Labour Co-ordinating Committee, *Labour and Mass Politics* (Labour Co-ordinating Committee, not dated).
50. Labour Co-ordinating Committee, *Labour and Mass Politics*.
51. D. Griffiths, 'Bridging the Credibility Gap', *Chartist*, no. 92, 1982, p. 25. See subsequent issues for a continuation of the debate.
52. C. Offe, 'Some Contradictions of the Modern Welfare State', *Critical Social Policy*, vol. 2, no. 2, 1982.
53. J. David, 'Walsall and Decentralisation', *Critical Social Policy*, issue 7, 1983, pp. 75–79.
54. *The Economist*, 14 May, 1983, p. 30.
55. D. Massey,'The Contours of Victory', *Marxism Today*, vol. 27, no. 7, 1983.

5 Women's Initiatives in Local Government

SUE GOSS

The early 1980s saw the establishment by several local councils of women's committees, to take up issues of equality, the representation of women and women's interests. In 1978 in fact, a Women's Rights Working Party had been established in the London Borough of Lewisham, but the main initiatives came after the GLC election in 1981 and the London Borough elections of 1982, following through manifesto commitments on issues relating to women. Confined so far to London authorities, women's committees or sub-committees have been set up by the GLC, and in Camden, Islington, Southwark, Hackney and Greenwich. More are being proposed and discussed in a variety of authorities in London and throughout the country. Committees have been backed by the appointment of specialist staff, 'political' appointments in a sense, drawing in some cases on an explicit socialist feminist commitment and experience, and by the establishment of spending budgets – ranging from £7 million in the case of the GLC for 1983/4 to a few thousand in some of the Boroughs. Other local councils, while not establishing separate committees, have made some commitment through the appointment of officers with specific responsibility for equal opportunities (though frequently linked with race issues under a general equal opportunities banner) or, as for example in Sheffield City Council's Employment Department, for women's employment issues.

These developments are linked to the more general progress of the women's liberation movement, and to struggles within the labour movement nationally to achieve greater priority for women's representation issues and concerns. They also reflect, changes in the Labour party at the local level through the 1970s. As more women gained confidence within women's groups and developed ideas, they began to move into more traditional arenas, local labour parties and the trades union movement, joining with women there. The major campaigns of the 1960s on pay and discrimination, around abortion and self-determination, and the growth of the women's liberation movement began, at least, to bring changes in the traditional spectrum. Within the Labour Party, previously moribund women's sections have begun in some places to develop as foci for discussing and bringing forward women's demands. Nationally, greater attention is being paid to the Women's Advisory Conference, although its resolutions remain only advisory. In 1982, motions were passed demanding that women's members on the Party's National Executive Committe be directly elected from the Women's Conference, that at least one woman should be shortlisted when selecting parliamentary candidates and that five motions from the Women's Conference be accepted on to the Party's Annual Conference agenda each year.

More generally, women have pointed out the lack of attention to the role of women, and the irrelevance to women of much left strategy. The labour movement's Alternative Economic Strategy in particular has been criticised for neglecting the 'issues raised by the women's liberation movement on what socialism is and who it is for,'[1] and failing to examine the implication of concepts such as 'full employment' or 'workers' control' for women. It has been argued that we need to start the other way round, by asking first of all 'how shall we care for and support our children' and then considering 'how to achieve a more equitable way of sharing between men and women society's resources on the one hand and its paid and unpaid work on the other.'[2] Some male theorist have begun to take these criticisms seriously,[3] and the 1982 Labour Party Programme does put forward policies on women's employment, child-care, welfare benefits and tighter legislation on sex discrimination.

The new women's committees, while reflecting the development of the women's movement and struggles within the labour movement nationally, raise important issues about the opportunities for and constraints on work within local authorities, and the priorities of socialist and feminist strategies at a local level. The origins of specific initiatives in different localities have varied considerably, as have the types of formal structure and representation which have been established and the issues that have been taken up. There are however common threads. This chapter sets out the initiatives which have been taken, looking in turn at the issues on which the new committees have focussed. These have included, first, the under-representation of women and women's issues in formal political structures; second, the particular place of women in the workforce; and, third, the relationship between women, the family and the welfare state. This leads on to a discussion of political struggles at a local level in the context of women's needs and demands, and finally an attempt to examine the issues and problems raised by women's initiatives in local government thus far.

Women's committees

By spring 1983, women's committees had been established in one form or another in the GLC and six London boroughs (summarised in Table 5.1). The first initiative dates from 1978, when women's groups in Lewisham organised around the local women's centre to demand that the Council took the initiative on equal rights for women. A Women's Rights Working Party was set up with a membership half of councillors and half of women from local groups, the latter elected from an open meeting at the Women's Centre.

TABLE 5.1 Women's committees in London

Authority	Set Up	Committee Status	Budget 1983/4*	Staff
Lewisham	1978	Women's Rights Working Party – now full Cttee	160,000	appointing
GLC	1981	full Committee	6,960,000	18
Camden	1982	full Committee	620,000	3 but expanding
Islington	1982	full Committee	100,000	4
Southwark	1982	full Committee	120,000	3
Hackney	1982	Sub-Committee of Policy & Resources	150,000	2
Greenwich	1982	Sub-Committee of Community Affairs	–	1

*Budgets to nearest 10,000

Because the Working Party reported directly to the main policy committee, and was co-chaired by the leader, its views were injected at a high level of the Council's policy-making process, despite its advisory status. Issues were raised either by the women's representatives or by local authority members or officers. The women's representatives did much of the research and prepared papers for the Working Party, meeting between the formal committee cycle to agree on action to be taken and to plan interventions at the next meeting. Over the past four years, the Working Party has dealt with mortgage policies, employment, child-care, housing allocations for single parents, leisure and recreation, the licensing of sex shops, training schemes and immigration, as well as successfully re-opening women's public lavatories in the evening. Recently, however, councillors have felt overtaken by the establishment in other authorities of full women's committees, and the new Labour administration is about to set up a full council committee, causing some bitterness among local women's groups who were not consulted, and who feel that in exchange for possibly greater influence, their working party will be swallowed up by the council machine. Under the new structure, the support group is to be expanded, and will elect six women who will be co-opted as full members of the Committee.

The second initiative came from the new Labour GLC in 1981. Commitments had been made to women's rights, and through the energies of a few feminists on the Council the new administration was persuaded, by a narrow vote, to set up a full Women's Committe. Of the eleven committee members eight are women and three are men, and of the seven Labour members only four are women. In its first year the Committee had a budget of £500,000 to set up a women's unit of fourteen staff, and to give grants to voluntary organisations totalling £300,000. In 1984, the budget has been increased to £6.961 million, of which nearly £6 million is to grant-aid new projects in London. The Committee has attempted to involve women from all over London by holding open meetings, and setting up working parties on employment, child-care, ethnic minority women, lesbian women, violence against women, women with disabilities, women and social work, planning and the police. A co-ordinating group brings the work of these groups together and discusses the work of the full Committee. Eight women from the open meeting have been co-opted onto the main Committee, with the agreement that of those eight, four should be black, one should be disabled, one a lesbian and two trades unionists. A wide range of reports have been presented on health workers and low pay, the economic status of women in London, women and housing, apprenticeship, training and female genital mutilation. Campaigning issues have been identified as health and the defence of women's health facilities, advertising and images of women, and unemployment. A women's 'signing on' campaign has been launched to encourage women to register as unemployed. A major and controversial part of the Committee work has been to give grants to women's projects – grants to *Spare Rib* and the Greenham Common Peace Camp have raised a political outcry from opposition members, although far outweighed by grants to creches, day nurseries, women's centres, health projects and hospitals. Child-care will form the centre of the Committee's grant funding for next year, with £3,647 million of the £5,954 million for new developments being grant-aid to child care projects in the voluntary sector throughout London.

The borough elections in May 1982 ushered in several new Labour administrations, many of which had followed the GLC in creating a democratic manifesto-making process and had made manifesto commitments to women's rights. Camden set up a Women's Committee immediately after the May elections as the first stage in a restructuring of committees. The Labour committee members are all women, but the Conservatives, with only two women councillors, had to add some men. With strong support form the Labour group and greater financial freedom than other London Boroughs. the Camden Committee has followed the GLC more closely. A Women's Unit was set up with three workers. The Committee had a budget of £300,000 in 1982–3, and £620,000 in 1983–4 of which £500,000 was for grants to the voluntary sector. A large public meeting in December 1982 agreed that women should be elected from an annual open meeting as co-opted members of the committee. Again, attempts were made to ensure the representation of black, lesbian, disabled and older women, as well as trades unionists. A co-ordinating committee was set up together with a wide range of working parties. A 'Women's Bus' has been funded to travel around housing estates, workplaces, and shopping centres as a focus for women's discussion groups and advice sessions. Camden already has a good equality of opportunities policy, but it has been extended to include an expanded staff day-nursery, job-sharing, revised maternity and paternity schemes and plans for screening all women workers for breast and cervical cancer – as well as affirmative action schemes. The Committee are also investigating housing allocations policies, promoting leisure and sports provision for girls and campaigning on low pay. A major campaign has emerged from the discussions of the working group on prostitution. A worker has been paid to observe the policing of prostitutes in the Kings Cross area, and proposals have been made on reviewing police procedure, refuges for prostitutes and counselling.

Islington also set up a full Committee of the Council with an all-women membership. After a considerable battle, a women's unit of four posts was established, and the Committee given a budget of £102,801 for 1983–84. Monthly open meetings are held on Sunday afternoons and four working groups have evolved, on under-fives, health, housing and employment. The under-fives group has initiated proposals for a staff nursery and for creche facilities attached to community centres. The health group has been campaigning over the possible closure of a local hospital and is working out plans to include mid–wives and health advisors in the decentralisation of council services. A women's employment officer is being employed, and housing allocations policies are being investigated for possible discrimination.

In Southwark a full Women's Committee was set up alongside Race Equality, Jobs and Industry and Community Affairs Committees. The Committee has nine members, all women – a budget of £120,000 per annum, including £60,000 for local women's projects, and a three-person women's unit. Southwark, as an overwhelming working-class borough lacks the feminist networks of Camden and Islington. Energy and thought has therefore gone into finding new ways of reaching women who are not yet organised. The Committee wrote to about six hundred playgroups, mothers' and toddlers' groups, old people's clubs, tenant's associations as well as women's groups asking to come and talk to them and inviting them to Committee meetings. Members have been round to talk to local groups about their needs and demands, and a day event where local groups can share and exchange information is planned. There are no formal open meetings or co-options as yet. Local women have expressed misgivings about these structures which I shall explore later, but all Committee meetings are open, and are attended by up to fifty women, all with speaking rights. The Committee has begun to campaign over the issue of women's safety – examining street and estate lighting, estate design, police attitudes, self-defence classes and safe women's transport, as well as monitoring sex and video shops. Housing allocations, housing design and policies towards the breakdown of relationships and domestic violence are under review. Southwark had hardly begun, before May 1982, to consider discrimination in employment, and a priority has been to create an equal opportunities policy for council employees, as well as examining planning and wider employment policies.

Hackney and Greenwich both have sub-committees concerned with equal opportunities. In Hackney a Women's Rights Sub-Committee of the Policy and Resources Committee was set up after the election in response to a manifesto commitment. Male councillors did not at first bargain for conferring more than an advisory or lobbying function, but eventually a unit of two staff with administrative support, and a budget of £150,000 was agreed. Indeed, because of support from the leader and male councillors, the Sub-Committee has powers similar to a full committee of the Council. A large open meeting was held in October 1982 to decide the priorities of the Committee – the issues raised included violence against women, child-care, education, pornography, health care, housing, employment and leisure.

In Greenwich the Women's Committee is one of five sub-committees of the new Community Affairs committee. It has no budget of its own or direct policy-making powers, but so far has found that the Senior Committee has been happy to rubber stamp its proposals. A women's advisor is being appointed. They have seen their first task as getting a wide group of women involved in the work of the Committee, sending details of meetings to some seven hundred groups. Early intentions to co-opt representatives on to the Committee have been shelved for a while, as there were worries about the unrepresentative nature of responses to their invitation. In the meantime, Committee meetings are totally open and informal, anyone can join in. Issues discussed have so far been referred by other committees or raised by women attending the Committee meetings – job-sharing, women's aid, women only sessions at leisure centres and safety.

Most of the new initiatives were set up as a result of manifesto commitments, but there the similarity ends. In the GLC and Camden, the Committees have been given considerably greater resources than elsewhere, although it is not clear whether this reflects a greater commitment or a more relaxed attitude to spending growth. There are clear differences between North and South London. The GLC, Camden and Islington have set up more formal structures, with co-options, open meetings and working parties. South of the river, committees have found fewer organised feminist groups, and have been concerned to experiment with ways to involve local working women.

So far, the women's committees have spent much of their time creating the tools they need to work with; money, staff, consultation structures, and so on, (all of which are preconditions for effective action) rather than taking action itself. Neverthless, the need for a separate space in local government for women has been challenged because of fears of 'ghettoisation' of women's issues, and because of a view that it is difficult to delineate clear women's concerns within policy areas (as well as the blunter view that women are doing all right as they are!). It is undeniable that many of the issues identified by the women's committees affect other groups – violence on the streets, pornography, even child-care. The arguments for women's committees are however linked to an analysis of the under-representation of women in political structures, the specific position of women in the workforce and in relation to welfaie provision, and the committees have pinpointed these three areas as the centre of a women's strategy in local government.

Women and representation

Women's committees have given priority to making links with and providing resources for local women's groups and constructing networks of communication and support, as well as funding women's projects. This has been linked to a commitment to consultation and an attempt to re-introduce women into structures of political representation. Women have been and remain poorly represented at all levels of political structures – there are only 19 women MPs and Jill Hills has shown that not only do women face discrimination in selection procedures, but when selected they are disproportionately chosen for marginal and hopeless seats.[4] At a local level women are massively under-represented, a survey in 1976 showing that only 17 per cent of councillors, and 12 per cent of council leaders were women.[5] Women face not only sexist assumptions but the problems of the unequal division of labour. 'It is only because men have so little responsibility in general for running the home and children that they can afford the time for political activity.'[6]

Under-representation extends to other organisations. Women are seldom leaders of tenants associations and trades unions, even when they make up the bulk of the membership. A survey by Anna Coote and Peter Kellner in 1980 showed that whereas 38 per cent of members in the unions surveyed were women, only 11 per cent of executive members, less than 6 per cent of full-time officials and under 15 per cent of TUC delegates were women.[7]

Women are under-represented in community groups where 'men do most of the talking'.[10] Women often have less experience and knowledge of political processes, and are less likely to be chosen to speak on behalf of groups or to attend meetings. This lack of women's representation distorts the issues that are put forward for political consideration. Priorities are chosen by men who assume that they are shared by everyone. The experiences and perceptions of women are missing.

Women's committees have thus been exploring new structures and ways of meeting that overcome the barriers women face. Open meetings, working groups, public meetings and co-options have all been attempts to bring women into the policy-making process. There has been an emphasis on informality, collective working and attempts to break down local authority hierarchies. Publicity has been carefully designed to reach and be understood by local women, and leaflets, day events, exhibitions, women's buses, and so on, have been experiments in reaching women that are not in organised groups.

Women and the workforce

Secondly there has been a stress on equality of opportunity, both within the local authority itself and in the local workforce. The

economic activity rate for women in London is now 65 per cent
(67 per cent in inner London).[11] Women's work is however very
different from men's work – a third of women work part-time,[12]
and even when they work full-time, women work shorter hours and
a far smaller proportion of their wages consists of bonus or
overtime payments.[13] Despite the Equal Pay Act, women's gross
average earnings remain only 65.6 per cent of men's, and after a
slight increase in women's relative earning between 1970–75, the
gap is again widening.[14] Women's work is also segregated into the
lower grade and lower status occupations – cleaning, catering,
service and clerical work. Women remain poorly organised and
concentrated in the non-unionised sectors of the economy. Only 39
per cent of eligible women workers were in trades unions in 1977,
compared to 62 per cent of men.[15] Home and child-care
responsibilities makes it harder for them to attend evening or
lunch-time meetings. The particular place of women in the work
force reflects the fact that the demands have never been represented
adequately by the trades union movement. Demands for shorter
and more flexible hours and for child-care, for example, have been
treated as 'soft' demands compared with 'hard' issues such as wage
rates or overtime bonuses. Free collective bargaining, central to
traditional union philosophy, has increasingly benefitted men over
women, and women, it has been argued, have done relatively best
in times of pay restraint.[16] This has been compounded by trades
unions' continued focus on the 'family wage' as the basis for pay
claims – the cost of keeping a worker, his wife and two children –
despite the fact that this image of the traditional male worker and
his family is increasingly unrealistic. The impact of this myth, in a
situation where only 18 per cent of households consist of a male
worker with a dependent wife and children – is to distort issues of
pay, and our perceptions of the structure of the workforce.

In the context of new economic initiatives in local government, it
is essential that local authorities analyse and respond to the needs
of the growing numbers of women in work, otherwise economic
and planning policies to develop jobs could misrepresent or distort
the employment needs of the community. In some cases, as in
Southwark, the local authority is the largest single employer in
the area, and thus their own employment policies are of considerable significance. As might be expected, women employed by
Southwark Borough Council are almost all concentrated in the

lower-paid manual jobs – care assistants, home helps, cleaners, and in the secretarial and administrative posts. Women's committees have therefore begun to examine the barriers to women within local authorities – policies on recruitment, training, promotion, terms and conditions of service, and so on, and to develop positive action programmes. Support has been offered to campaigns over home working and low pay and the barriers to job-sharing. Work place nurseries, maternity and paternity pay and more flexible working hours are being explored. 'Good employer codes', covering sexual and racial equality as well as union recognition, have been used to assess the elegibility of local companies and voluntary organisations for grant aid. Local authority provision of transport and child-care and welfare services for dependents all crucially affect women's position within the work force, and are being examined by working parties and committees.

Women and welfare services

Thirdly, there has been a concern to examine the way welfare services relate specifically to women. Cockburn argued that the family 'is the unit to which state services choose to relate, which is reinforced and structured by local government'[17], and that local government uses the family as a central part of a management system which attempts to control women within the home. The family has been inscribed at the centre of the welfare state, with inequalities written into state provision *because* of women's position within the family. Thus the forms of health, social services and public housing provision are all constructed on the ideal of a male wage and female domestic servicing. Many (male) writers have assumed that it is the state that provides the majority of welfare services – Gough's important book *The Political Economy of the Welfare State* contains only two-thirds of a page on the family![18] But by far the greatest proportion of personal needs are met by family units, and within the family, women. Laura Balbo shows that, for example, less than two per cent of those over sixty-five in England and Wales in 1975 were living in private or state institutions, the rest were being looked after or helped by their families, by wives if they lived as a couple, or by daughters or daughters-in-law. Welfare services such as home helps or meals-on-wheels were provided only once or twice a week, and families had both to fill the gaps and provide the organisation to make access to other services possible.[19] In London, while there is some form of provision, public or private, in playgroups and nurseries, with child-minders for over a third of children under five, there are only places for twenty-five children in every thousand in local authority, full-time day nurseries.

There is not one 'welfare' system but two, or rather, three – the family, the state and the commercial private sector. The relationship of the state to the family has thus been profoundly ambivalent. On the one hand, women have benefitted from the provision and extension of local authority provision, midwifery, maternity care and family allowances, but the construction of welfare provision has cemented women into a particular place within the family. On the other hand, the growing independence and self-determination of women and their movement into the workforce has been dependent on the provision of nurseries, day centres and a minimum level of state benefits, which are increasingly under threat. The effects of political struggles won or lost is to shift provision from one sector to another and, (as shown in Chapter 9) the last few years have seen a sustained attempt from the right to 'roll back the state' – to shift welfare provision back from the state towards the private sector for the better-off and towards the family for working people.

Many women experience the growing intervention of the state in their lives as oppressive, and it has been seen as an encroachment on the autonomy of the family.[20] In some ways, however, the power of patriarchal structures has led to a preservation of male control within the family, and a denial of individual citizenship to women. 'The state frequently defines a space, the family, in which its agent will not interfere, but in which control is left to men.'[21] Hence the reluctance of police or government to interfere in cases of marital rape or domestic violence. What is seen from one dimension as interference in women's lives is, from another, an extension of state responsibility for welfare services and an extension of women's rights as separate citizens. The family, while identified as the site of women's oppression, remains the centre of people's emotional lives, offering intimacy, affection, comfort and support, which creates another area of real ambivalence. And yet, as shown earlier, only a minority of the population live within the traditional family and, therefore, to continue to centre social policy on a structure that is so unrepresentative is to lose touch with reality. It is the powerful *ideology* of the family and not the actual structures within which people chose to live which need to be challenged. There is a need for 'a major social transformation that will displace the family as the sole and privileged provider of moral and material support and spread these good things more widely through the community.'[22] At the same time, new forms of state provision could provide real choices about caring for children and the elderly, challenging the assumption that emotional ties lead to total welfare responsibility or that these responsibilities fall on the shoulders of women within the family.

Women's committees have therefore examined assumptions about family structures inscribed into local authority housing and planning policies – the predominance of three-bedroomed family housing, the absence of housing choices, for example, for single parents wishing to share a home, and the separation of 'family' housing from other sorts. Policies that privilege nuclear families in, for example, housing allocations, are being challenged, as are traditional assumptions about 'family' social and leisure provision. Community nurseries and child-care has been made a central area of policy, with stress on creche provision for leisure, education and social activities. Some committees have also begun to look at the problems of those caring for elderly or disabled relatives. More crucially, the structure of welfare services needs to be re-examined as part of overall left strategies for decentralisation, discussed in Chapter 8, to find forms of provision that meet needs for support and resourcing but do not manage or structure peoples' lives.

The role of women in local political struggles

The issues of women's representation, their place in the workforce and their relationship to welfare provision raise a number of questions of political strategy, which have to be considered in discussing initiatives at local government level. The specific position of women has implications for questions of collective provision and of political alliances in local political struggles. Historically, local government played a key role in the development of welfare provision. It was the early Labour councils that initiated health-visiting clinics and maternity care, that opened baths and laundries and began to build public housing. Local government has historically been vulnerable to working-class control in a way that other state structures have not,[23] and in the early twentieth century, Labour councils could and did exert their powers in the interests of local people, providing collective services that could not be offered in the private sector.[24] Since then, there has been increasing centralisation of services, and since the 1940s major shifts in consumption patterns which have eroded the base of support for collective provision, with increasingly private provision of housing and transport.[25] Analysis of the changing demand for collectively provided services have, however, largely failed to take account of the specific position of women.

Both Saunders and Dunleavy, in their opening chapters, have challenged a crude analysis which identifies a single working class with a common or unitary interest in local government struggles. But by analysing the local level in terms of sectoral interests, or competing consumer groups, both have sidestepped the question of divisions based on gender (or on race). Women form neither a distinct sector within the economy, nor do they constitute a specific consumer group. Because of the specific roles to which women are constrained, they have a specific relationship to local government service provision, employment and political representation. Male theorists have consistently failed to come to terms with the patriarchal structures of discrimination and exploitation. Some feminist theorists, beginning with Shulasmith Firestone have seen gender as the fundamental antagonistic division in society. 'Unlike economic class, sex class springs directly from a biological reality, men and women were created different and not equal.'[26] Such an account has been criticised for 'biologism' and for failing to explain the differences between women. More recently socialist feminists have described two processes (the development of patriarchy considerably pre-dating capitalism) that intertwine. Capitalism creates 'empty spaces' – tasks that must be performed to ensure the reproduction of the economic system, but it is the structures of patriarchy that ensure that some spaces are filled by women and some by men. And it is the systematic oppression of women that ensures that the spaces occupied by women are the lowest in status and the least rewarded.

Thus in Southwark, 90 per cent of single parents are women, and

67 per cent of pensioners; women rely disproportionately on public transport and even when the household owns a car it is mostly used by the man.[27] Households headed by women are disproportionately housed in the public sector and 59 per cent of single-parent families are council tenants, compared with only 26 per cent of two-parent families.[28] This is in part because they are disproportionately represented in the poorest sections of the population. Women are also doubly dependent on welfare services, the vast majority of jobs in these sectors are occupied by women, and it is predominately women who would take over the burden of these services if they were not provided collectively. For many women, a range of provision for children elderly or handicapped relatives is necessary before they can enter the workforce. Cuts in these services, or crucially, a failure to keep up with the expansion of demand, means that the family (women) takes up the slack. Although women are not being forced out of the workforce,[29] they face a lengthening double shift of paid and domestic labour, and an increasingly exhausting process of 'making do' with part-time jobs and long journeys to child-minders and work on inefficient buses.

As the resources of inner city areas are drained by the government cut-backs and financial penalties described in Chapter 9, the choices between raising rates and cutting services become increasingly untenable. There are potentially major conflicts and dislocations if services benefit only certain sectors of the population, but their maintenance depends on the willingness of the rest of the community (for whom private provision has become increasingly important) to continue to subsidise them in higher rates. Strategies based on building campaigning alliances and confronting central government have to take account of the different material interests of different groups. I have argued that the exclusion of women from local government and trades union representation has distorted the demands made of government. But if women are to be brought into defensive and developmental struggles, women's priorities will have to be taken seriously enough to reshape the total demands on local government.

Saunders sees local struggles as inevitably fragmented, because they are consumption struggles rather than class struggles, and suggests the need to demarcate a sphere of class politics.[30] It does not seem adequate, however, to limit class struggles to the sphere of labour–capital conflicts within the workplace, and situate all other struggles within pluralism, as Saunders does. This is not the place (thank god!) to re-examine theories of class, but what seems important is to look at how the social system is fashioned by processes of division and separation – class, gender, race, and the consumption-based struggles cited by Saunders and Dunleavy – and to examine how these divisions congeal to create shared consciousness and identification. Analyses of class based on economic relations in the workplace have meant that the 'working class' has been constructed so as to exclude the work experiences of women. At the same time, women have been excluded from the self-definitions and cultural traditions of male workers. Other groups 'excluded' from the working class include black people, the elderly, the disabled, the unemployed – leaving precious few white men in work to carry struggles forward. What is needed is a process of redefinition and alliances based on negotiated programmes that will collectively meet the aspirations of exploited sections of the community. In this process, demands that have been traditionally assumed to be put forward 'on behalf of the working class' will have to be displaced to make room for the priorities of previously excluded groups. In relation to town-hall unions, for example, we will have to recognise that 50 per cent of the workforce are women in most councils, and ensure that the interests of home-helps and cleaners are given equal weight to those of dustmen and building workers. The absence of women and women's demands is a crucial weakness of any campaign around collective provision.

The new committees – criteria for success

It is too early to tell whether the new women's committees represent a radical reorganisation of priorities within left Labour authorities, or merely a token gesture to some noisy and active Labour women! Indeed to some extent the attention paid to radical local government initiatives on women, race, employment and decentralisation has followed on from recent theoretical accounts of the 'local state', which imply that at worst such initiatives are an exercise in co-option and at best are unsustainable. It is therefore important for socialists and feminists to develop some sort of criteria from which to judge the new initiatives which are not uncritically supportive. Sarah Roleoffs has argued that women's committees should be judged by the extent to which they have been able to practise 'feminist' democracy, to campaign to defend women's rights and to indicate a feminist alternative.[31] In this section, therefore, I want to raise several issues that emerge from these sorts of criteria, and from the working of the women's committees so far: questions of representation and democracy, appropriate forms of organisation within a local authority, and of the location of power. Finally, I want to suggest alternative criteria which assess the possibility of women's committees achieving the reconstruction of radical policies for local government that I have discussed.

Roleoffs raised many doubts about the GLC Women's Committee. She welcomed the fact that:

'feminist democracy' with its particular emphasis on accessibility, participation, maximum involvement of the maximum number, non-hierarchical structures with a distribution of authority, rotation of tasks, sensitivity to different women's needs, abilities, development and competence, diffusion of information and equal access to resources has been attempted in a very big way ... the idea was mass involvement and for women themselves to make decisions.[31]

But on crucial occasions, the views of the open meetings have been rejected by the committee and the Labour group. 'Came the time when the women decided, but the GLC elected representatives disagreed, the women were reminded in no uncertain terms who called the tune and paid the piper – the GLC and the GLC alone.'[32] The elaborate democratic structures hide the fact that the women themselves have no effective power – the working groups are autonomous but powerless. Another writer describing the Camden Women's Committee says that 'the labour councillors have the final say which can never be truly democratic'[33] – what is obviously missing is a shared definition of democratic.

Women's committees have confronted the issue that has been ducked throughout the new manifesto-making process – when does participation mean consultation, and when does it mean power? The worst that can happen, has happened, is that the committee sees the process as consultation while the groups themselves assume real power has been devolved. There is already in some ways a clash between the 'constitutional' view of local authority practises, whereby an elected body makes policies on behalf of its constituents and is accountable to them – and the reality that party groups operate within a disciplined whip system. The new left administrations have been elected on democratically agreed and binding manifestos, and are committed to making councillors accountable to their local Labour parties. On to these systems have been grafted structures for involving previously excluded groups without any resolution of the resulting conflicts. Should people who are not strictly accountable to the electorate make decisions on committees? Should the Labour Party abandon its majority control over the political process to other groups? Should 'liberal' policies be enforced at the centre at the expense of devolved power? Roleoffs suggests that committees need to clarify what is being offered, and if women's meetings and working parties can only be advisory this must be made clear, to avoid demoralisation and disillusionment. Meanwhile the Left has some hard thinking to do about the realities of devolved power. In some ways the new structures add up to a 'left-corporatism' – the selection of certain groups for direct involvement in policy making structures superceding pluralist processes at a local level. Because of the systematic bias of traditional political structures this can be positive – but the question of which groups or individuals are chosen and which are excluded and by whom becomes all important.

It is also important to consider forms of representation. Because of the systematic under-representation of women, feminists have developed a whole series of new ways or organising, described as 'feminist democracy', ways of ensuring that everyone is given a chance to speak, that women do not too easily speak on behalf of women in general, that everyone is involved in the work to be done, is supported and given space to develop her ideas. These are not so much 'pre-figurative' forms as Keith Bassett describes them in Chapter 4, but a direct result of women's exclusion from traditional structures and an attempt to create a form of politics in which more than the élite few could function. But these structures fit very badly into traditional local government notions of political practise, and import some of the sticky problems that many of us have experienced within the women's movement. The women who come to open meetings or working groups can find themselves expected to 'represent' the interests of women from a particular location, and to approve or comment upon the women's committee proposals. Women who have been co-opted as committee members are expected to throw their weight for or against political decisions, when they sometimes have little background informaton and may have no opportunity to consult their colleagues. Where co-optees have been accountable to an open meeting, they have found that both the attendance and the decisions of these meetings shifts from week to week. One way out proposed by Hackney and Lewisham is to ask for representatives from specific organisations, but again, the political decision is which groups are invited to send representatives and which are not.

Inevitably, the new committees have tended to attract women already involved in women's rights or in the voluntary sector. The GLC and Camden have linked into the feminist networks that exist, and attempted to respond to feminist demands. The structure of open meetings means that they can be and have been taken over by groups that are organised enough to hold caucus meetings in advance. The domination of the open meetings or co-ordinating meetings by groups such as Wages for Housework has led frustrated politicians to draw distinctions between the 'feminists' and 'ordinary women', when they perceive the demands made to be unreasonable. It seems important to affirm feminist analysis and demands at a local level while remaining aware of the self-selected nature of the groups of women involved. Open meetings held in central London in the evening must inevitably attract women who are articulate, who are used to, and able to, travel around London at night, and who have no child-care difficulties. They run the risk of being 'middle class'. This criticism extends to the committees themselves; the new councillors heading women's committees and the majority of officers in the new women's units are young professional women. For local authorities in largely working-class inner city areas there is a danger of missing out entirely the majority of local women. The committees in Southwark, Hackney and Greenwich in particular have been aware of this and have set out to involve local working women. But there are very real reasons why women have not been drawn into organised politics – baby-sitting difficulties, the lack of public transport and the dangers of walking anywhere at night mean that many women are virtually imprisoned in their homes in the evening – and the stresses of full-time child-care or the double shift leave women precious little time for theoretical debate. Women's committees have the double task of creating new ways of meeting and contacting people, and of achieving material results to make it worth women's while.

These sorts of issues raise the question of how far women's committees are or should be feminist structures. As local authority initiatives, they should not be confused with the wider women's movement or be seen as the centres of women's organisation. Otherwise committees may concentrate on things they do relatively badly and neglect things they could do well. Local authorities are poorly adapted, as yet, to take on a major campaigning role, and although they have an important part to play in resourcing and supporting campaigns, there is a danger they can slow them down or take them over. Roleoffs stresses the need for political activity outside the state, and then criticises the GLC for not organising it. There needs to be political activity outside of and separate from, women's committees. This feeling of being absorbed has led to suspicion from feminist groups, who are wary of an opportunist Labour Party which has done little enough for women in the past, and what could be seen as a 'hypocritical attempt to co-opt us and direct our energies'.[34] Feminists who have analysed the state as directly involved in repressing and co-ercing women 'into their primary task as adults . . . the task of reproducing the workforce'[35], are wary of new attempts by local government to absorb and manage them. Those of us who have been involved in setting up women's committees have nevertheless felt that local government, which intervenes directly in women's lives, is an important site of struggle and change. The women's movement has in practise directed many of its demands to the state. Jan Parker sees women's committees as having 'the potential power to affect all policy and practise on every issue a council has to deal with'.[36] Nevertheless, there are real fears that the independent organisation of women will be absorbed into council machinery, and women's energies will be drained into an endless series of council meetings. There is also a danger of centering the women's movement on local authority administrations with an uncertain future. The new committees can potentially act as a bridge between feminist and labour movements, without one attempting to absorb the other.

In any case, as I have argued earlier, women's committees have specific tasks to perform in relation to local government – to shift the focus of employment policies within and outside the council, and to alter the framework of service provision. Local authority women's committees have to change the form of intervention in women's lives the council already makes, and have to achieve some sort of tangible improvement in women's lives. That requires a fundamental change in the way local government functions. It will be important for the new forms of organisation to transform the structure of the local authority, and not be merely added on. Attempts in Southwark to make the Women's Committee meetings themselves accessible to local women have been clumsy – aims of ensuring everyone knows what is on the agenda, introducing everyone, ensuring everyone has space and is encouraged to speak square uneasily with the need to get through a thick agenda by eleven p.m. Still, women keep coming, and we are learning skills to take into other parts of the council. If new forms of organisation are meaningful they must make meetings accessible to inex-perienced and unorganised women as well as the articulate and practised groups. If women are to participate constructively, they must also have information in advance, and have time to discuss issues with their colleagues and formulate ideas. Local groups meet irregularly and rely on voluntary support, and will be quickly alienated if they find themselves called to meetings at a few days notice, or find that decisions have already been taken.

Most important of all, if women's committees are to achieve material results they must have political power. There is, of course, the question of whether real power resides in elected members at all – but within its limits, local government is one of the few state institutions where elected members do have executive power. But realistically, the extent to which women's committees can carry through policies depends on the level of support from within the administration as a whole, from both members and officers, and on the level of pressure exerted on councillors from women outside the council. The effectiveness of the committees so far has depended on the level of support from leaders and other key councillors, and on the influence that women councillors can wield within Labour groups. Committees with only women members have found themselves dangerously isolated where few women are in positions of leadership in the council as a whole (or where the ones there are fail to provide support). There is always a danger that separate committees become ghettos to which issues relating to women can be consigned, leaving other committees free to carry out the 'serious' work of the council. The mechanisms for referring decisions to other committees need therefore to be effective, and women's committees need the power to ensure that other committees and departments not only implement their proposals, but begin to re-assess priorities themselves. That is, perhaps, where the new initiatives are at their most fragile; the labour movement and Labour councils have not yet come to terms with the new priorities raised by women, and issues such as child-care, safety, and women's jobs are often still seen as 'soft' or marginal compared to 'hard' decisions on wages and finance, or housing repairs and rents. The new conferences, festivals, newsletters and campaigns are all an important part of a feminist alternative, but there must be bread as well as circuses.

I would suggest that the women's committees give us important new opportunities at a local level and that the aim must be to ensure that:

- the demands and priorities of women are brought to the forefront of local authority decision-making;
- women's committees act as a resource to, and support, women organising in their areas while respecting their autonomy;
- the new forms of representation and organisation developed challenge and change the political organisation of local government as a whole;
- material changes are made in women's lives by responding to the new assessments of employment or service provision.

It is success in meeting these sorts of objectives which will enable us to evaluate not just the new women's committees but the seriousness with which left administrations take the issues they raise, and their willingness to develop new local government strategies in the 1980s.

Notes and References

1. CSE Sex and Class Group, 'Plenary Paper of CSE Conference' (CSE, 1981) p. 6.
2. Anna Coote, 'The AES: a New Starting Place', *New Socialist*, 2, Nov/Dec 1981, p. 6.
3. See A. Sharples, Women and Economic Strategy, CSE Conference Paper (CSE, 1982).

4. J. Hills, 'Candidates – The Impact of Gender', *Parliamentary Affairs*, Spring 1981.
5. Department of the Environment, *Findings of the Committee of Inquiry into the System or Remuneration of Members of Local Authorities*, vol. 2, table 16, p. 13.
6. J. Hills, 'Candidates – The Impact of Gender', p. 223.
7. A. Coote and P. Kellner, 'Powerlessness and How to Fight it', *New Statesmen*, 7 November 1980, p.8–11.
8. C. Cockburn 'Why Women get Involved in Community Action', in Mayo (ed.), *Women in the Community* (Routledge and Kegan Paul, 1977).
9. A. Gallagher, 'Women and Community Work' in Mayo, *Women in the Community*.
10. C. Cockburn, 'Why Women get Involved in Community Affairs'.
11. GLC, *Economic Status of Women in London*, (GLC, 1982) Table 1b, p. 3.
12. Table 4a, p. 9.
13. Ibid, tables 8 & 9, pp. 16–18.
14. Ibid, table 10, p. 9. Gross earnings overstate this position because of the widespread practise of overtime among men – but even if we take manual workers' average hourly earnings, women's earnings are still only 72.6 per cent of men's.
15. G. S. Bain and R. Price, *Profiles of Union Growth* (Blackwell, 1980), table 2.1, p. 37.
16. See B. Campbell and D. Charlton, 'Work to Role' in *Red Rag*, 1979, and B. Campbell 'Power Not Pin Money', *New Socialist*, July–August 1982. For a critique of this position see A. Weir and M. McIntosh, 'Towards a Wages Strategy for Women', *Feminist Review*, Spring 1982, p. 12.
17. C. Cockburn, *The Local State* (Pluto, London 1977) p. 61.
18. I. Gough, *The Political Economy of the Welfare State* (Macmillan, 1981).
19. L. Balbo, 'The Servicing Work of Women and the Capitalist State', *Political Power and Social Theory*, vol. 3, 1982, p. 263.
20. See for example J. Donzelot, *The Policing of Families* (Hutchinson, 1980); for a critique of Donzelot see M. Macintosh and M. Barrett, *The Anti-Social Family*, (Verso, 1982).
21. M. McIntosh, 'The State and the Oppression of Women' in Kuhn and Wolpe, (eds), *Feminism and Materialism* (Routledge and Kegan Paul, 1978) p. 257.
22. M. McIntosh and M. Barrett, *The Anti-Social Family*, p. 133.
23. For a longer exposition, see J. Dearlove, *The Re-Organisation of British Local Government* (Cambridge University Press, 1979) and S. Duncan and M. Goodwin, 'The Local State and Restructuring Social Relations – Theory and Practice', Urban and Regional Studies Working Paper (Sussex University, 1980)
24. See for example N. Branson, *Poplarism 1919–1925: George Lansbury and the Councillors' Revolt* (Lawrence & Wishart, 1979)

25. See P. Dunleavy 'The Urban Basis of Political Alignment', *Britsh Journal of Political Science*, vol. 9, 1979, pp. 409–443.
26. S. Firestone, *The Dialect of Sex* (Morrow, 1970) p. 16.
27. GLC, *Economic Status of Women in London*, table 30, p. 49.
28. *General Household Survey* 1980, see table 3.9, p. 50 and table 2.19, p. 24.
29. See recent evidence in L. Segal, 'A Question of Choice', *Marxism Today*, Jan 1983.
30. See Saunders, this book, p. 31.
31. S. Roleoffs, GLC Women's Committee – Democratism or Feminism' in *London Labour Briefing*, April 1983, p. 18.
32. Ibid., p. 18.
33. J. Watson, 'Takeover Town Hall', *Spare Rib*, April 1983.
34. J. Parker in 'Takeover Town Hall', p. 6.
35. L. Wilson, *Women and the Welfare State* (Tavistock, 1977) p. 8.
36. Parker, 'Takeover Town Hall', p. 7.

6 Local Authority Race Initiatives

HERMAN OUSELEY

Since the end of the 1950s, local authorities have been responding to their local black inhabitants in a variety of ways. Two and a half decades later virtually all local authorities are still unclear about what they are doing. Initially it was sheer blatant discrimination: most local authorities did not employ black people or accept that they had legitimate or justifiable housing needs. Blacks were denied access to services and facilities. Later on they were offered the menial and low status jobs, and tenancies in the worst publicly-owned slums, even when more services were available. Judging from the 'blacklash' of anger at the way in which the social, health and education services have failed them, it is clear that black people regard many of those services as irrelevant to their particular needs.

Around the late 1970s a number of progressive local authorities started developing race equality initiatives. These all happened to be Labour-controlled authorities, but then most black people tend to be concentrated in the most deprived parts of the main cities and these have been the areas with a Labour following. Such authorities included Haringey and Camden who both launched major initiatives in 1978, the Inner London Education Authority more or less around the same period, Lambeth in 1979, and a cluster of others soon afterwards. In London, these included Brent, Hackney, Newham and the GLC. During 1983, Southwark, Islington and Greenwich joined the fray. The only Conservative-controlled authority to display a stomach for such initiatives was Hammersmith and Fulham. In addition, both Lewisham and Tower Hamlets were engaged in a variety of race relations initiatives. A schedule of known local authority activity in the

Greater London area is set out at the end of this chapter. In other parts of England, initiatives were being developed in Bradford, Leicester, Coventry, the West Midlands and Greater Manchester.

The responses have been prompted at different times by different circumstances. Political expediency, the black electorate, community relation's pressure and the 1981 street uprisings have all prompted local authority action. The responses have been varied: sometimes enlightened and innovative, other times tokenistic, but generally all marginal in terms of effectiveness.

The confused response after two and a half decades is largely a result of racism, intensely institutionalised and endemic and still not understood, even by those authorities who are described as 'progressive' because of their new found enlightenment in developing race equality policies and programmes, and their desire to politicise ethnicity. Added to racism, the confusions are located in a misunderstanding of what local government is all about, who it is intended to serve, who runs it and for whose benefit. Local government in those areas where blacks predominantly reside – the inner, depressed parts of the major conurbations – is largely controlled by the middle classes, who see themselves as running a service for the poor and deprived. These poor and deprived sections of the society are often popularly described as the working class, even though increasingly they are to be found on the unemployment register, many without apparent hope of ever working again.

It is not unreasonable to say that local government is largely run by the middle classes, even though many new elected members nowadays claim empathy with the working classes because of their own similar background to those of the communities they claim to serve. But do they run the service or is it the paid officials! Certainly over the years, the chief officers, the senior officers and the middle managers have built up incredibly strong power bases, safe in the security of a new professionalism (which means they are considered as the only people 'qualified' to make certain decisions). They are often not accountable to anyone for decisions made, and over the years have built up structures, customs and practices which give them the capacity to maintain control. Nor should it be forgotten that they are the long term custodians of the local state apparatus. Elected members come and go, but the paid officials can be there until retirement. In some instances, the elected members are regarded as so transient that they have been described behind the scenes as 'fly by nights'. That would explain, in part, why some senior officers greeted the recent introduction of race policies in the sphere of local government as 'the flavour of the month'. They argue that new policies and new gimmicks are often tried by new administrations but fundamentally nothing really changes. Superficially yes, but deep down, no! Or so the story goes, so far.

Those middle managers, senior and chief officers are the people therefore who wield a considerable amount of power. They are largely middle class, they have 'made it' in materialistic terms, and they have frequently suburbanised their existence. Not all have lost their empathy with the poor and the deprived, and in fact most will diligently work on behalf of the disadvantaged sections of the community. But because they have moved on and moved away from the problems, many have lost the conviction and determination to be part of the solution. To do so would fundamentally challenge their own position and could result in an erosion of their power and resources. As elected members try to impose their authority with new forms of approaches including decentralisation, full-time councillors, alternative bureaucracies, privatisation, and so on as ways and means of defining, in their own terms, what local government should be all about, the dilemmas of adding the race of dimension becomes clearer.

Given black people's extensive social, political and economic disadvantages, some sociological experts and social scientists contend that they are forming a new underclass. So how does local government deal with the race dimension, given black people's underclass status? As efforts are made, through the local state, to equalise opportunities for the black communities the task appears to be defined as giving black people an equal share of the poverty and deprivation that makes them no worse off than poor whites. It cannot be more than that with so many poor whites qualifying in increasing numbers for supplementary benefits. It has little to do with control of power and equal access to all resources. The conflicts and dilemmas of local government, and its role in raising the living standards of the poor and the deprived remain crucial for resolution as far as ordinary people are concerned. The efforts of the local state in seeking to introduce new approaches for responding to mass unemployment, the housing crisis, deteriorating health and social services and increased social stresses, must be put into perspective with a recognition of the central conflicts, the loss of considerable amounts of central government revenues and an unsympathetic central state. Given the role of central government in enacting racially discriminatory legislation, such as the Immigration and Nationality Acts, and its reluctance to acknowledge the existence of institutionalised racism, the local states' efforts to tackle racism face massive obstacles.

Conflicts and confrontations

Very few local authorities have actually attempted to deal with all aspects of racism within their activities. Where this has happened, it has required and continues to demand a total confrontation with long-established and cherished traditions of custom and practice. It requires skillful, perceptive and committed anti-racists operating within their local state structures and performing acts of challenge. This in turn requires further support and commitment from both political and other officers.

Race policies in local government owe their introduction to a very few people. Usually it is easy to identify the policy with an individual – the race relations committee chair, a black councillor, or the leader of the council. This can polarise the issue on political lines, although in some cases such as Bradford, Lambeth (for part of 1982) and Hammersmith and Fulham some evidence exists of bi-partisan approaches to the implementation of race equality programmes. Nevertheless, it is virtually always left to a handful of individuals to do all the battling, to generate the conflict, to resolve the difficulties, to challenge obstinacy and to highlight resistance. Race now appears more frequently in the manifestos of the political parties and predominantly, though not exclusively, in Labour Party programmes. Once again, the responsibility for its inclusion and development rests with very few concerned individuals or small groups of activists.

Commitment to tackle racism, to set up specialist committees, appoint advisers, and monitor housing allocations has spread, but most party members or elected members have no real understanding of the realities of dismantling racism. That they are well intentioned there is no doubt, but they expect race equality to just happen without causing them any consternation. They don't really want to get involved. After all 'that's why we've got our race relations committee and we've got our race relations advisers!' Or something along those lines. And so race policies become synonymous with the race relations adviser.

Advisers have to carry the can: they make most of the running; fight all the battles, negotiate with the workforce, take the challenge to management, seek to carry the trades unions with them, and accept the reaction when things go wrong, as they invariably do. They have to operate in a status-conscious industry (local government) but in most cases they have to operate at middle management or senior management levels. Very rarely at chief officer level, where negotiations have to take place. Thus they have to be as sophisticated and capable as their counterparts at the top level but without the status. Because many of them are black, advisers can be regarded as a new breed of interventionists, almost alien to the local government profession, and, perhaps transitory, in keeping with the gimmickry attached to this new area of policy development. They tend to become isolated in the organisation. They must either work at the customary snail's pace in bringing about changes or face accusations of going 'too fast, too soon'. Either way they are on to a loser. If progress is not apparently being made, other black staff lose confidence – assuming they ever had any – and black community organisations may feel the policies lack credibility. On the other hand, warnings of a 'backlash' are often given, especially by the very same people who trigger off such reactions. Failure to bring about success then breeds further isolation.

The new tendency therefore is for advisers to begin surrounding themselves with proven allies. Black workers groups, NALGO Black Members Sections, and community-based support groups can counter isolationism as well as sharing the confrontations. Thus alliances are central to the success of rolling back the benign neglect, the years of complacency and the resistance to change for the sake of change. After all, those who run the services have had much experience of ruling, and it is inconceivable that they will wish to lose their power and control overnight.

The new mood

If so much is owed to so few, and so little has been achieved despite the conflicts and the confrontations, the alliances and the political commitments, why is local government being deluged with a plethora of exhortations about race relations? There are five main reasons why recently local authorities have been making attempts to develop race equality policies and programmes. Firstly, some local authorities have accepted that they must be seen to be doing something, whether or not effective or relevant. Secondly, in response to the growing pressure from their local black communities, authorities often argue that 'we must be seen to be doing something', often dictated by the strengths and cohesiveness of the community's demands. Thirdly, political changes in the Labour Party have heralded the prominence of black councillors in increased numbers in local government, and they have put race issues high on the agenda. Fourthly, and more recently, the effects of the 1981 street uprisings, followed by Scarman and other official reports on racial disadvantage, prompted a wave of new responses. Fifthly, there is Section 71 of the Race Relations Act 1976, which in theory places a duty on local authorities to make race equality a reality. Most local authorities however regard Section 71 as meaningless exhortation and therefore ignore it without fear of challenge; others take it more seriously and genuinely try to develop anti-discriminatory policies and programmes. Most of these innovative authorities have been ill-prepared for dealing with the enormous conflicts generated when institutional racism is confronted. As a consequence, good intentions either go wrong, or take an extraordinarily long time to be converted into good practices, or become secondary when compared to other dilemmas facing local government, not least of which are its recent conflicts with central government over expenditure control.

The most progressive local authorities on race matters would probably be aiming to:

- adopt an equal opportunity policy statement;
- implement such a policy with positive action programmes;
- establish a race relations committee of elected members (or some other equivalent);
- appoint special race/ethnic advisers;
- agree codes of practice covering personnel matters;
- run anti-racist or racism awareness training for existing staff;
- introduce race/ethnic dimension into policy-making procedures;
- conduct consultation programmes/arrangements with local black/ethnic minority groups;

- monitor equal opportunity by race/ethnic origin in employment;
- review services take up/relevance/access/for black and ethnic minority consumers;
- support programmes for black self-help initiatives (usually through grant-aid);
- influence public opinions on race matters through promotional, information and publicity programmes.

Most authorities however still regard the issue as irrelevant to them,while others have marginalised their responses within the context of special programmes (for example, Urban Programme, Section 11). Only a handful have extended beyond these responses and are attempting to deal with the effects of institutional racism.

The facts of racial disadvantage are now beyond dispute and recognition of institutional racism is now an urgent and essential pre-requisite to the formulation of effective policies and pro-grammes which will lead to equality for black people and other racial minorities in Britain. Understanding institutional racism is important. It is not simply a description of deliberate or direct discrimination, and many people who reject it as non-existent in British society mistakenly misunderstand the term. It is, instead, a description of policies, practices, structures, procedures, rules and regulations which have developed over time and are embedded in the customs and practices of the institution. Their development is steeped in the notion of traditionalism and developed by people in powerful positions (predominantly male and white) who have themselves been conditioned by racism. The history of British racism has conditioned the white British to the notion of race superiority, to stereotypical images of black people and other foreigners, and to regard most ethnic minorities as 'immigrants' with the stigma of 'undesirablity' and 'problems' that go with that tag.

Contemporary race issues have polarised around the immi-gration debate (obsessions about numbers and 'swamping') and racial disadvantage. Deliberate confusions, such as Scarman's enthusiasm for positive discrimination,[1] have diverted attention from the reality of what has to be done to create a society without racial divisions, to lengthy fruitless discussions about the natural fears of the 'indigenous'. It is that reality which local government has to face up to in the 1980s if street conflict in pursuit of racial justice is to be avoided. Given that racism is woven into the

institutional structures, the responses must be both comprehensive
and radical if an impact is to be achieved. Thus local government
must operate in future within the context of a nationally-directed
race equality programme that is underpinned by an anti-racist
strategy.

The central/local government relationship

Central government needs to develop and lead with its own race
equality strategy and programmes. So far this has been sadly
lacking. In its relationships with local authorities, the Government
must offer financial inducements to local authorities who draw up
race equality strategy plans in accordance with the detailed
framework described later in the chapter. The two most important
financial factors are the annual Rate Support Grant (RSG) and
the Housing Investment Programme (HIP). All RSG and HIP
settlements should reflect needs, demands and responses on race
and be based on explicit statements on ethnic minority housing
needs, as well as all other main programme service provision. Local
authorities must be discouraged from using marginal programmes
such as Section 11 (which should be phased out anyway). Race
equality strategy plans which contain explicit costed programmes
would be prepared by local government and submitted to central
government, to qualify for funding within the context of the
government's overall anti-racist and race equality strategy plan.
Since the June 1983 election there has been no evidence whatsoever
to suggest that a second term of Thatcherism will do anything to
alter the status quo.

Race equality strategy plans

There is no reason why local authorities should not develop such
plans now. These should be prepared by each local authority to
accord with the statutory duty imposed under Section 71 of the
Race Relations Act 1976. Guidelines should be issued by the
Government about the minimum requirements acceptable as a
Section 71 response. If necessary, legislative backing must be given
to secure local authorities' compliance with such requirements.

An important concept to be utilised by local authorities in the race equality strategy statements will be that of 'equality targets'. These will not be quotas but minimum specified goals which can be exceeded, unlike quotas.

Such specified goals will be determined according to the facts of under-representation and non-representation as currently allowed in the Race Relations Act 1976, using demographic data for determining proportionality and measuring representation as well as progress. An example would be an authority setting a recruitment equality target of 20 per cent ethnic minority employees at every level as part of its workforce, to reflect a 20 per cent ethnic minority composition of the population within the local authority and general recruitment area. Equality targets have, to date, been developed and utilised by the London Boroughs of Lambeth and Hackney and are being considered for implementation by other authorities, including the GLC.

The *objectives* of the race equality strategy plans would be to secure for ethnic minority groups: equal shares of jobs and training opportunities, equal access to resources, services and facilities, and equal involvement in decision-making. In drawing up such plans local authorities should:

- assess general needs in the area, setting out demographic information including ethnic data, highlighting special needs of ethnic minority groups, identifying racial disadvantage and its extent;
- describe what structural arrangements (such as corporate planning approaches, departmental race adviser, ethnic minority or race relations units, special committees) are being made to assess, evaluate and continuously monitor the impact of services on its deprived racial groups. Describe steps taken to avoid discrimination, particulary indirect forms, and to make service provision relevant and accessible to their black and other disadvantage minority communities;
- devise positive action plans incorporating equality targets, to utilise the provisions of the Race Relations Act 1976, particularly:

Section 5(a) – general occupational qualifications
Section 35 – special needs provisions
Section 37 – training, educational provision
Section 38 – employment and training provisions.

These provisions are at present inadequate for redressng imbalances but, until improved legislation is enacted, should nevertheless be fully utilised.

- describe how the positive action plans would be implemented through the main programmes of the authority, supplemented by the availability of the Urban Programme and Partnership resources while these exist. Positive action plans should have time-specified equality targets spread over a three-year implementation period, with annual reviews and more frequent monitoring. The intention of the plans and equality targets would be to redress current imbalances within a target period;
- devise and state in detail positive action plans and equality targets covering both employment and service provision applicable to all expenditure headings for each departmental activity, so that the race equality strategy plan represents a comprehensive document covering all local authority activities;
- describe the role and funding arrangements for local voluntary initiatives including the Community Relations Councils, black and other ethnic minority organisations, and self-help as well as anti-racist initiatives;
- draw up local anti-racist programmes to challenge and dis- courage all racist activities, materials and harassment, promoting at all times the black and other minority communities and their cultures prominently and positively;
- describe the consultative and participative arrangements for black people and other racial groups to be involved in drawing up the strategy plan with the local authority, and also for continuous involvement in evaluation and monitoring. All race equality strategy plans should be the subject of consultations between black and other ethnic minorities and the local authority, and should only be regarded as satisfactory when endorsed by the deprived racial groups themselves;
- draw up enforcement arrangements for anti-discrimination conditions on grant-aid, contracts, tenders and purchasing.

Marginalism

The preparation of local authority strategy plans could achieve a lot, but there would still be the need for a strong lead from central government. Central government resources would have to be put into spearheading a nationally directed anti-racist strategy and into local authorities to implement race equality strategy plans; stronger anti-racist legislation would be needed to give effect to the desired goals of equality. No government has yet pledged itself to get rid of racist legislation, and such reform is a pre-requisite for tackling institutionalised racism. Instead, marginalism has been the order of the day, manifested in the notion of special programmes, including the Urban Programme and Partnership authorities, MSC initiatives, Educational Priority Areas and Section 11 of the Local Government Act 1966. Section 11, as it is affectionately referred to, is the ultimate in marginalism. It was the government's answer to the race problem in 1966 and is still regarded today in 1983 as the only Central Government direct grant-aid to local authorities for tackling racial disadvantage. In 1983, over £90 million gross is being spent nationally on special posts for work with 'New Commonwealth Immigrants'. Many local authorities have, however, used Section 11 as a topping-up fund. This has been particularly true of educational authorities providing language teachers, multicultural teachers and inspectors, as well as other specialist teaching posts. Many still do so and cannot identify the posts being specifically funded. An increasing number of local authorities are seeking Home Office approval for posts such as race relations advisers, liaison officers, ethnic housing officers and specialist social services practitioners. As more local authorities seek to get funding through Section 11 for newly-created posts to work with 'New Commonwealth Immigrants', they are now finding a more vigilant Home Office vetting all bids and being very careful not to give too many approvals, particularly on any new innovative posts, so that unspecified cash limits can be maintained.

Many of these specialist postholders are expected to achieve herculean feats. One or two black specialist social workers (with special responsibility for the Afro-Caribbean or Asian communities) will be expected to carry excessive case workloads, and to become the focus for the 'race problem'. Yet virtually all of these postholders tend to be isolated, on relatively low grades, frozen out of policy-making processes, and thus completely marginalised. They are expected to be loyal to the department, not 'rocking the boat' on issues such as racism, nor having alliances with black community organisations or local individuals; in other words, to be just another employee within the line management processes, except when it comes to 'difficult' clients.

Section 11 has therefore reinforced marginalism and frustrated the contributions which many specialist workers could have made and still would, given the political will and correct deployment of such skills and experience. Challenging bureaucratic elitism and local government professionalism are interwoven in the struggle against institutionalised racism. None of these forces can be weakened sufficiently to allow community-controlled local services without a major restructuring of local government, in which these workers are allowed to play more meaningful and independent roles within the framework of race equality and anti-racist strategies. On top of the cosmetic layer of special posts have been added race relations advisers, ethnic minorities units and similar-sounding structures. A schedule of action taken by the London Boroughs is set out in Table 6.1, at the end of this Chapter. Once again, Section 11 has been used in part to finance these. Although most of these units or advisers have been able to influence policy changes there are nevertheless many obstacles. They have been:

- grafted onto structures which neither accept that changes in practices are necessary nor that racism exists;
- created with the expectation that they will make changes in policies and practices necessary to achieve race equality, yet there is no real understanding by decision makers of institutionalised racism, how it operates and what is required in the way of resources, will-power, and attitudes to remove it;
- established on low grades, with low status, yet they are expected to relate to all levels within the authority. Given the status consciousness of local government hierarchies, it is impossible for race advisers to exert pressure and influence without an involvement in decision-making at officer level;
- set up, like specialist workers, so as to make them easy targets for bureaucracies to isolate, thus reducing further their potential and scope for getting close enough to power structures to challenge them.

Benefits

What then is the value of race equality policy, given the constraints of racism and elitist power structures? There can be some measurable benefits and indeed there have been. The new race equality policies are being created with much conviction, resolve and sincerity. On the whole, however, overall strategy is lacking. People making staffing decisions, such as managers and personnel officers, also have to be trained so that they interview without bias and make decisions without prejudice. However, that by itself only prevents discrimination from happening in the future; it does not compensate for previous discrimination. That is why local authorities such as Brent, Islington, Lambeth, Hackney, Haringey and the Greater London Council have made commitments to redress the balance through positive action. It sounds like a mechanism for reverse discrimination. And that is how it is seen by the reactionary traditionalists, who are quick to point out how 'non-racist' they are, while doing nothing to give black people a 'second chance' (or indeed a first chance!).

The claims of positive discrimination in favour of blacks are wholly misunderstood, representing a clear outcome of racist conditioning. The Race Relations Act 1976, although never fully tested or extended, has very limited scope for dynamic positive action. Black people can be offered help with training, with education and with welfare in respect of their special needs. To do more is unlawful. Thus at the point of selection it is unlawful to discriminate against a person on the grounds of race. This means an employer cannot discriminate against white or black at the point of selection.

In spite of the legal constraints some local authorities have assisted with traineeships, access courses, apprenticeships and career entry posts, as part of their positive action programmes to offer enhanced opportunities for job acquisition. Lambeth, Brent, Hackney and the GLC are four authorities who have done so. It is a slow process, not helped by an over cautious CRE and an over-zealous Home Office. The latter has been anxious to challenge too liberal an interpretation of key sections of the Act, such as Section 38, which provides an employer with the opportunity to offer training to people from a particular racial group not represented or under-represented as part of that workforce, so that they can equip themselves with the essential qualifications to make them suitable for available jobs. However the constraining interpretations make it difficult, if not impossible, to make real progress.

Monitoring must also be a major part of equal opportunities policy. Most authorities cannot even reveal how many black people they employ, what they do, how they fare in terms of promotion and whether progress is being made with implementing equal opportunities policy. Yet it is apparent that most local authorities employ far fewer black people than would be expected given the proportion of black people in the local population. Those who are on the local authority payroll are generally to be found in low-paid, low-grade jobs. Certainly, a quick look around GLC's County Hall shows major over-representation of black women among cleaning and catering staff and a virtual absence of blacks among senior and chief officers in the corridors of power.

Where ethnic or race monitoring of jobs and service provision has taken place, it has provided startling facts and enabled progress to be charted. For instance, Lambeth Council was able to show, after introducing race monitoring in 1978, that through positive action it had doubled the percentage of black employees from 8 per cent to 16 per cent over a two-year period, albeit mainly in lower-paid jobs.

Training

Progressive authorities have tackled training in two ways. The first has been to train existing staff who are involved in key decision-making to observe equal opportunity commitments, as well as to develop and implement equal opportunity policies and practices. The second has been to provide training opportunities for potential as well as existing staff, so that they could attain appropriate qualifications or skills to compete for certain jobs as well as to develop their careers.

Equal opportunities training comes in many guises. It can take the form of straightforward familiarisation with anti-discrimination legislation. In some cases it goes beyond that, and examines the nature of and scope for positive action as a means of redressing imbalances, responding to special needs and compensatory recognition for previous racial discrimination. Linked to these two aspects of equal opportunities training would be the practical changes which have to take place in order to implement equal opportunity policies. That means training staff on new procedures and practices to give effect to advertising in the specialist newspapers and publications serving black people; circulating community networks with details of job vacancies so that they can be made more acessible to black unemployed people; objective interviewing; giving adequate weight in selection to the experiential qualifications of black applicants and recognising the specialist skills which they can bring into the public services by virtue of their race experience, particularly in areas with large black populations; assisting with the career development of black staff; monitoring progress through confidential race data analysis; implementing objective grievance procedures which would provide black staff with the opportunity to have racism against supervisory staff dealt with; and finally, invoking disciplinary rules to deal effectively with all racist behaviour.

The latter two aspects in particular must be seen as crucial. It has certainly been so for a number of authorities. Where new independent grievance procedures have been introduced to deal with racism, these have resulted in more black staff bringing forward complaints against managers, supervisors and other colleagues, where before it had proved a waste of time. There was no point in complaining about the boss when the boss investigated the complaint himself or herself and suppressed it. Equally, it was and still is likely to lead to victimisation, further harassment and being branded as a trouble-maker. Also, complaining to the trades union representative did not always resolve such problems; it would not be unusual to find situations where union representatives or stewards were also in supervisory positions and often regarded complainants of racial discrimination as 'over-reacting' or having 'chips on their shoulders' or in cases of being overlooked for promotion as being 'too ambitious'. When new procedures for dealing with such grievances have been introduced, they have had to have an independent component and safeguards to protect staff from victimisation and stigmatisation. The effectiveness of such a system and confidence in it have both depended on results. There is nothing like success to breed success.

Revised disciplinary codes have provided equal opportunity employers with some insurance against their policies being flouted. Implementation is once again the key factor. Enforcement of anti-discriminatory behaviour and practices is more likely to be effective when staff are made aware of the consequences of default. Thus, the realisation that dismissal would be a possible consequence of racial discrimination or racial abuse becomes a real deterrent for most staff who might otherwise avoid compliance with the new arrangements.

At a general level, in-service training is crucial to familiarise staff with all new policies and practices and the behavioural expectations of the employer. Training for existing employees also surrounds the daily experiences of staff. For instance, the sorts of training offered to park-keepers would be different from that for social workers, and these would again differ from those offered to receptionists or refuse collectors. The workplace problems are different, yet the race factors are basically the same. Racism awareness training is a relatively new innovation, which is regarded by an increasing number of professional trainers and specialist race workers as an effective means of dealing with the issue of racism per se. Some local authorities have introduced varying degrees of racism awareness training, as well as what is also described as human awareness or race sensitivity training, so that their white staff can have their racism exposed and confronted before attempting to implement race equality policies and programmes. The harsh reality underpinning the concept of racism awareness training is that racism is a white problem which has to be resolved by white people themselves. The training provides the opportunity to identify racist conditioning and facilitates exposure of individual biased conditioning as well as processes and conditions for change.

The final aspect of training offered under the heading of race equality programmes is the resources made available for black staff to improve their career prospects. 'Not qualified' is a frequent reason offered for overlooking blacks for promotion or appointment into professional positions. Specific qualifications can be acquired if assistance is given to black staff through access to training and study courses.

Service provision

Perhaps the two most important services provided by local authorities as far as black people are concerned are education and housing. Both have been the subject of much criticism; volumes have been written about racism in education and housing allocations and have provided irrefutable evidence of racial discrimination. A look at social services and a range of other services also raises a number of issues.

Education

Early race issues in education surrounded the campaigns to get black children out of the Educational Sub-Normal Schools, and the bussing of black children (particularly Asians) out of their local areas to 'prevent their over-concentration' in schools. Thus racism in education was a major factor in the 1950s and 1960s as it is today in the 1980s. Now however, multi-ethnic and multi-cultural education are in vogue, which has basically meant adding black history and culture to the margins of the curriculum. Marginal approaches yet again in the form of special projects (black studies), multi-cultural teachers, and special language classes have dominated. The debate around the educational underachievement of black children coming out of the state schools has, however, brought racism in the education system firmly back on to the agenda. Although parent pressure mounts, very few authorities are now pursuing anti-racist education.

The new movement starts with an unequivocal identity of racism, locating its responsibility with the white community, acknowledging its divisive and damaging effects and committing resources to its removal. Initiatives being pursued by progressive education authorities include recruiting black teachers at all levels, seeking anti-racist declarations and commitments from the teaching profession, incorporating racist behaviour as a serious disciplinable offence, removing all racist publications from schools, using only anti-racist and multi-racial materials, monitoring black children's progress academically and involving black parents as governors, on parent–teachers associations and as activists in helping to shape education policy for the whole community. The Inner London Education Authority and the London Boroughs of Brent and Haringey are three authorities who have attempted some or most of these initiatives.

Housing

As is well known, a very high percentage of black households are concentrated in some of the worst inner-city areas, with Asian households mainly in (substandard) private ownership and Afro-Caribbean households increasingly in council housing, particularly the oldest and least desirable estates. The Runnymede Trust study of the Greater London Council in 1976[2] and, more recently, the Nottingham study confirm racial discrimination as a major causatory factor.[3] When Lambeth Council monitored its allocations policies and practices in 1978 and 1979 it showed very clearly that black households, irrespective of their housing needs, were predominantly being allocated old pre-war and inter-war 'undesirable' accommodation, whereas white households were getting the new housing units (mainly houses with gardens). Some policies designed to meet different housing needs (for example, high priority for sons and daughters, transfers, and length of time on waiting-lists, low priority for homeless families) had an indirect discriminatory effect on black households, and were amended accordingly. Beyond this, however, there were more than strong suspicions of individual discriminatory practices, although they were substantially unproven. Much of the remedial action concentrated on changing both policy and practice. Certainly, by setting equality targets and monitoring these, Lambeth Council was able to show that whereas only 2 per cent of black households got the best quality accommodation in 1978, more than 30 per cent did so by 1981, thus exceeding the target. So-called 'positive discrimination' had not been used. Instead, the Housing Department's Race Relations Adviser was involved in pre-allocations monitoring to ensure that offers were being made in line with needs and entitlements. More generally in the housing field, the most progressive councils are making sure that all services offered (rent rebates, mortgage advances, improvement grants, housing improvement programmes) are monitored to ensure equality and fairness, black staff are recruited at all levels, black households get access to a fair and equal share of new and existing resources, and that effective policies and procedures for dealing with racial harassment on council estates are developed and implemented.

Social services

The social services are beginning to experience the same sort of backlash once reserved for the education system. It is black families themselves who are in the forefront of challenging racist policies and practices developed over the past two decades as a result of paternalism, maternalism, traditionalism, cultural misunderstanding and professionalism. When mixed with deep-seated racism the results are, not surprisingly, disturbing. Disproportionate numbers of black children in care, family relationships fractured through misguided intervention, wrong pleadings on behalf of juveniles before the courts, and disturbingly large numbers of admissions into the mental institutions. The issues are complex and it is true to say that, through social and community work, many professional workers have become dedicated to assisting black families experiencing problems in their community. However, without the recognition, understanding and countering of racism it was inevitable that mistakes would be made.

Putting in black professionals has not proved to be the answer, because there have been relatively few and most have been unable to influence policy-making. More effort to change the outlook and challenge racism would help. However, a closer involvement with and understanding of the new black community networks (self-help initiatives have been mushrooming all over the place as alternatives to inadequate state-run provision) would necessitate new radical approaches for dealing with black families and individuals with needs. With such influences, the challenges to existing institutional caring arrangements, whether for children, adults or the elderly, would have to accede to culturally beneficial alternatives such as giving greater support to sustain extended family networks where these can be preserved with sensitive state support.

Other service provision

Without doubt, all local authority services have the potential for adverse impact on black people. Because of racism, constant and continuous attention has to be given to all service provision to secure fairness and provision relevant to all needs of black people. Progressive local authorities have been making explicit arrangements for their black communities in recreation, sport, the arts, libraries, employment promotion and job creation, town planning, environmental health and consumer services.[4]

Recent innovations, especially in London in the form of women's committees, police committees, community affairs committees and employment committees, have major implications for race equality and anti-racist policies. Those authorities with these new committees are more likely to have race committees anyway. Employment committees can assist directly with the creation of jobs for black people by imposing conditions of grant or financial assistance to firms which make it impossible for them to discriminate. In addition direct assistance to existing and potential black employers can have a similar desired effect. Women's committees should have anti-racist stances alongside their anti-sexist commitments, involving black and other ethnic minority women from the outset in all activities. The London Borough of Camden and the GLC are two authorities with these dual objectives.

Another potentially productive area for anti-discriminatory work is through contract compliance activity. This entails local authorities not trading with firms who do not pursue equal opportunity policies. Such firms would be removed from approved lists of tenderers, suppliers and contractors if they refused to comply with reasonable requirements for recruiting black people (as well as other groups of employees such as women at all levels and disabled people in appropriate jobs). This is a relatively new area and although some local authorities already impose anti-discriminatory conditions, few follow up compliance because of resource implications. Some authorities like Sheffield and Lambeth have anti-apartheid stances and would not deal with any tender, supplier or contractor with links, however tenuous, with South Africa. Sheffield in fact have gone further than most and designated their area an 'anti-apartheid zone'.

Local authorities can use their spending powers strategically to fight racism and inequalities, by imposing conditions on grants to secure equal opportunities and non-oppressive practices, described in the previous paragraph; placing advertisements in publications which show bias to racial minorities; and actively trading and dealing with firms with proven anti-racist commitments. 'Purse power' can and does make things happen, whereas monitoring or exhortation without clout is virtually meaningless. So far only the GLC has made available a reasonable amount of resources to back its newly established contract compliance, and it remains to be seen how successful it will be given the constraints and limitations of Britain's anti-discrimination legislation compared to the USA.

Grant aid

To some extent the assistance provided by local authorities to encourage and sustain voluntary initiatives to meet the needs of the disadvantaged groups in their localities should be seen as a cost-effective means of providing some services of benefit to black people. Sadly though, this has not been the case. Instead, progressive local authorities have had to be very vigilant in persuading voluntary sector groups to fulfil their equality under-takings to involve black people and respond to their particular needs. Furthermore, this has had to be supplemented by programmes of specific financial assistance for black self-help programmes and projects. These have mushroomed over the past decade, because of the failure of both statutory and voluntary sectors to respond effectively to their particular needs. Thus grant-aid is another specific area of policy development requiring an anti-discriminatory approach, and should therefore be placed within the context of an anti-racist strategy.

Consultation and participation

Involving black people in policy development and implementation is an essential prerequisite for developing effective anti-racist and race equality strategies. If equality existed, the number of blacks selected and elected as members of authorities, the number of black chief officers and senior officers, black involvement in pressure group and voluntary sector activities (for example, tenants' associations) and black involvement in local authority consultation programmes would be proportionate to the representation of blacks in the community as a whole. Alas, this is not the case. In the circumstances, while efforts have to be made to achieve larger numbers of black councillors and senior managers, the efforts of progressive authorities have been to increase black involvement in consultation programmes and special programmes relating to race equality, the urban programme and black self-help projects.

Black people, by and large, will feel that any special initiative developed by an authority is not really in their best interests unless they were involved in its initiation, development and implementa-tion. Not that this ideal arrangement ever works in reality.

Inevitably, consultation tends to involve a minority, usually the most articulate and active members of a local community, who are not necessarily representative of mass views or indeed necessarily sensitive to views other than their own. Whatever the arrangement, those who are not involved regard any new 'race' initiatives with suspicion and even contempt.

Effective consultation is where views are sought, nurtured and developed, and where proposals are formulated before authorities have devised their own ideas. There are not many examples of ideal models, although general structures of note can be identified. There is support for a Joint Consultative Committee in Haringey, and Lewisham has set up a Joint Working Party on Race Relations. Some other authorities, for example Greenwich and Hackney have relied on co-options on to committees, although in Southwark co-option was attempted but failed because of imprecision and confusions about membership. Southwark in fact spent over a year (1982–3) without sorting out its consultative and participatory arrangements for black people. The Inner London Education Authority spent nearly two years trying to reach some agreement about consultative arrangements which would give black people power, by placing them at the decision-making table as well as creating supplementary arrangements for wider involvement in policy and other education issues on a divisional level as well as London-wide.

The issues are fraught with dangers and even after time-consuming and seemingly endless rounds of discussions, there are always groups of people trying to discredit such arrangements. Some authorities such as the GLC have in fact avoided fixed arrangements. Instead, the GLC, through its Ethnic Minorities Committee has gone for consultations based on issues (health, unemployment, youth, the elderly, arts) and with specific commitments, for example, to Afro-Caribbean people, youth, migrants, gypsies and travellers, Asians and Irish. During an eighteen-month period over thirty such meetings have taken place, with over 3,000 people participating in different forums. One consultative conference on the theme 'Challenging Racism in London', in March 1983, attracted over 850 people. Not only was it one of local government's largest gatherings but it was a unique occasion for local government in anti-racist terms. The main purpose of such arrangements are to get the black communities and other identified ethnic minority groups to assist with the shaping of policies, to be involved through the exchange of information and ideas in the implementation of race equality programmes, and to monitor progress.

At the end of the day, it must be conceded that there is no flawless system of consultation. Certainly none is known which harnesses both the aspirations and frustrations of the black communities. The recognition that information is one of the keys to power, and that black people are generally powerless in relation to the control of institutions such as local government should, however, help local authorities to start meeting their obligations to their black inhabitants. Because racism is very much the result of white power, the challenge to racism is inevitably aimed at the whites who hold the power, the very same people who oppress powerless whites. Thus, any shift of power towards blacks in terms of institutional control must be done with the understanding that a new form of non-oppressive local authority provision is now necessary to make local authority services meaningful for those most in need.

That is why the new mood among the progressive local authorities must be to locate all race equality programmes within an anti-racist, non-oppressive context. Few authorities in Britain so far have captured the new mood or even accept that any other initiatives, however well-intentioned, are more or less doomed to the same fate as all other marginal programmes. It remains to be seen how much resistance the anti-racist strategies meet. If the media and government responses to the GLC's anti-racist strategies are anything to go by, there are major problems ahead. The June 1983 General Election confirmed that the four million or so unemployed had passively accepted the resolute approach as the way forward to solving the country's economic ills. That being so, the challenge against racism seems destined to be fought out in compartments of marginalism in the foreseeable future.

A very few local authorities have indicated an acceptance that marginality must be rejected. They are, however, up against a centralist state that is determined to thwart local government under the guises of expenditure controls, rate reductions and even abolition. It so happens that the most vulnerable authorities are those showing a new determination to dismantle racist structures from their institutions. Meanwhile, the state is nurturing the

emergence of a new black middle-class élite while making sure that
the state's public control apparatus is better equipped to deal with
any further uprising from the oppressed no-hopers.

Notes and References

1. *The Brixton Disorders 10–12 April 1981*, report of an inquiry by the
   Rt. Hon. the Lord Scarman, OBE, Cmnd. 8427 (HMSO, 1981).
2. *Race and Council Housing in London* (Runnymede Trust, 1975).
3. *Stacking the Decks* (Nottingham and District CRC, 1981).
4. *The System*, a study of positive action in the London Borough of
   Lambeth, 1981 (available from Runnymede Trust).

TABLE 6.1 London borough race initiaves, July 1983

Borough	Maj. Party Labour/ Conservative	EOP Comprehensive Employment	Member Structure	Officer Structure	Adviser Posts	Ethnic Records	S.11 – use (1980/1) £	NCWP Population % 1981 Census
Barking	L	–	–	–	–	–	71,461	4.1
Barnet	C	–	–	–	–	–	302,201	12.6
Bexley	C	–	–	–	–	–	–	4.2
Brent	–	Comp.	Race Rel. Sub-Committee	Race Unit	Principal Housing, Social Services Personnel Libraries	All Depts	2,002,269	33.0
Bromley	C							3.6
Camden	L	Comp.	Race Rel. Committee	Equal Opp. Monitoring Group	Principal Housing Social Services Training	Some Depts	71,0749	10.1
Croydon	C						550,922	11.9
Ealing	C						2,004,512	25.0
Enfield	C						199,571	13.9
Greenwich	L	Empt	Race Rel. Sub. Comm.	–	Principal (2) Housing	Agreed but TU opposition	130,091	7.9
Hackney	L	Empt	Race Rel. Sub-Committee	–	Principal Housing Social Services Personnel Leisure	Personnel	131,107	27.5

TABLE 6.1 Contd.

Borough	Maj. Party Labour/ Conservative	EOP Comprehensive Employment	Member Structure	Officer Structure	Adviser Posts	Ethnic Records	S.11 – use (1980/1) £	NCWP Population % 1981 Census
Hammersmith & Fulham	C	-	Race Rel. Committee	Officers' Group	Principal Business	-	20,087	14.8
Haringey	L	Comp.	Consultative Committee	-	Principal Business	-	1,744,345	29.4
Harrow	C	-	Community Affairs Sub-Committee	Officers' Group	-	-	271,187	15.2
Havering	C	-	-	-	-	-	-	2.4
Hillingdon	C	Empt	-	-	-	-	117,032	6.5
Hounslow	L	-	(Finance & General Purposes)	-	(PA to Chief Executive)	-	386,169	16.9
Islington	L	Comp.	Race Rel. Sub-Committee	Working	Principal Housing Social Services Leisure	Housing	45,791	16.5
Kensington & Chelsea	C	Empt	Community Rel. Committee	-	Community Relations	-	81,088	8.9
Kingston	C	-	-	-	-	-	-	5.3
Lambeth	L	Comp.	Community Affairs	Race Rel. Unit	Principal Housing Leisure Personnel	All Depts	116,681	23.0

Borough								
Lewisham	L	Empt	Race Rel. Committee	-	Housing Social Services (¾ corporate planner)	Personnel Housing	29,612	15.0
Merton	C	Comp.	-	Community Affairs Sub-Committee	-	Personnel	138,828	10.6
Newham	L				Principal Housing	Housing	750,116	26.5
Redbridge	C	-	-	-	-	-	270,057	11.0
Richmond	C	-	-	-	-	-	-	4.5
Southwark	L	-	-	Race Equa.	Principal	-	96,362	16.2
Tower Hamlets	L	Empt	-	Working Party	Social Services	-	99,600	19.8
Waltham Forest	C	-	-	-	-	-	929,597	17.3
Wandsworth	C	Empt	-	Working Party	Housing Personnel	Housing Personnel	23,785	18.4
Westminster	C	-	-	Ethnic Min. Committee	Principal Services Arts Employment Personnel	Personnel	14,442	11.5
GLC	L	Comp.						
ILEA	L	Comp.	Equal Opp. Unit		Principal Inspectorate			

7 Local Economic and Employment Strategies

MARTIN BODDY

Since the early 1970s, local authorities have become increasingly involved in economic development activity directly related to production and investment. As unemployment soared, provision of industrial sites and premises, advertising and promotion, and provision of loans and grants became an established part of mainstream local government activity. Then, following political shifts in the early 1980s and with unemployment headed towards three million, several Labour authorities, Sheffield, West Midlands County and the GLC in particular, started to develop more radical economic and employment strategies, exploring socialist alternatives. This chapter focusses in particular on these more radical initiatives, the forms they have taken and their potential and implications. First, however, and by way of context, the more traditional approaches can be usefully outlined.

Mainstream approaches

Many authorities around the country have some history of economic development activity through, for example, municipal trading estates. The early 1970s, however, saw a rapid expansion in levels of expenditure, the number and type of authorities involved and the range of activity and innovation. Action has fallen into three main areas.[1]

1. *Sites and premises.* Provision of sites for industry is a traditional area of involvement which expanded markedly from the early 1970s, while the building and letting of factory units,

160

particularly small or 'nursery' units mushroomed. Three-quarters of respondents to a 1974 survey had sites available and over half had premises.[2] Environmental work, derelict land reclamation and industrial improvement area initiatives have been widespread.

2. *Promotion, advertising and advice.* General promotion of particular localities, marketing specific sites and premises, provision of property lists and information or advice services are important in a wide range of authorities, some of which are big spenders in this field. Much activity, usually focussed around Economic Development Officers, aims to attract firms expanding or relocating from elsewhere in the country or abroad, or to promote new businesses in the area.

3. *Finance.* Some authorities, particularly in the main con-urbations and the less prosperous regions, provide loans on 'soft' terms and, less commonly, grants, mainly to small businesses. These relate mainly to acquisition of sites and premises but possibly to plant, machinery and operating costs. A third of respondents to the 1974 Survey were active in this area, but most on a very small scale.

These broad headings encompass a great variety of activity and scales of involvement in different authorities. This has been accompanied in many cases by organisational changes and the establishment of economic development committees and units within local authorities. Activity has been funded through a variety of means including the Urban Programme, Section 137 of the Local Government Act 1972,[3] the Community Land Act (1975 to 1980) and by drawing on authorities' own rates balances, capital receipts and main programmes. Joint schemes with private developers and financial institutions have become common.[4] More generally the 'policy environment' in many authorities, particularly in the areas of planning, transport and infrastructure provision, increasingly reflected a commitment to facilitating 'enterprise' and economic development.

The initial expansion in economic development activity was largely a response to rising unemployment and economic decline, particularly in manufacturing industry, and their consequences in the wake of the oil crisis and the massive rise in interest rates. As the crisis deepened, however, authorities responded to rising unemployment in the historically more prosperous parts of the country, the Midlands and South East and the inner areas of the major conurbations including London. Local government reorganisation, the rise of strategic planning and corporate management and increasing concern to implement strategy, coinciding with accelerating unemployment and economic crisis, further stimulated policy development in many authorities. Local economic policy, moreover, received some support from the government in *Local Government and the Industrial Strategy*,[5] while the Inner Urban Areas Act, 1978, recast the Urban Programme in more of an economic development than social welfare mould, which subsequent central government policy has reinforced.[6] Regional policy, on the other hand, while remaining important has been running down. Spending was almost halved in real terms from 1975–6 to 1979–80, Industrial Development Certificate refusals are now insignificant and the designated assisted areas have been substantially cut back, although Development Agencies remain important in Wales, Scotland and Northern Ireland.[7]

Underpinning private enterprise

Despite the variety of activity and emphases, local authority economic development activity since the early 1970s tends to share a number of key characteristics. First, activity has been *property led*. The main emphasis, growing from authorities' traditional planning and estates activity, has been on providing sites and premises, and financial assistance has also related mainly to land and premises. This implies the very questionable underlying assumption that shortage of land and premises is a major constraint on economic activity, or at least the main constraint on which local councils can get leverage. In a 1982 survey of one hundred small firms, only five mentioned inadequate site or premises as a constraint on output, while more generally there is a glut of industrial property throughout the country.[8] Central government policy has also encouraged this property-led emphasis, through the way inner city policy has been implemented, Urban Development Grants and Enterprise Zones.[9]

Second, local authorities have been *market and business related*. The overall aim has been to stimulate or attract in private enterprise by creating the preconditions for profitable investment. Policies have thus relied on the independent decisions of individual firms in the market and on subsidising the costs of private capital. Policies, aid and promotional activity have been oriented to business, the manager, the investor – the ethos and image of economic development officers is that of enterprise and big business.

Third, while jobs have been the ostensible aim and unemployment the initial stimulus for much of this activity, the main focus has been on economic development and *employment has been secondary*. It is assumed that benefits will 'trickle through' to the labour market, with little concern to target policies to benefit identified disadvantaged groups, women, ethnic groups, the low paid or long-term unemployed. Sustained by a general belief in the benefits of economic development, the link from economic policy to the labour market has been largely taken for granted.

Fourth, in attempting to attract what few firms are expanding or relocating from elsewhere, local authorities have been competing one with another in an uncoordinated way playing 'beggar thy neighbour'. Competing in a limited market and duplicating expenditure on promotion, provision of sites and premises has undoubtedly been wasteful and inefficient, at best shifting jobs around like deck chairs on the Titanic rather than securing real economic growth. Little attention has been paid to retaining employment in existing firms, but some authorities have directed their attention overseas (more distant 'neighbours'?) or to stimulating new indigenous enterprise.

Finally, many authorities have placed considerable emphasis on new or existing *small firms*. In part, this reflects the scale of resources available and the local orientation of small firms which gives authorities a handle at this scale, but it also draws heavily on seedbed or acorn ideology, laying the foundations for future prosperity. This however simply ignores the lack of real evidence to link new business creation or a successful small firm sector to significant employment creation. Single closures of medium and large local employers wipe out the equivalent of tens or hundreds of small firms at a stroke, while in terms of quality of employment, small firms are frequently characterised by low wages, lack of unionisation and training, poor working conditions and job insecurity – the new sweatshops.[10]

Mainstream approaches have thus been property-led, business and market orientated and competitive, with economic develop-

ment rather than employment the primary focus, and with an
emphasis on small firms. The impact of this activity is, however,
hard to assess even on its own terms. Evaluation tends to be based
on sites or premises developed and let, numbers of enquiries
received from firms or numbers of loans given, together with the
numbers of jobs involved in these cases rather than on hard
evidence of what would have happened *without* local authority
involvement, how many firms set up in the local area and how
many jobs were created or retained as a *direct* result of local
authority activity, and the extent to which these firms or jobs were
lost by other localities.[11] Local government has in effect ended up
underpinning private enterprise, and taking on part of the burden
of production costs.[12] Different activities have related to different
elements of private capital. The emphasis on small firms has linked
local authorities to small – often local – capital. Promotional
activity, provision of larger sites and infrastructure has been
directed to national and international enterprises. Links with
property capital have been established through the development of
estates and premises. Local authorities have thus become
increasingly involved in the 'socialisation' of production costs,
ensuring the general conditions for private production and facilitating the profitability of private investment, without change or
challenge to existing relations between labour and capital. This
socialisation of production costs should not, however, be seen as a
necessary or inevitable process, as implied in some accounts of
growing state involvement in production. And to argue, as Chris
Pickvance does in relation to regional policy, that the range of state
policies is 'in principle limited by the need to secure the continued
domination of the capitalist class'[13] would be to gloss over the
variety of political structures and the balance of political forces at
the local level, and the question of how far local government is
inevitably a part of the capitalist state, sharing what Pickvance calls
the 'built-in link' of the state to the capitalist class.

The shared characteristics of mainstream local economic policy
reflect more than simply need, necessity or the inevitably capitalist
nature of the state. Although underpinned by the basically
capitalist nature of the production system and of the state,
explanation lies more in the combination of the ostensible aims of
policy as it has emerged in particular local authorities, in response
to, in particular, unemployment, the limitations of finance, powers

and other resources; and a context for policy of a predominantly private, market-orientated economic sphere, reinforced by a
dominant ideology which places the public sector generally and
local authorities in particular in a subordinate role to private
capital.

Nor is it a question of one-sided support for capital, since state
policy reflects the balance of political (including class) forces.
While it cannot reasonably be argued that local government
economic policy is a response to direct working-class demands
placed on local councils, the extent to which different councils have
responded to rising unemployment and the particular scale and
character of policies they have pursued does reflect the varying
balance of political forces and interests in different localities, as
well as the wider economic, political and ideological constraints
within which they have developed and operate. Mainstream
approaches have, however, done little to challenge these
limitations, to push beyond a context of support for private
enterprise or to challenge existing relations between labour and
capital. It is in this respect that the radical strategies now being
pursued in Sheffield, the West Midlands, Greater London and
elsewhere are particularly significant. So while the traditional
approaches discussed above will be dominant in most localities over
the next few years, with changes of emphasis, innovation and the
incorporation of successive central government initiatives, it is the
questions raised by these radical alternatives, the possibility for a
real change in direction and their relation to wider economic and
social strategies at local and national levels which I want to pursue
here.

Radical alternatives

In the early 1980s a number of local authorities, Sheffield City,
West Midlands County Council (WMCC) and the Greater London
Council (GLC), in particular, set about developing radical
economic strategies which broke away from the mainstream
concerns of the 1970s. In part, these moves reflected the local
impact of accelerating national unemployment, which had broken
the two and a half million mark by April 1981. As the cold winds of
the recession were felt in these traditionally more prosperous areas

of South Yorkshire, the Midlands and the South East, the shortcomings of mainstream policies became increasingly obvious. More significant, however, were political developments. In 1981 Labour took control of both WMCC and the GLC from the Conservatives, with a strong radical element represented on both Labour groups, while in Sheffield, traditionally Labour controlled, a younger, more radical group gained control in 1980. Important at a more general level were re-evaluation of the National Enterprise Board, experience gained through the Community Development Projects and other local action and resource projects, the Lucas Aerospace campaign to develop alternative products and forms of work organisation, other trades union initiatives and the producer co-op movement and, finally, attempts on the Left to develop some form of alternative economic strategy.[14] Manifesto commitments, policy development and key personnel were drawn in part from this background and all three councils started with a commitment not only to tackle job loss and the immediate crisis, but also to explore the possibility of developing socialist strategy in the economic and employment field in the longer term.

Sheffield

Sheffield City Council set up an Employment Committee and Department in 1981. The aim was:

> to co-ordinate everything the City Council can do (alongside trades unions, employers' and community organisations), (i) to prevent further loss of jobs in the City, (ii) to alleviate the worst effects of unemployment and to encourage the development of new skills, (iii) to stimulate new investment, to create new kinds of employment and to diversify job opportunities, (iv) to explore new forms of democracy and co-operative control over work.[15]

The initial motivation was the 'rapid rise in unemployment and the crisis facing Sheffield's industry', but 'the longer-term aim is to try to gain more direct, local democratic control over employment, and to impose a greater degree of social planning upon the structural and technological changes taking place in Sheffield'.[16] The broader aim is to ensure that 'a future socialist government has working models available of socialist planning and how this can be implemented'.[17] The Department became fully operational in May 1982 with an initial staff of thirty, about half recruited internally and the rest from outside, including personnel with specialist skills and individual experience drawn, for example, from the Community Development Projects and the Lucas Aerospace Combine. Additional staff have been recruited since and the total may reach sixty. The Committee's initial budget of £2.5 million was provided under Section 137 of the Local Government Act, 1972.

Sheffield's employment policy

1. Planned growth led by the public sector.
2. Regeneration of the local economy under local determination and control, with wide consultation from the bottom up, releasing the resources and skills of the community.
3. An emphasis on direct intervention to preserve existing employment and create new jobs, in contrast to an indirect approach through the property market.[18]

Broad areas of work identified at the outset included: developing an economic analysis and investment plan for Sheffield; investigating ways for the council to use its powers as an employer, a consumer and a provider of services to maintain and expand employment; monitoring, research and information disemination; work on new technology to prevent job loss, promote control over its introduction, and pursue job creation and product development to meet social needs; small-firm promotion, particularly co-ops and other new forms of ownership and control of work; training initiatives including working with Manpower Services Commission schemes; and promoting equal opportunities for women in particular, ethnic groups and the disabled.[19]

The City's previously high-profile promotional activity, including overseas efforts, have been down-graded and the 'open door' approach to financial assistance, responding to individual requests, has been revised with a view to directing assistance more in accordance with investment plans developed by the City Council in consultation with unions and other groups. Assistance will be linked to planning agreements, tailored to particular cases but

covering fair wages and rights to union membership, and implemented through checks, reviews of forward plans and liaison with
unions. Activities in the early months included an investigation of
the background and economic and social implications of the
proposed merger of public and private steel making in Sheffield, in
conjunction with shop stewards and the servicing of the Steel
Campaign's Committee; a detailed analysis of the future of the
cutlery industry; a feasibility study for a combined heat and power
system; financial support for several co-ops, including three
engineering co-ops formed in the face of planned closure; and
investment in a computer systems firm.

Priorities for work in 1983–4 gave increasing emphasis to public
sector employment including: campaigns against expenditure cuts
and privatisation, which threaten local authority employment and
service provision; projects relating to local authority employment
including positive action programmes for equal opportunities, a
low-pay campaign, promotion of high quality training using the
Youth Training Scheme, and the development of new technology;
the Council's role in the local economy, particularly its employment implications; and projects linking provision for unmet social
need and employment creation. Priorities relating to private and
nationalised industry included aid and assistance for small firms,
workers' co-ops and equal opportunities initiatives; attraction of
private sector finance in support of public sector schemes; and the
provision of research and resource facilities for workers.[20]

West Midlands

West Midlands County Council has established a dual strategy of
investment and income support under its Economic Development
Committee. Central to the overall strategy is the West Midlands
Enterprise Board (WEB) which aims to invest in selected companies
which have potential for long-term growth and employment
creation, and which meet the Council's economic strategy
objectives. The Board operates alongside an Economic Development Unit responsible for industrial strategy and monitoring as
well as income maintenance, training, Council purchasing policy,
co-ops and other economic initiatives which relate more to income
support and redistribution. Set up in early 1982 but not fully

staffed until later in the year, WEB is currently financed from the rate fund. The objective is however to secure finance from, in particular, pension funds including the Council's own fund to encourage direct investment in West Midlands firms.[21] The Board has been set up as an independent company with directors appointed by the Economic Development Committee, operating on a day-to-day basis at least at arm's length from the Council.

West Midlands Enterprise Board: Objectives

1. To preserve or create employment: this is to be seen in terms of the need to plan the future of enterprises facing financial and other difficulties.
2. To invest where there are long-term prospects of viability: here we are referring to the need to plan for the long-term future of the West Midlands and not to be restricted by short-term considerations.
3. To invest primarily in existing medium-sized firms (of 100 employees upwards): this means identifying viable parts of larger groups as well as independent firms in need of support.
4. To provide financial assistance through equity, loans and loan guarantees, as operated by a public development agency, in order to maximise the range of support which can be provided. Equity investments are particularly appropriate for firms where loan repayments would be excessive, as well as providing ratepayers and pension funds with a share in profits in exchange for taking the risk. Shares in firms will be sold when circumstances are appropriate – for example, if other local investors appear, or if the firm's management or workforce want to buy out our stake; this would enlarge the local ownership of firms.
5. To ensure accountability through planning agreements and other conditions which specify investment and employment targets, projects planned, union recognition and wage levels; planning agreements and all other conditions and investment should be agreed in conjunction not only with managements, but with unions too wherever possible: the Council views this emphasis on union involvement as in the best long-term interests of the firms concerned.

6. To invest in the interests of the community: this means that it is not just a matter of creating jobs doing anything, especially if the work may sooner or later put others out of jobs or may be environmentally or socially harmful.

7. To take into account, when calculating the rate of return on investments which use rate fund money, the cost to the community in terms of lost rate income, increased social services etc. which would have occurred if the investment had not been made. This social accounting approach should be used when looking at the returns to the Enterprise Board on all its investments; the result will be a higher rate of return to the community as a whole than to any single investor.[22]

Attention will focus on medium and large firms since this is where the greatest job losses occur, and which small or new firms can do little to offset, and the Council hopes to have adequate resources to make this feasible. The case is, however, seen for supporting unemployed workers attempting to develop products where it is important to retain active skills – co-operatives are seen as relevant here and are to be supported primarily for this reason. Land for industry and property development, like technology and training, are seen as related to the overall strategy rather than as ends in themselves. Indigenous firms in danger of closure or contraction because of cash-flow problems, but with long-term growth prospects, are singled out as investment targets since it is argued that 'many firms are affected by the decline of a sector or of a larger group of companies while remaining viable themselves if they can attract sympathetic investors'.[23] The emphasis is on identifying firms with long-term commercial viability unable to find backing among traditional institutions with short-term views and the main principle behind Enterprise Board investment is:

the positive commitment of the investor to the productive process, rather than an interest in short-term money management. Through planning agreements, involvement of unions and organisations like the shop stewards' movements (with their ideas for retraining and building on workers' engineering and production skills), the investments would be part of a new approach to the planning of production with finance firmly linked to a long-term view of the productive process.[24]

By late 1982, the Board was negotiating with ten pension funds including the County Council fund, which was considering a proposal to invest 10 per cent of its money in the West Midlands. The Board's allocation from the rate fund for the year was £3.5 million out of a total economic development budget of £7.4 million, and by March 1983, £3 million had been invested in, or allocated to, ten companies. The first major investment provided £450,000 in equity capital to save an aluminium casting company, Sage Aluminium Products, employing 140, which was threatened by the debt burden built up by its ultimate owners. Sage was one of Ford's two suppliers of high-quality castings, with the prospect of contracts for the new Sierra which would otherwise have been met from overseas. Short-term returns for WEB are unlikely, but the prospect is of long-term growth and defensible employment, and a planning agreement covering employment, training, health and safety, equal opportunities and trades union recognition has been concluded together with cost savings and management changes. As in Sheffield, it is intended to base investment on sector analyses and a study of the ferrous foundry sector was initiated in 1982.

GLC

Following the 1981 election, the new Labour-controlled GLC established an Industry and Employment Committee, an Economic Policy Group with an initial staff of five to advise the Committee and draw up a London Industrial Strategy, the Greater London Enterprise Board (GLEB) and a Greater London Manpower Board (sic–subsequently retitled as Greater London Training Board). The Enterprise Board is the main vehicle for implementing the strategy, with three main functions: *Investment to provide strategic or structural change* to include municipal and public enterprise and industrial co-operatives; *general investment* in enterprises newly starting up, at risk of closure or operating in areas or trades with high unemployment; *development* of factory sites.[25] GLEB was established as a limited company in July 1982 and is funded from GLC's own resources with an initial budget of £25 million for 1982–3, under Section 137 of the 1972 Local Government Act, but with the aim subsequently of tapping GLC and other pension-fund money. Financial support will normally take the form of loans and equity and levels of support will relate among other things to job creation. Investment is conditional on agreements with the company and unions concerned covering employment policy and future patterns of employment and investment, while leases of GLEB premises will include clauses covering minimum wages and working conditions, Inducements to firms seeking to move from regions of high unemployment are ruled out. One section of GLEB is responsible specifically for encouraging and assisting new producer co-operatives. The Manpower Board was a Council committee but with representatives from the unions and employers and the Manpower Services Commission. Its initial role was to draw up a London Manpower Plan, advise on manpower planning and labour market problems, and promote and develop training in co-ordination with other agencies in relation to labour needs, and the GLC's industrial strategy. As in Sheffield, traditional promotional activity has been wound down, signalled by the closure of the London Business Centre set up by the Tory GLC to advise small firms and promote London as a place to invest – its offices are now occupied, symbolically, by the Economic Policy Group.

The GLC approach: jobs for a change

1. bring wasted assets – human potential, land, finance, technological expertise and resources – into production for socially useful ends;
2. extending social control of investment through social and co-operative ownership and increased trade union powers;
3. development of new techniques which increase productivity while keeping human judgement and skills in control.[26]

Putting these into practice is centred around two themes, 'popular planning' and 'technology networks'. Popular planning aims to develop effective community and workplace involvement in both strategy and the implementation of the Council's industry and employment policy, making the economy more accountable to the people who live and work in London. This involves greater public control through GLC's own policies, involvement of unions and community-based organisations in policy development, extending industrial democracy through 'local planning agreements', and the extension of popular control through new forms of social ownership, including co-ops. A key element is the attempt to in a sense generalise the approach of Lucas Aerospace workers, encouraging proposals for socially useful production and services, going beyond traditional defensive strategies.[27] Unlike indicative planning backed by incentives or command planning through direct intervention:

> The main feature of a popular approach is that although the general principles of economic strategy are laid down by the elected political authority, the more detailed plans and priorities are developed through trade union and community groups participating in a planning process, supported, co-ordinated and implemented through the elected authority or one of its instruments.
>
> Moreover the *implementation* of the plans drawn up through this broadly based planning process is carried out in consultation and negotiation with the trade union and community groups directly concerned, for example through planning agreements. Like the command approach it is premised on the failure of existing market relations adequately to match resources with needs and wants. Unlike the command approach however, it does not assume that political authorities *on their own* can provide the best means of overcoming the deficiences of the market.[28]

Initial steps involve support for research, education, cultural projects and the development of local organisational bases to support the development of popular planning. A booklet, *Jobs for a Change* which sets out the approach in an attractive and accessible format was produced and widely distributed, and a newspaper of the same name was started up in April 1983.[29] Linked to popular planning is the attempt to promote technological innovation in a way which meets socialist objectives. Technology networks to link facilities and expertise in, particularly, polytechnics and universities to trades unionists and others developing employment plans, new forms of enterprise and socially useful products are central. First examples being explored include a 'Jobs from Warmth' plan, linking employment strategies to public sector heating needs; proposals for GLC involvement in cable television and the 'wiring up' of London:[30] and a 'Jobs from Child-care' plan linked to an expansion of GLC funding for child-care centres, to improve opportunities for women to participate in the formal labour market and reduce the burden on women of domestic labour.

More immediate activity has been stimulated in the face of threatened closures and redundancy with requests from workers for help. In the case of Austin Furniture, a large East End furniture factory which was in the hands of the Receiver, 150 jobs out of 400 were rescued. GLC offered to buy the factory for £1.25 million and provide 18 months revenue grant on the basis of £20 per job per week, on condition that plans for future business were negotiated with the unions and GLC. A buyer acceptable to the unions was found and the factory reopened. Revenue support was to be given quarterly, subject to GLC and the unions being satisfied that the management is meeting its employment commitments, while provision was made for the workers as a collective to share profit when the company became viable. The factory union organisation has a place on the management board, as does the national union to back factory shop stewards with national resources. In the case of Associated Automation, a GEC subsidiary producing coin-operated telephone boxes which was threatened with closure, the GLC was prepared to buy the factory and machinery and provide start-up capital to enable a form of cooperative organised through the union to maintain production, saving 182 jobs. Though profitable in the short term, future viability will depend on new product development. Finally, when Lee Cooper Jeans transferred production to Plymouth with the loss of 200 jobs, the Council facilitated the establishment of a small co-op among twelve women machinists, manufacturing children's clothes in consultation with potential customers on a nearby council estate. The economic rationale for investment, as explained by Ken Livingstone, is that: 'The Council provide finance up to a grant limit of £20 per job per week, on the grounds that an average industrial worker produces £160 value each week, stimulates a further £40 worth of London production through a multiplier effect, and furnishes a return to the public exchequer of an average of £70 per week'.[31]

Radical initiatives have thus developed on two levels. They have involved responding to the immediate crisis in the face of threatened job loss and intervening with the unions on the side of labour, in contrast to the management orientation of mainstream approaches. The attempt is also being made, however, to develop democratic socialist strategies through promoting union and locality-based involvement in bottom-up popular economic planning, the development of new forms of work organisation and control through municipal enterprise, local planning agreements and producer co-ops, the pursuit of socially useful production and service provision, and utilisation of new technology. New committee and organisational structures have been created, involving politically appointed and committed officers working closely with elected members who have been and remain centrally involved in the development and implementation of new strategies. Enterprise Boards have been established, albeit on somewhat different lines, in the West Midlands and Greater London financed initially by council funds, but aiming to draw in pension fund and other money. Promotional activity has been scaled down, the emphasis has shifted towards indigenous, mainly medium to large, firms, with property development facilitating rather than leading economic and employment objectives.

Towards a socialist alternative?

Defensive action

Faced with the immediate impact of the recession in terms of soaring unemployment and restructuring, much of this activity is essentially defensive, firefighting, trying to rescue something positive out of crises and immediate threats of redundancy and closure. Equally relevant, however, is the form taken by defensive action. By intervening on the side of labour in crisis situations, councils may be able to boost morale and provide public support, to work with unions in campaigns and preparing proposals and to back workers' struggles with political support and financial resources. WEB's backing of Sage Aluminium and other companies, Sheffield's work with the steel unions and GLC's work with Austin, Associated Automation and Lee Cooper are examples. And although these were essentially defensive actions, it has been possible to some extent to secure greater control for labour or new forms of work organisation out of the ashes. Different situations will however offer different possibilities depending on the specific causes of job loss,[32] ownership and funding structure, union organisation, the sector involved and the stage of development which capital–labour relations have reached. The development of sector studies, technology networks and new forms of financing, while central to longer-term strategy, are also important as a basis for effective defensive action.

Exploring and illustrating alternatives

While responding to immediate crises will, justifiably, take up considerable time and resources, it is seen as important that defensive, reactive activity contains the seeds of more general socialist principles and is linked to broader policy aims and the development of planned rather than *ad hoc* initiatives. In Sheffield, for example, it was felt that:

> In the early months of the Department, much of the work has been 'firefighting', responding to many requests for urgent help. There is now a need to go beyond this short-term crisis work and to develop a more planned and preventive strategy, in which the City Council takes the initiative and intervenes actively to prevent the loss of jobs, to identify new kinds of employment opportunities, and to explore all kinds of ways of bringing the local economy and employment under more direct democratic control.[33]

Radical employment policies offer the possibility of exploring and illustrating in a very practical way the alternatives and principles of socialist production, and can at least put socialist alternatives on the agenda in a way which mainstream policies avoid. Practical exploration and experiment, albeit in a less than favourable context, are essential to the development of socialist alternatives, which do not spring fully grown from the seedbed of theory. Illustrating the alternatives is essential to develop support for socialist principles, illustrating what they mean and how they relate in a practical way to working people's lives. In this sense bottom-up, popular planning, involving union and locality-based groups, new forms of work organisation and control, and the exploratory work in relation to new technology and socially useful production, are central. Much of this activity will operate at the level of building people's awareness and possibly involvement, what Hilary Wainwright of GLC's Economic Policy Group has called 'propaganda by example'.[34]

The particular commitment of WEB to equity finance and the attraction of pension fund money offers the opportunity to explore the possibilities for ownership and control of industry being achieved via financial institutions. This represents a working model for the sort of national strategy set out by Richard Minns,[35] an early member of WMCC Economic Development Unit, now policy advisor to WEB. He argues that take-over of financial institutions and pension funds in particular would provide an effective stake in British industry and a means for implementing some form of AES based on long-term investment by the institutions in accordance with socialist principles. The importance of WEB thus lies in part in its prefiguring this form of national strategy, representing even in the short term a more direct challenge to existing economic structures and power than other forms of 'illustrative' initiative effectively developed on the basis of subsidies.[36]

Alternative Economic Strategy and the regional dimension

The evolution of local initiatives has, however, a wider significance in relation to debates around the development of some form of Alternative Economic Strategy (AES) to be implemented by a future Labour government. For much of the debate has envisaged a centrist, top-down strategy based around nationalisation, industrial democracy and, in some versions, selective import controls while the debate has largely ignored issues of women's employment in particular and distributional questions in general.[37] Radical local authority initiatives have a potentially vital role in developing, and securing support for a democratically accountable decentralised AES, genuinely reflecting and building on union participation and locality-based organisations. As David Blunkett has argued:

If we genuinely believe in social ownership and democratic control of economic and industrial activity through direct intervention, then logically, local government as well as, and not instead of, central government should be a vital tool in this process ... Anything done at local level should not be seen as an alternative to bringing about a dramatic shift towards democratic socialist change from national level. Clearly, the international and national ramifications of economic and industrial activity outweigh any possibilities of socialist change taking place in isolated pockets in individual local areas. It is therefore as part of a total national jigsaw and not as separate endeavours, that local community responses must be seen. However, it is also vital to recognise that national plans, planning agreements, sector working parties and a range of activities associated with National Enterprise Board type initiatives have and will continue to fail unless they ensure the involvement of the people for whom they are supposed to be working.[38]

Local authorities would have a key role in putting such a strategy into practice, via Enterprise Boards combined possibly with regional bodies based on local authority and union representation, going beyond the Scottish and Welsh Development Agency model, which Labour's 1983 Members suggested might be extended to other regions. Something along these lines is suggested in the Labour Party's *Alternative Regional Strategy* discussion paper;[39] This proposes democratically accountable regional assemblies, regional planning boards, the scrapping of geographically-defined Assisted Areas, a regionally structured public expenditure programme, and a reconstituted National Enterprise Board linked to a network of regional or local enterprise boards.

Integrating economic and social strategy

Building economic and employment strategy from a local authority base also offers the opportunity of re-integrating economic and social policy. The development of economic and employment functions alongside local government's traditional role of service provision is, to some extent, breaking down the central government/economic and local government/social separation discussed by Peter Saunders in Chapter 2, a split which centrist alternative economic strategies have tended to reproduce. To the extent that radical strategy at the local level can successfully break with the corporate style of politics and policy, typifying economic policy at Central Government level and imported along with mainstream economic development policies to the local level, they may form a basis for combatting the priority accorded to economic, rather than social, strategy by most variants of an AES. As Walker has argued, the political relevance and radicalism of the AES is diminished by its preoccupation precisely with the economic, and acceptance that growth is a prerequisite for redistribution – an assumption shared across a wide political spectrum. This reifies the crisis as fundamentally economic, rather than relating it to a particular form of social organisation, power and interests. It also emphasises the centralism of the AES and ignores the fact, that popular support is most likely to be mobilised around the felt needs of citizens, the social components of an alternative strategy and people's direct experience of the state including, significantly, local authority services.

An emphasis on popular planning, social accounting and socially useful service provision and production within alternative economic and employment policies could go some way towards this goal. But it would also require the integrated development of social strategy, emphasising community participation rather than service delivery, and here the decentralisation of traditional local authority functions discussed in Chapter 8 is particularly relevant. Any split between economic and social policy as, for example, implied in the distinction which WMCC made early on between 'Investment in firms' and 'Redistributive policies'[40] may undermine longer-term strategy. Integrating economic and social strategy is also fundamentally important for the relevance of policy to women, given the particular relationship between local government and women both in the domestic sphere and the labour market, and also to black people.

This, in turn, has implications for how committees, strategy groups and personnel working in these areas relate to economic and employment initiatives.

Possibilities and pitfalls

What can be achieved?

If it is accepted that the recession, restructuring and job loss reflect international processes exacerbated by national government policies aiming to drive down wage costs, weaken the power of labour and facilitate restructuring in favour of capital, then there are severe limitations on what can be achieved at the local level in an immediate sense. Resource constraints merely re-emphasise this. Against the flood-tide of restructuring and job loss, gains in a tangible sense won through defensive struggles will inevitably look insignificant – by the end of 1982 around 785 workers had benefited through WMEB initiatives although the Council's target is to save up to 5,000 jobs a year. About 600 jobs were involved in GLC initiatives up to early 1983. If, however, radical strategies are to command and build credibility, resources and political backing, it is important that they are seen to be at least as effective on the same terms as mainstream approaches in the short run. It is important that the councils involved can, for example, point to lists of action taken, the number of firms assisted, jobs saved or training places established, if such claims are as valid as the traditional claims of economic development officers.

The objective must be, however, to go beyond these numbers games. In the shorter term at least, the main achievement is likely to be in terms of exploring and illustrating the alternatives with a view to the wider development of socialist economic and employment strategy. The potential for learning, for changing agendas and building support behind relatively limited practical alternatives should not may be underestimated. Lessons may be drawn from the impact of the Community Development Projects and of very limited experiments with new forms of socialist organisation, Lucas Aerospace and various trades union initiatives, and with much greater resources and a political base, local authority initiatives must have considerable potential.

Underwriting or undermining capital?

This raises the crucial question of how far 'radical' initiatives are dependent on local authority subsidy and whether this negates any direct challenge to capital. Robin Murray, for example, has argued in relation to the GLC, that the financing of new initiatives can be separated into commercial components – in which external funds such as pension fund money can be incorporated – and sub-commercial components – which would require revenue subsidies to meet the difference between expected performance and the normal rate of return.[41] This sub-commercial (subsidy) element allows the possibility of restructuring for labour rather than capital and as Murray argues, for the social rather than purely market valuation of individual projects, involving calculation of wider economic and social costs and benefits rather than basing evaluation purely on profitability in narrowly financial terms, at the level of the capitalist enterprise. This approach then, which seems to underly the GLC strategy in particular, allows space for the exploration and illustration of alternatives which do not show a commercial return narrowly defined, while providing for external funds to be drawn in.

The dilemma is that although exploratory and illustrative initiatives are insulated from commercial evaluation, they therefore represent no direct challenge to the existing economic structure and the power of capital, while the longer term gains from such exploration and illustration are inevitably nebulous and uncertain. As Richard Minns has argued therefore, a more fundamental attack on the economic power structure is necessary, via in particular the pension funds – a road on which WEB represents a first exploratory step.[42] The idea is that this does not involve subsidising capital, with the attendant risk of marginalising radical initiatives. Investment via enterprise boards should provide funds with an acceptable return, without any call on local authority funds. This involves putting together investment deals which funds themselves are not equipped or are unwilling to do, demonstrating that rates of return on investment via enterprise boards offer returns which meet funds' criteria compared with the alternatives, and arguing for the importance of longer rather than short-term results. In particular, this involves the enterprise board in identifying firms which, though non-viable in the short-run, are profitable in the longer term offering long-term capital growth.

The danger here is that the enterprise board simply ends up meeting a gap in the capital market and contributing to the better management of capitalist enterprise – municipal capitalism rather than municipal socialism. This may not be a problem. Barry Hindess, for one, has suggested 'the successful management of the British economy is an important and worthwhile political objective for the Labour Party' and that 'what is most disturbing about dominant strategies for a Left Labour government is that they seem designed to ensure that Labour doesn't get the chance to manage capitalism at all'.[43] More specifically, Minns has argued that such proposals 'basically add up to capitalism ... But intervention can at the same time be based on the advancement of socialist principles, such as greater accountability of capital (industrial and financial) to the workforce and to the community, and the greater planning of investment and production in Britain which is less wasteful of human and environmental resources.'[44] This much, he suggests it might be possible to get away with on the grounds that it is responsible investment and in the long-term interest of the firm. 'If we want to advance anywhere near controlling the financial institutions for productive investment, then that is the political reality'[45] and to achieve even this there are still tremendous obstacles to be overcome in convincing trustees, managers and members. Control through ownership, effective planning agreements and new forms of work organisation and control which represent a real change in capital–labour relations will nevertheless be crucial if enterprise boards are to be more than enlightened merchant banks.

Whether this can be achieved will in part depend on the political control and accountability of enterprise boards, and while there may not be any immediate problem in this respect in the West Midlands or GLC, the shortcomings of the National Enterprise Board signal the possible dangers. Whereas Sheffield, with secure Labour control of the Council, have kept direct control of policy and implementation close to the Employment Committee and Department, WMCC and the GLC set up Enterprise Boards as arms-length organisations with political control of WEB ensured by Labour councillors holding the majority on the Board and in the case of GLEB through detailed and legalling binding guide-lines, close working with the Economic Policy Group and the appointment of appropriate Board members. This structure was, in part, dictated by the desire to attract pension fund and other money through the Enterprise Boards. It might also be argued that this form of semi-autonomous, single-purpose agency might be freer to pursue effective policy and is more likely to survive a change of political control in some form. The problem, which may become more apparent as other authorities seek to establish 'enterprise boards', is that as an organisational form, boards can be harnessed to very different policies and principles. For example, 'while GLEB itself cannot be described as prefiguring socialist production except perhaps in its methods of investment appraisal and its unit responsible for municipal and co-operative enterprise, it has the potential to support, sustain and protect such prefigurative and defensive projects, if the political and industrial initiative is there to create them.[46] Control and accountability of enterprise boards and the structure of representation are therefore crucial if the narrow path to socialist principles is to be followed, if planning agreements and changes in capital–labour relations are to be achieved and if initiatives are to be built up with the full involvement of unions and locality-based groups, rather than through negotiation with managers and bankers.

Co-ops: socialism in one company?

Particular dilemmas are raised by producer co-operatives which seem to form an obligatory part of most radical litanies, despite the misgivings of many on the Left. Many examples of co-ops reproduce the worst features of small businesses in general in terms of pay and conditions, though bolstered by some form of socialist vision rather than small business ideology. More specifically, problems arise because co-ops are largely dependent on the market for sales and to some extent funding. As the GLC Economic Policy Group have recognised, they may operate as

> a new means for controlling labour within the workplace on behalf of financial captial: The market pressures on co-ops, as on any firm, are to increase the productivity of labour, and to expand profit. But with co-ops the danger is that the profit generated will be lost to those that produce it, either because they are forced to sub-contract at low prices, or because it flows out in the form of interest paid to money capital. Where private capital has run into resistance to expanded productivity from labour in private factories, co-ops may be one way of overcoming this resistance by breaking up the workforce into small groups of legally autonomous units who work harder because they appear to be working for themselves, but who are still tied into the imperatives of capital accumulation.[47]

The GLC is nevertheless,like many other councils, committed to supporting co-ops, offering finance, advice and technological aid. If as the GLC in fact argue it is possible, even on a very limited scale, to increase working people's control over production while, more generally, establishing successful examples of alternative forms of work organisation, then it might be worth insulating co-ops from some of the rigours of the capitalist world by providing a market for products linked possibly to other council initiatives, aid with funding, or premises, even though the central problems cannot be addressed.

Organisational issues

The process of building links with unions and locality-based groups and the concept of 'popular planning' from the 'bottom-up' itself contains problems, particularly when set against issues of political leadership. It is a question of how far the form and pace of policy development is genuinely determined by popular involvement rather than by councils setting out to implement manifesto commitments and their own strategies and seeking the support and involvement of unions and local groups in the process. The more general dilemma faced, for example, in relation to decentralisation, of how far local councils can pursue programmes and open themselves up to the real popular control is particularly relevant to the economic and employment field. The assumption behind popular planning from outside the council is that needs can genuinely be met by working through the local authority. The danger as one critic has observed is 'that the energies of extra-parliamentary organisations become policy oriented and divorced from their base struggles.'[45]

Within local authorities as well, there are problems of building support for radical economic and employment strategy and integrating this with other policy areas. The appointment of politically-committed strategy officers with particular skills and experience acknowledges the problems of developing and putting into practice radical policies within traditionally structured and socialised departments and committee frameworks, recognising the need for a specific focus. If, however, policy groups and committees remain isolated and unsupported by the main departments – planning, finance, estates, personnel and so on – much of their effort may be frustrated, for these policies need to draw on the entire resources of the local authority. In this sense, the status accorded to the policy in Sheffield through the creation of a full department and committee is important, contrasting with the much smaller Economic Policy Group in the GLC. Close working between members and officers will be particularly important with members fully involved in policy development and implementation but also confident in officers' ability to maintain the political commitment of this work on their own account. This goes well beyond traditional officer–member roles and relationships, however, and undoubtedly puts pressure on both.

Timescale

Underlying all these debates is the question of timescale. With the GLC and WMCC for example facing elections in 1985 and continued Labour control by no means certain, not to mention the likelihood of abolition, the importance of tangible gains in both a defensive and illustrative sense is doubly important. Such uncertainty underlines the obvious importance of electoral success to the effective development of radical strategies particularly in the longer term. It may to some extent be possible to establish structures and policies resistant in the short-term at least to dismantling – WEB, for example, might well gain some political support beyond the current ruling group which could ensure survival in some form. More important, however, may be the practical and political experience carried forward from current initiatives. Hilary Wainwright has spoken of the GLC creating 'a plan to haunt capital in London for years to come'.[49] Here the development of durable initiatives extending outside of the local authority will be particularly important – community and trades union research centres, technology networks and other forms of 'popular planning'. Propaganda and political education are likely to be more important in the longer term than the short-term gains in terms of firms and jobs created or saved on which they are grounded. In Sheffield, with secure Labour control ensured for the foreseeable future, the timescale for policies to prove themselves is less immediate, such that more attention can perhaps be paid to developing alternatives and building up links with unions and other groups in the locality than to outright propaganda or immediate results. As suggested earlier, however, tangible results are still likely to be necessary to ensure continued financial and political support from the Labour group.

Central government

At a different level, real progress beyond isolated examples and localities is unlikely without the sort of measures which a Labour central government, committed to the role of local authorities in economic and employment policy, might introduce. This would involve giving local authorities freedom to pursue economic and employment policies, possibly via general powers to carry out whatever activities are not expressly forbidden by statute, thus removing restrictions under Section 137 of the Local Government Act 1972 and constraints on municipal enterprise. An expansion of central government finance via increases in block grant, coupled with the removal of expenditure ceilings on local authority spending would be needed. Specific measures at national level to encourage or enforce contributions by pension funds and other financial institutions, possibly via a national investment agency would provide a firm base for the operation of local enterprise boards – without this, local boards are unlikely to develop on a wide scale nor get much beyond the initial steps being taken by WEB. More generally a context of reflation, expansion of public expenditure and a commitment to reversing the squeeze on the public sector would provide a fertile environment in which local initiatives could develop. It would be important, however, to ensure the full integration of local and regional initiatives as a component of national economic, social and employment planning and avoid lapsing back into the usual centrist strategies.

Back home

Finally, while radical and innovative initiatives will inevitably attract attention, funding and staff resources, it is vital to set alongside these new initiatives the potential of local authorities' own role as employers, purchasers and providers of goods and services on a massive scale – potential for exploiting authorities' more traditional roles in new ways. And there are massive shortcomings in even the most radical authorities. On the employment front, there is a very long way to go in breaking down rigid hierarchies of career structure and control, achieving equal job opportunities and rewards for women and black people, providing work – place nurseries and creches and providing training opportunities, before local authorities can be held up as examples. Yet local authorities are major employers – often the single largest employer in their area – and thus have the ability directly to affect the position of large numbers of workers in their own employment, and to themselves explore and illustrate alternatives as a model against which to measure other employers, to develop policies to be pursued outside the authority, and provide examples and encouragement for unions in other public sector bodies and in the private sector. The development of radical personnel policies, possibly with key 'political appointments', which directly challenge the structure of local authority recruitment and internal mobility in which sexism, racism and professionalism are endemic, should be central to any radical economic and employment policy. Implicit in this is the need also to secure real changes in union structure and practices.

Resistance to privatisation of local authority provision also has obvious employment implications in an immediate sense, and must be seen as a key element of economic and employment policy. Resistance needs, however, to be linked specifically to the benefits of local authority as opposed to private provision, rather than simply built around the employment issue – effective provision to meet socially defined needs coupled with the maintenance and expansion of employment should be the aim, linking, where possible, the interests of the producers and consumers of local authority goods and services.[50]

This raises the point that at present, 'popular planning', community involvement and accountability in relation to local authority goods and services are minimal in terms of both the producers and consumers, with a limited number of authorities only just starting to explore what these might mean in practice – one thing that decentralisation in effect offers is the opportunity to develop 'popular planning' in relation to local authority provision (see Chapter 8).

Given local authorities' massive purchasing power, the use of clauses in contracts to enforce compliance with policies relating to employment and the use of approved supplier or contractor lists which meet criteria laid down by authorities is a potentially important influence over employers in the outside world, which a number of authorities are starting to explore. The GLC for example set up a Contracts Compliance Unit in 1983 to develop this area.[51]

It is important to recognise, finally, that marginal changes to the pattern and level of local authorities' main programme spending, both capital and revenue, might have a much greater impact on employment in the locality, at least in the short term. The use of several million pounds of an authority's own resources to fund innovative economic initiatives where, it might be argued, the connection between expenditure and jobs is at best uncertain and the political impact something of a matter of faith, has to be carefully weighed against the jobs that could have been directly created by using these resources to expand the authority's workforce in some worthwhile way. Marginal expansion, say, to education committee budgets, might allow an increase in nursery provision thus improving women's place in the job market. Similarly, any underspending on capital programmes will have a significant impact locally, on construction industry employment particularly. Administrative resources devoted to maintaining expenditure target can thus have important employment implications, while arguments over the revenue implications of capital expenditure levels must also take these into account, particularly if revenue budgets include provision for economic and employment initiatives, the impact of which is uncertain.

Notes and References

1. For more detailed accounts see in particular M. Boddy, *Local Government and Industrial Development*, Occasional Paper 7 (School for Advanced Urban Studies, University of Bristol, 1982). K. Young and C. Mason (eds), *Urban Economic Development* (Macmillan, 1983), provides an excellent and up-to-date analysis of mainstream approaches. See also N. Falk, *The Role of Local*

Authorities in Industrial Development, paper represented to the Association of Industrial Development Officers Conference 1978; R. Gaunt 'Economic Development by District Councils', *Initiatives*, November 1982, pp. 13–15.

2. N. Falk, 'The Role of Local Authorities in Industrial Development'. In 1982, over 80 per cent of district councils were providing sites and over half providing premises (Gaunt,) 'Economic Development by District Councils'.

3. This allows a local authority to spend up to the equivalent of the product of a 2p rate, 'in the interests of their area, or part of it, or all or some of its inhabitants'.

4. M. Boddy, 'Changing Public–Private Sector Relationships in the Industrial Development Process', in K. Young and C. Mason, *Urban Economic Development*, pp. 34–52.

5. Department of the Environment Circular 71/77 (1977).

6. Department of the Environment, *Review of Tradition Urban Programme: Consultation Document* (DoE, 1980), guidelines issued by letter to partnership and programme authorities by the DoE, July, 1981.

7. J. Mawson, 'Changing Directions in Regional Policy and the Implications for Local Government', *Local Government Studies*, March–April 1981, pp. 68–74. J. Mawson and D. Miller, *Agencies in Regional and Local Development,* Occasional Paper 6 (Centre for Urban and Regional Studies, University of Birmingham, 1983).

8. R. Tym and Partners, *Monitoring Enterprise Zones: Year one Report* (Department of the Environment, 1982).

9. Ibid.

10. P. Brimson, *Small Firms: the Solution to Unemployment?* (South East Region Trades Union Congress, 1981); *Small firms and the London Industrial Strategy*, Economic Policy Group, Strategy Document, no. 4 (Greater London Council, 1983).

11. T. Bovaird, 'An Evaluation of Local Authority Employment Initiatives', *Local Government Studies*, July–August 1981, pp. 37–52. D. J. Storey, 'Local Employment Initiatives in North East England: Evaluation and Assessment Problems', in K. Young and C. Mason, *Urban Economic Development*, pp. 184–209. D. J. North and J. Gough, 'The Impact of Local Authorities on Manufacturing Firms: Recent Experience in London', in K. Young and C. Mason, pp. 155–183.

12. C. Pickvance, 'Policies as Chameleons: an Interpretation of Regional Policy and Office Policy in Britain' in M. Dear and A. J. Scott (eds), *Urbanisation and Urban Planning in Capitalist Society* (Methuen, 1981) pp. 231–66.

13. Ibid., p. 232.

14. See M. Ward, 'Job Creation by the Council: Local Government and the Struggle for Full Employment', Pamphlet no. 78 (Institute for Workers Control, 1982), pp. 16–24.

15. Job advertisement, January 1982.

16. *Employment Department: An Initial Outline* (Sheffield City Council, 1982).
17. D. Grayson, 'Sheffield's Employment Department', *Initiatives*, (February, 1982), p. 22.
18. Employment Department, Sheffield City Council, *Report* (September, 1982).
19. *Employment Department: An Initial Outline* (Sheffield City Council, 1982).
20. 'Strategies for the Employment Department 1983/84', Employment Programme Committee, Sheffield City Council, July 1983.
21. *A Proposal for Pension Funds and Other Institutions to Invest in the West Midlands* (West Midlands Enterprise Board Ltd, 1982). R. Minns, *Take Over the City* (Pluto, 1982) pp. 93–106.
22. G. Edge, Priorities for Economic, Development in the West Midlands', paper to WMCC Economic Development Committee, November, 1981.
23. Ibid.
24. R. Minns, *Take over the City*, p. 96.
25. Ibid., p. 93.
26. 'A Socialist GLC in Capitalist Britiain?', Editorial Collective, *Capital and Class*, 18, 1982, p. 125.
27. Ibid. See also H. Wainwright and D. Eliot, *The Lucas Plan* (Allison and Busby, 1982).
28. 'Popular Involvement in the Council's Industry and Employment Strategy and Its Implementation', Industry and Employment Committee, GLC Report IEC351 (1982).
29. GLC Economic Policy Group, *Jobs for a Change* (GLC, 1983).
30. Economic Policy Group. 'Cabling in London', Industry and Employment Committee, GLC, *Report* IEC586A (1982).
31. K. Livingstone, 'Monetarism in London', *Report to the Council,* GLC, 5 October 1982.
32. See D. Massey and R. Meegan, *The Anatomy of Job Loss* (Methuen, 1982), who distinguish between job loss due to rationalisation, intensification and technical change.
33. *City of Sheffield: Employment Department* (Employment Department, City of Sheffield, 1982).
34. 'A Socialist GLC in Capitalist Britain?' *Capital and Class*, Editorial Collective.
35. R. Minns, *Take over the City*.
36. R. Minns, 'Pension Funds: an Alternative View',·*Capital and Class*, 20, 1983, pp. 104–115.
37. A. Walker, 'Why We Need a Social Strategy', *Marxism Today*, September 1982, pp. 26–31. J. Gardiner and S. Smith, 'Feminism and the Alternative Economic Strategy', *Marxism Today*, October 1981.
38. D. Blunkett, 'Local Enterprise: How It Can Help the Alternative Economic Strategy', *Pamphlet* No. 79, (Institute for Workers Control, 1982) p. 12.
39. Parliamentary Spokesman's Working Group, *Alternative Regional*

Strategy (1982). J. Mawson and D. Miller, 'A New Look at Regional Planning', *Town and Country Planning*, January 1983, pp. 14–15.

40. Edge, 'Priorities for Economic Development in the West Midlands'.
41. R. Murray, 'Pension Funds and Local Authority Investments', *Capital and Class*, 20, 1983, pp. 89–102.
42. R. Minns, 'Pension Funds: an Alternative View', p. 114.
43. B. Hindess, *Parliamentary Democracy and Socialist Politics* (Routledge and Kegan Paul, 1983), p. 156.
44. Minns, 'Pension Funds', p. 112.
45. Ibid.
46. 'A Socialist GLC in Capitalist Britain?', *Capital and Class*, p. 126.
47. 'The Development of Co-operatives in London', Industry and Employment Committee, GLC *Report* IEC478,(1982).
48. J. Mitchell, 'Popular Planning Has a Lot of Meanings', note to conference 'London as it Might Be', GLC, 2–3 October 1982.
49. H. Wainwright, 'Local Authorities and the Fight for Jobs', paper to a conference 'Local Politics and the State', School for Advanced Urban Studies, University of Bristol, September 1982.
50. D. Whitfield, *Making it Public* (Pluto, 1983).
51. GLC Economic Policy Group, *Jobs for a Change*.

8 Decentralisation: Socialism goes Local?

COLIN FUDGE

Introduction

Proposals to decentralise local services and devolve political control to neighbourhood committees followed manifesto commitments and electoral success in the early 1980s. In Britain, such initiatives are being pursued by Labour councils, in opposition to the electoral success and apparent popularity of the Conservative Party and their policies on public spending and local government. However, it is also the failure of a centralised, statist socialism to match expectations, the declining reputation of council services and workers, and the waning of public support for the Labour Party that has led to the emergence of a new left grouping, with decentralisation of the local state as one of its political directions.

At the political or ideological level, they reflect the Left's concern with the socialist potential of local government. This concern embraces two main elements. The first is the idea of using 'the local state . . . as an example of what we could do as a socialist government at national level',[1] thereby creating local illustrations of socialism which provide positive experiences for people at the grassroots. The second is the notion of local government as an arena for contesting cuts in public expenditure, defending local social programmes and opposing Thatcherite policies.[2] Through these two elements, it is hoped that support will be mobilised and a new coalition with the traditional labour movement formed.

During the last two decades, there has in fact been considerable discussion and experimentation with new forms of political organisation at the local or neighbourhood level, in response to social and

192

economic problems and issues relating to the role of the local state. Three aspects of political organisation may be recognised at the neighbourhood level. The first has been identified as urban social movements, community action, community politics, urban struggles or micro-politics and involves community groups, tenants' associations or interest groups.[3] The second category of neighbourhood politics is party political intervention, usually as an element in a strategy to gain electoral support and broaden the popular base of the party. The 'community politics' of the Liberal Party provides a good example in Britain.[4] The third kind is more difficult to define, but would cover 'officially' sponsored neighbourhood management and community development schemes.

Clearly, in particular situations the distinctions between these three aspects of local political organisation are less specific; the different types of intervention merge in a complex pattern of neighbourhood political activity. The merging of different types of organisation and intervention has led to a number of approaches to change existing political and administrative moulds, and move towards 'new' forms of neighbourhood democracy. As well as a vast growth in attempts to involve the public[5] and the development of community work, there have been various experiments in area-based approaches to local government management and service delivery. The 'area management trials,'[6] for example, developed from the Urban Guidelines Studies of 1973,[7] and particularly the recommendations for area committees and neighbourhood offices and officers in the Sunderland Study.[8] The area management trials are significant since it is these authorities: Stockport, Newcastle and Liverpool who went on to attempt different forms of decentralisation in practice. This concern with neighbourhood autonomy and popular democratic control has emerged in more recent initiatives taken by the Labour Group in Walsall, and now being developed further in some of the Labour-controlled London boroughs, notably Hackney and Islington, but also Camden, Haringey, Brent and Lewisham.[9] Other authorities, for example, Sheffield and Southwark, whilst not rejecting the strategy outright have been concerned that pursuing decentralisation may deflect people away from strategies to defend, maintain and develop existing levels and approaches to service delivery.

Although the concern here is with decentralisation in parts of Britain, similar initiatives in neighbourhood politics can be observed in Italy, where party political intervention is provided by the actions and strategies of the Italian Communist Party;[10] in the United States where there are numerous examples of government-backed neighbourhood management schemes;[11] and in Norway and Italy, where in Oslo, the model neighbourhood councils[12] and in Bologna, the model *'consigli de quartiere'*[13] have been established. The growth of neighbourhood political activity, and consequent attempts to democratise and decentralise local authority services, is not just a British phenomenon but rather is international, albeit with considerably different underlying objectives and ideologies.

Thus it is in the context of deepening world economic crisis and a newly mandated, radical Conservative central government in Britain committed to reducing public expenditure in local government, and a number of Labour councils equally committed to defending and improving services and local democracy, that decentralisation in Britain has come to some prominence.

Proposals for decentralisation, and struggles around attempts to implement them raises a number of issues – the effective provision of services, local democratic control, accountability of politicians and bureaucrats, the breadth of the local political base, new forms of managerial and administrative efficiency, opportunities for illustrative or prefigurative forms of local control and self-management, diversionary practice from real struggles – of which some may be complementary, and others clearly contradictory.

This chapter reviews and attempts to make sense of decentralisation at the level of political practice and meaning. It does this by first describing the strategies and forms of decentralisation adopted in Walsall, and being proposed in Hackney and Islington. It then discusses the broader political meaning of decentralisation and the socialist potential of local government.

Strategies and forms of decentralisation

Whilst 'decentralisation' may be used to signify certain common objectives, the strategy for decentralisation being pursued in one local authority and the form it takes may be considerably different from that being pursued in another. The form of decentralisation refers to the range of services to be decentralised, the kind of activities to be undertaken by local authority staff, and the political organisation and life to be developed in the neighbourhood and the local authority area as a whole.

It is possible to limit decentralisation to a single service. This may not be decentralisation to some, but this is the kind of approach with which local authorities are already familiar. For example, ever since the *Seebohm Report* of 1968, which emphasised the importance of community-based social work, there has been a strong emphasis on area-based working within social services departments – an approach given renewed legitimacy by the recent *Barclay Committee Report* on social work which stressed the value of localised or 'patch' working.[14] Another service which, in many authorities, is organised on an area basis is housing management, with area housing managers and their staff operating out of area offices. Similarly, in a number of local authorities town planning has also been organised on an area basis, but with officers located centrally in area divisions. At the other extreme, it may be possible to decentralise all council services to local offices giving local control. Given that many authorities will already have some existing area arrangements, what strategies and forms are currently being pursued? Three, in particular, can be seen in practice which aid our understanding of decentralisation, although there are no doubt many more in the grey areas in-between. Here, each of these strategies is looked at in turn using the experience in three local authorities, Walsall, Hackney and Islington.

Walsall

The first strategy is to start with a particular service, develop it from its current form and then progressively extend the scope of decentralisation over time to other services. In Walsall,[15] the initial emphasis was almost wholly on decentralising housing functions (for example, rent collection, waiting-list registrations, repairs) which had hitherto been highly centralised. When the Labour Group took control of the Borough Council in May 1980, they set about implementing their proposals for neighbourhood democracy. By the time they had lost overall control in May 1982, they had been able to introduce a number of significant changes to the way services were delivered. Thirty-two neighbourhood offices were established, offering a comprehensive housing service for both public and private sectors. The original Housing Department was dismantled and about a hundred and fifty of its central staff of two hundred were allocated to neighbourhood offices. It had also planned to decentralise other services – social services, environmental health, leisure and education – and, in fact, the decentralisation of the Social Services Department was well advanced when implementation was halted by the incoming coalition of May 1982.

Walsall Borough Labour Party argued that 'people should be continually involved in decision making about themselves, their neighbours and their town'.[16] They suggested that 'people', 'councillors' and 'officials' need to work together if local authority services were to be made more effective.[17] The May 1980 manifesto promised a programme of 'community Housing Services Offices' (20–25 in number) and the setting up of 'Community/estate-based offices' for social workers, which ideally should be linked with the Housing Offices. The philosophy underlying both was that; 'socialism is most likely to be achieved in this country through participative democracy'.[18] Decentralisation, they argued, will break down the remoteness of local government, spread knowledge of how the system can be controlled locally, and increase people's experience and confidence to participate and make decisions. Thus through these changes it was argued a 'knock-on' effect, leading to democratisation of other capitalist and state organisations, would take place.

The Walsall approach

Service Objectives:

1. Services physically more convenient.
2. Services more informally presented.
3. Services more responsive to clients' needs.
4. A more comprehensive service.
5. Each area base as autonomous as possible.
6. Enhanced skills in dealing with public.
7. Reduced role of councillor as caseworker so can concentrate on policy role.

Community development:

1. Inject information into the neighbourhood.

2. Inject goals/services to make the most visible impact.
3. Generate increased participation.·
4. Provide local community with a 'unit' they can exploit to influence policy.

Relationship between council officials and public:

1. Attempt to stop 'buck-passing'.
2. Change attitudes towards public.
3. Allow 'front-line' staff to stay in that role.
4. Place 'people skills' above administrative ability.
5. Develop a more client responsive attitude throughout the staff by secondment to neighbourhood offices.

The approach in Walsall involved three sets of objectives. To facilitate this approach to decentralisation, Walsall under Labour appointed 70–80 new 'sympathetically-minded' officers to run the neighbourhood offices. Indeed it was this strategy that attracted considerable political controversy, with criticism from the Prime Minister that the appointment of such officers undermined the traditional 'neutrality' of the executive.[19] The very fact that Walsall found it necessary to employ such officers to work in the neighbourhood offices demonstrates the Labour Group's awareness of the problems of trying to introduce a more open and responsive service, and in overcoming the dynamic conservatism of the existing organisation. Indeed, in the Housing Department, staff went on unofficial strike for a period over the decentralisation proposals. This strike was only settled when the Labour Group agreed to a NALGO representative being present at all discussions.

To implement the initial aspects of decentralisation, the Labour Group formed a powerful Policy and Resources Sub-Committee which met twice weekly to produce the initial plans. In addition, the Chairs of all main committees met informally at weekly meetings. The councillors in the majority group needed to display considerable initiative, energy and expertise (as those in Nottingham and Brent had done in trying to implement their manifestos[20]), to overcome administrative conservatism and speed up the process of political and organisational change. The timescale envisaged by the Labour Group was a problem. Senior officers expected a much longer implementation period. The chief executive had forecast that it would take three years to set up the first neighbourhood offices. In the event, thirty-two were established in a year. The thirty-two, open-plan neighbourhood offices operated normal hours, plus one evening a week and Saturday mornings. The staff were required to respond to all issues. There was no receptionist. The main functions carried out at the neighbourhood office were rent and rate collection, housing management, housing and community services, the management of a small budget, and an information and advice service including a local newsletter. At the same time, the authority's own Direct Labour Organisation was completely reorganised and decentralised. This service was based on a mobile caravan system, operating in an area the size of three or four neighbourhood offices.

The main arguments in favour of this gradual approach based on one service at a time were first, in a pragmatic sense it was possible politically to achieve the objective and second, it gave the authority time to learn and adapt in the light of experience. The main arguments against were that it diluted the impact of decentralisation, and that the form and style of decentralisation was over-influenced at the outset by the nature of a particular service. For example, there is no reason to suggest that a housing- or social services-led decentralisation would necessarily produce the best overall model of decentralised services for the authority as a whole.

A second, more comprehensive strategy is to pursue the decentralisation of *all services*, unless sound arguments can be put forward for retaining a centralised approach in any service area. At the time of writing this is the strategy being pursued by the London Borough of Hackney.

Hackney

An extract from the draft *Redprint*[21] written by members of the Council's Decentralisation Working Group sets out their main criteria for decentralisation.

The Hackney approach

These common criteria bind together and give an overall coherence to the specific proposals for each service. They have emerged in discussion and debate over the past 9 months (since

May 1982) and may be said to make up the basic philosophy of the kind of decentralisation we wish to carry out. The main criteria are as follows:

(i) all services should be controlled from neighbourhood centres and exceptions to this rule need specifically to be justified,
(ii) power and decision making in the management of services and staff should be vested in a neighbourhood management team,
(iii) the staff of neighbourhood centres would be accountable to a democratically elected body of local representatives, which would play an increasingly important role in controlling the Council's services and resources,
(iv) the Council's main committees would provide broad policy guidelines within which local committees would work, but giving considerable room for local autonomy.[22]

In meeting these criteria for decentralisation, Hackney propose about thirty Neighbourhood Centres. Each ward will have one, some for geographical reasons will have more than one. Each Neighbourhood Centre will be the place where the Council services are co-ordinated. The Centres will be designed to be 'friendly and welcoming' with facilities for 'meetings, catering, listening to music, reading newspapers and books, duplicating, looking after neighbourhood workers' children as well as those who use the centre, emergency child-care facilities, as well as the normal facilities for the neighbourhood workers to carry out their work'. The centres will be open beyond nine to five and at weekends.

The work at the neighbourhood level will be carried out by a number of teams, some providing front-line services, others carrying out important back-up functions. The key team in the Neighbourhood Centre would be the neighbourhood co-ordination and information team. Other teams housed in the Neighbourhood Centre would be:

1. *The family and personal support team.* Responsible for generic social work, home-help services, meals-on-wheels, luncheon clubs, the provision of residential care, occupational therapy, fostering and adoption, and intermediate treatment.

2. *Community resource team.* Responsible for day nurseries,

child-minding service, community play schemes and all aspects of play provision, community arts, school holiday programmes, community liaison and community centres, support for local sports clubs, development of cross-cultural links, exhibitions, local library services and exhibitions of local works of art and decentralised exhibits from the central Art Gallery.

3. *Housing support team.* Advisers to both public and private sectors on all housing matters, responsible for seeing that essential maintenance and repairs of Council's housing stock are carried out. This support team would also be responsible for the operation of the Council's housing list and allocation of points to people on the waiting list, letting of short-life properties, approval of loans to housing associations, preparation of decanting, rehousing homeless families (subject to some central overview), improvement grants, administer the multi-occupancy scheme and be responsible for aspects of environmental health relating to upkeep and maintenance of housing.

4. *Environmental improvement team.* Responsible for all environmental health matters and environmental improvement. On environmental health this includes pollution control, clean air, trading standards shop and food hygiene, animal diseases, registration of hairdressers and barbers and licensing of pet shops and stalls. On environmental improvement this includes planning and open spaces, processing planning applications, protecting the environment and historic buildings, co-ordinating highway planning, preparing groundwork on borough plan, inspecting street markets and highways, preparing schedules of dilapidation, preparing compulsory pruchase orders and dealing with valuation of property.

5. *Local service teams.* These are also envisaged in the Redprint. One would provide for building and maintenance in local neighbourhoods, and would include present building trades operatives, dealing with conversions and improvements, and specialist trades such as joinery, plumbing and heating, electrical and ventilation. This team would also be responsible for running an emergency repairs service, the security of leisure areas, maintenance of paly equipment, public conveniences and laundries. Other teams would include legal services and personnel.

6. *A common administrative service.* This would support all these teams in typing, support services for local representatives, collect rents and rates, manage money, keep records, link up with

central administrative services and use computerised systems for information storage and retrieval.

In the draft *Redprint* it is recognised that it may not be possible – or necessary – to have equal numbers of people in every centre. For example, a small professional group of, say, planners may be located in one centre, but serve the area covered by three centres.

All local services run from the Neighbourhood Centre will be managed by a *neighbourhood committee*. Under them will be a team of neighbourhood co-ordinators, drawn from the various teams employed in each Centre who will co-ordinate the day-to-day work of the neighbourhood. In order to have executive powers rather than purely advisory functions, Neighbourhood Committees will have to be formal Sub-Committees of the Policy and Resources Committee (as per the Local Government Act 1972, Section 102 S). Each committee would be responsible for all decisions in its ward relating to every council service and function delegated to its purview.

The intention is that Neighbourhood Committees will comprise, in addition to the present ward councillors *ex-officia*, a basic core of 'street representatives' supplemented by other local community representatives. The maximum possible membership of a Neighbourhood Committee may therefore be forty-eight members but in most Neighbourhoods Committees will be about thirty members. A notional breakdown of membership from the draft *Redprint* is given below:

TABLE 8.1   **Neighbourhood committee: a notional maximum membership**

Representative	Political Base	Number
Ward councillors	*ex officia*	2/3
Street	Residental 'patches' involving tenants' and residents' associations	15
Council workforce	Neighbourhood centres and other council establishments, local field workers, trades unions	5–10 (non-voting)
Community	Ward-based interest groups and user groups	say, 20
Total membership		42–48

The draft *Redprint* envisages that neighbourhood committees will be given delegated responsibility and powers to run all local services including the administering of 'area budgets', engaging staff and all local disciplinary and grievance matters. But if most of the power and the decisions are to be moved to the neighbourhoods, what will happen at the centre? What kinds of borough-wide administration, support and decision making will be maintained? The draft *Redprint* suggests that at this borough-wide level there could be four kinds of function:

1. *Policy and resources groups.* One for each service or programme area, to provide support for their respective service committees in relation to borough-wide analysis of needs, advice and information on possible policy developments, advice on resource allocations, assembling and co-ordinating borough-wide programmes, monitoring, and so on, external liaison and supporting borough-wide voluntary organisations. The Council and its Policy and Resources Committee will also obtain similar support in co-ordinating borough-wide policies and programmes.

2. *Secretariat and administration.* Supporting the new political structure; the Council, Policy and Resources Committee, Service/Programme Committees and Neighbourhood Committees.

3. *Borough registry and reference services.* Provided to the Borough as a whole and considered best located centrally. These include births, marriages and deaths, electoral registration, specialist library services, some licensing and registration.

4. *Specialist support groups.* Providing professional or technical advice and support for the neighbourhoods. It is envisaged that these groups will be accountable to the Neighbourhood Committees on a 'contract' basis and will work in Neighbourhood Centres, but not working solely on matters in that neighbourhood. The main groups involve architects, design engineers, quantity surveyors, valuers, clerks of works, some builders.

Subsequently Hackney Council Decentralisation Working Group prepared a second draft *Redprint*,[24] considerably modified from the one described above. This proposed a more limited decentralisation of services into Neighbourhood Centres. The Neighbourhood Centre would house 20–40 workers, depending on the demand for services and would have 'core' workers in housing, social services, environmental health and administrative support. As in the Islington model, other services and workers would form 'clusters' around the core teams. Very little mention is made in the second *Redprint* of the democratic forms of control associated with the decentralisation of services. A full account of the politics of decentralisation in Hackney up to mid–1983 is given in a research report from the School for Advanced Urban Studies.[25]

Islington

The Decentralisation Sub-Committee, at its meeting in July 1982, accepted that the main objective of decentralisation should be to improve the services available to the people of Islington.

The Islington approach

(i)   Having locally based non-bureaucratic services able to respond directly and quickly to the demands of Council tenants and the needs of local people;

(ii) the provision of co-ordinated and immediate advice, accompanied by direct action where possible on welfare benefits of all kinds, and

(iii) the provision of a local focus for community development and community information, so far as possible under local control.[26]

The emphasis in the first phase is on improving service delivery, with moves towards community control developing on the back of an improved service function. The Council have opened up for discussion the number and location of the Neighbourhood Offices. However, their own costings and preferences seem to be based on twenty-five, that is one for each ward.

The central concept in the Islington approach is the Neighbourhood Office with 'core functions' of housing, management and repairs, social services, environmental health and community development. Other functions would 'cluster' around this core or be integrated within it. Islington have expressed their approach and terms diagrammatically (see Figure 8.1).

The Neighbourhood Offices, Islington argue, should be open and welcoming places with secure areas for collection of rents, some private offices, interviewing space and a main reception area with carpets and comfortable chairs. Within this area would be office services available to local groups and amenities such as a

FIGURE 8.1   The neighbourhood office – basic framework

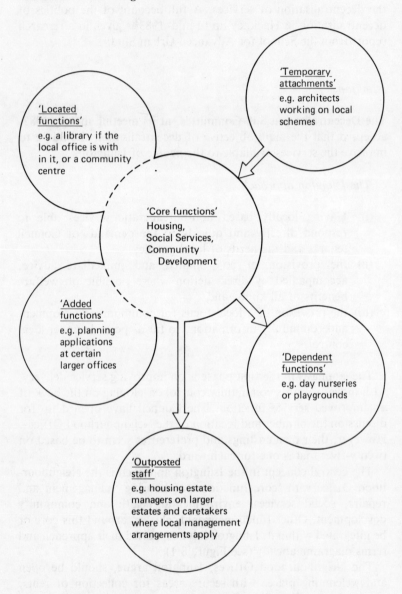

Source: *Committee Report*: Decentralisation Sub-Committee July 1982, London
Borough of Islington.

payphone and drinks dispenser. Few of the Council's existing local offices measure up to these standards. Within such an office, staff would need to work flexibly, requiring adequate training to fulfil their new roles and adequate support in terms of computerised information systems. For the purposes of consultation, in April 1983[27] the following outline of core functions and staff located in the Neighbourhood Offices was suggested:

1. *Housing.* Each office would provide the full range of estate management services for Council tenants, repair ordering, requests for transfers, rent queries and problems and the liaison on local rehabilitation or improvement schemes. Vacant properties would be let locally; and caretakers and porters would work within and would be responsible to the neighbourhood struture. Islington Council made it clear that local responsibility for lettings would only operate within a Council-wide policy. Housing advice to private and public tenants and to owner occupiers would be locally available and, where appropriate, linked to advice on welfare rights. In addition, the Direct Labour Committee considered the improvement of the repairs service on an area-orientated maintenance team basis. The aim was for multi-trade operations at local level, which would regard a minor repair task as a single project with all associated works connected in one cycle.

2. *Social Services.* Each office would have a number of social workers responsible for a generic case load. The existing area teams would disappear. As far as sheltered and domiciliary services are concerned, staff at each office would be responsible for the elderly and handicapped and co-ordinating home-helps, meals-on-wheels, holidays, volunteers and good neighbourhood schemes.

3. *Environmental Health.* The functions of the environmental health inspectorate, except for pollution control and fire inspection, would also be located in the Neighbourhood Offices, and these staff would then deal with improvement grants as well. The integration of this function was felt to be important in moving towards a comprehensive service at the local level.

4. *Community Development.* Within each neighbourhood area, there would be staff responsible to the Neighbourhood Management Officer for helping community groups to formulate and present their ideas. These workers would be community workers in social services, tenant liaison officers and some neighbourhood workers. As well as helping local groups, it was also suggested that

some support staff might require a technical background to help groups formulate detailed plans and programmes. It was envisaged that through such staff, local environmental programmes, for example, would be formulated and implemented.

5. *Information, Advice and Welfare Rights.* In place of receptionists, there would need to be staff in each office properly trained in dealing with housing advice, welfare rights and general queries. These staff would deal with rent and rate rebates and would need to be able to pursue cases on behalf of people with a claim to welfare benefits. Although this is a specialist advice activity, it would still be necessary for all others in the neighbourhood office to be trained in basic advice since most would be expected to handle initial enquiries. The systems necessary to support advice of all kinds, and particularly the use of computers, are seen as essential supports, if the neighbourhood office is to operate effectively.

6. *Administrative Support.* Each office would need a finance/ staffing officer responsible directly to a Neighbourhood Management Officer. Typing and clerical support would also be available. Cashiers needed for the collection of income would also act as finance assistants.

This suggested outline of 'core' functions of a Neighbourhood Office did not at this stage cover the potential decentralisation of planning, refuse collection, street sweeping and road maintenance. Nor did it cover the relationships with recreation, employment, the Inner London Education Authority and District Health Authority. Further work on these aspects was continuing at the time of writing.

The Brief for Consultation stated that 'the nature of local control over the work of management of neighbourhood offices is critical to their success ... in improving services available to the people of Islington'.[28] The Council's main commitments for local democracy included control over local budgets, the ability to influence Council policy and decisions, and the encouragement of a partnership with Council staff at the local level. In March 1983, the Council put forward a number of possible models of local democracy. The neighbourhood council, with a number of different forms of electoral procedure, would form the main elected focus for democratic processes. An alternative form would be user groups such as tenants' associations, community groups, or interest groups. A third form would be a mix of neighbourhood councils and user groups, linked together through representative systems and working practices.

As far as area budgeting and localised power is concerned, the Council's Consultancy Control Working Party's view in March 1983 was that power could be handed-over in the following areas:

1. Money and budgeting.
2. Staff and some personnel matters.
3. Policy and organisation of a particular service.
4. Allocations and user policies for particular services.
5. Alterations to fixed capital.

In practice, however, the Council stated that the handing-over of power would depend on whether or not there were user committees and neighbourhood councils and how these two types of organisation related. Furthermore, the Council stated that it would retain control of the allocation of overall resources and would insist that many services follow particular policies and guidelines. It would also only give limited control over staffing matters. In the early phase of decentralisation, neighbourhood councils might have largely advisory powers and as their confidence (or conformity?) increases they may feel capable (be allowed?) to take on greater powers. Finally, it is clear that as far as the Council is concerned, the local democratic arrangements need not be uniform across the borough but could and should be adapted to suit local needs, experience and circumstances.

Discussion

The general problem facing the introduction of a decentralised approach to local government is that it requires the various actors to play substantially different political roles. In a nutshell, there are likely to be (and have been) severe problems in producing the implied adjustments and actions of actors involved in the politics of decentralisation. In particular council employees, professionals, white- and blue-collar workers, their trades unions, Party activists, councillors and the public will experience considerable changes in attitude and role if the vision of populist democracy is to become a reality.

In Walsall and Hackney, crucial parts of the workforce and the white-collar trades unions were unsympathetic to the new style of administration and the process by which it was introduced. By mid 1983, NALGO in Hackney has still not lifted its ban on work for decentralisation by its members. At present, the proposals in Hackney are no more than provisional in nature, and even then are hedged around with qualifications which will ensure that the parameters of neighbourhood decision-making and service delivery are strategically governed and guided by the constitutionally-elected Council.

In Walsall, Councillors and Party workers faced other challenges as well as the task of changing the administration of local government. In particular, the decentralist concept requires a new relationship with the public. The Labour Group hoped that they would be able to concentrate on developing policy in their wards together with 'their' public. However, as in Hackney and Islington, there appeared to be some uncertainty about which decisions, which policies, and discretion over what areas, should remain with the councillors. As Shannon has commented, the local councillors were not sure what their own future role would be and many feared that neighbourhood control would lead to 'dubious interests' manipulating them.[29]

Feelings of powerlessness and alienation from local government cannot be overcome without considerable effort, and traditional attitudes to local politics cannot be changed quickly. So, although the public in all three locations have been encouraged to participate and get involved, it is unclear what this really means. Are those that get involved just the politically active? It is difficult to tell in Hackney and Islington whether the public involvement is with the public in general, or the extra-Council Left. In addition, as a new style of political involvement is promised and develops so public demands may also rise. As the Walsall Labour Group acknowledge: 'The involvement of the people of Walsall in their Council must become a reality not a dream. The difficulties of creating a three way partnership – between officers, councillors and the public – should not be underestimated.'[30]

The three attempts to translate the socialist ideal into reality at the local rather than the national level, expose a number of ambiguities and dilemmas. The idea of a decentralised local socialism clearly can be developed in different ways and in different forms. The general point is to suggest that there is a range of issues which are and need to be confronted in relation to decentralisation – about power, interests, accountability and participation. These issues raise further important questions about the relations between local people and Party activists, between local communities and the local authority and its controlling Party, and, between local government and the state. The final part of the chapter discusses these local political initiatives and the implications of a local, decentralised socialism.

Socialism goes local?

Decentralisation initiatives have been underpinned by three principle arguments. First, the populist divide between the 'people' and the 'power bloc' has emerged, in the British situation, in terms of a close association between neighbourhood politics and public disenchantment with the established political and administrative institutions of the local state. Second local government is an important locality for both *defending* local democracy and self-determination in terms of welfare provision and social pro-grammes, *experimenting* with new forms of community enterprise that may provide experiences through which people can learn about new possibilities for future society and developing socialist strategies, forms and organisation at the local level. Third, building on these first two arguments, it is argued that socialists will be able to reconstruct a new majority coalition in alliance with the traditional labour movement. It is these arguments that are behind what may be loosely termed a political tendency that Gyford has called the 'new urban Left'[31] with, as discussed in Chapter 1, a variety of specific origins.

Decentralisation has in this context become a political slogan and idea around which alliances can be made, and support mobilised. As *London Labour Briefing* put it in August 1982: 'One of our hopes for decentralisation of council services should be that it will help develop a political awareness among more people that the struggles of council workers and 'the community' over cuts in jobs and services are a common anti-capitalist struggle against economic oppression.'[32]

The origins of the idea of decentralisation and the commitment to it are quite complex. Whilst it is seen by the 'new urban Left' as valuable in and of itself, it is simultaneously one of a number of tactical ploys in a strategy designed to mobilise a new 'anti-capitalist' coalition. At the same time, it appears that the existing form of organisation and structure of local authority and other welfare state institutions are believed to be an obstacle to such a strategy – a counter-force. This sort of view seems to predominate in Hackney, where Council Leader Anthony Kendall gave his views in a discussion which appeared in a *New Statesman* article: 'Kendall subscribes to a widely held view on the left: that the Tory 1979 election victory represented an anti-State, anti-bureaucracy rebellion. Welfare state institutions were rejected as faceless, inept and uncontrollable. In this atmosphere, traditional calls to 'defend our services' and 'fight the cuts' fall on deaf ears.'' [33]

The question posed is how can the manual working class, the core of traditional, socialist Labour parties which is contracting and disaffected with local authority and welfare institutions, be encouraged to change their perception and loyalty? Who within the electorate will join them in providing a new broad alliance – a 'new proletariat'? The kind of coalition envisaged, based on differences of class, generation, lifestyle, race, culture, housing tenure, job status, family circumstances and issue orientation, seems difficult to hold together and represents a considerable contrast to the traditional view of a mass party based on a homogeneous working class with a tradition of collective action. But as Ken Livingstone observed (see Chapter 10):

> The Labour Party, whether it likes it or not, has become a party that can only win power if it actually maintains its skilled working-class vote, but also attracts the votes of the really poor and of those without work experience, in a way that it has not done successfully. To try to appeal to both wings is really very difficult and the Party hasn't really given it any thought. I think most people in the Labour Party aren't even aware that this is the future. [34]

Clearly then, mobilisation and coalition building are important elements in moves towards increasing support for socialist advances at the local level. What is not so clear is just what is meant by 'mobilising the people for socialism'. Whilst this seems to imply the existence of an offensive political strategy based on local government, the overriding objective, in fact, given the context of Thatcherism and the economic situation, appears to be the defence of local authorities and the future of the welfare state against the further attacks, both selectively and across the board, proposed by the Conservative Government in the Queen's Speech. 'Legislation will be brought forward to provide a selective scheme to curb excessive rate increases by individual local authorities, and to provide a general power, to be used if necessary, for the limitation of rate increases for all authorities.'[35] Yet again, from the arguments already given, it is acknowledged by many in the new urban Left that up till now it has still been calling upon those dependent on local services to defend what may be indefensible, to turn their feelings of powerlessness, dependence and cumulative disenchantment to feelings of comradely support.

Dilemmas like these, it is hoped, would be overcome through the popular involvement of local people in the control of local services, matched to local needs and delivered by a workforce that is committed to providing services sensitively and in a non-bureaucratic manner. But it is dilemmas like these that also give rise to a wider problem; the understanding of contradiction. Contradictions exist in the material world and are reflected in the world of ideas. Local government and other welfare state institutions can be envisaged both as functional to the needs of capital and as the result of the political struggles of the organised working class and other disadvantaged groups. In drawing conclusions on decentralisation, it is difficult to walk the tightrope between a crude functionalism and what might be utopian, popular democracy – between seeing local government as oppressive and seeing it as an oasis of socialism within a capitalist economy. Decentralisation is perhaps being advocated as the process through which these dilemmas can be resolved or at least mediated.

A further dilemma remains to be discussed. Decentralisation, to some Labour authorities, represents a diversion from the key struggle to defend and maintain existing programmes and public sector jobs against central government intervention. These authorities have argued that, whilst decentralisation seems an attractive initiative to popularise local government, the setting-up costs and the effective deployment of resources and political energy at a time of severe cuts and broader threats to local democracy, must be seriously examined. They are also questioning whether the different model of democracy implied by decentralisation is more democratic than the existing focus on elected councillors. This kind of position poses the further question of whether reluctance to decentralise services and power is more a function of a desire to maintain the status quo and the power relations that currently exist, or whether it represents a responsible and protective position in the face of a considerable challenge from the Thatcher government?

Decentralisation proposals are still being pursued in Hackney and Islington, and many more Labour-controlled authorities are considering their own forms and strategies for improving services and the political control over their delivery. Meanwhile, the local government context is changing rapidly, with the prospect of rate capping and central control of local expenditure.

Obviously, local government faces a turbulent period. And the development of decentralisation has not gone far enough to have necessarily broadened local opposition to further cuts in expenditure and services. What remains unclear is whether the challenge to local democracy and the opposition to it, will further stimulate decentralisation or draw resources and political energy away from it. The more fundamental question is whether, following decentralisation, the forms of alliance and mobilisation do in fact provide the stimulus and strength to advance socialist transformation remains to be seen.

Notes and References

1. D. Blunkett, 'Towards a Socialist Social Policy', *Local Government Policy Making*, vol. 8, no. 1, 1981, p. 102.
2. See the resolution carried at the 1980 Labour Party Conference: *Labour Party Annual Conference Report* 1980, pp. 111–12.
3. 'Community action' is a term used in Britain (e.g. P. Leonard (ed.), *The Sociology of Community Action*, Sociological Review Monograph No. 21 (University of Keele, 1975). 'Urban social movements' and 'urban struggles' are derived from literature produced by the Continental Left (e.g. M. Castells, *City, Class and Power*, Macmillan, 1978). 'Community politics' is the term often adopted by members of the Liberal Party (e.g. P. Hain (ed.), *Community Politics*, Calder, 1976). And the term 'micro-politics' is used in D. Donnison and D. Eversley (eds), *London: Patterns and Problems* (Heinemann, 1973).
4. For 'further understanding of Liberal Party views on 'community

politics' see T. Greaves, 'Problems of Self-Government in Rendle' and P. Hain, 'The Future of Community Politics', in P. Hain (ed.), *Community Politics*; and Association of Liberal Councillors, *How to Fight Local Elections and Win*, A.L.C. Campaign Booklet No. 8 March 1978, and other A.L.C. Booklets, particularly the *Community Politics Manual*.

5. There is a vast literature which emphasises the fact that in out society, participation, representation and community concepts are problematical. Good discussions of participation are provided in A. Richardson, 'Thinking about Participation', *Policy and Politics* 7(3), July 1979 and N. Broaden *et al.*, *Public Participation in Local Services* (Longman, 1982).

6. See T. Mason *et al.*, *Tackling urban deprivation: the contribution of area-based management* and K. J. Harrop *et al.*, *The implementation and development of area management* (Inlogov, University of Birmingham, 1977 and 1978).

7. Department of the Environment, *The Sunderland Study, The Oldham Study, The Rotherham Study*. Published as the 'Making Towns Better' series (1973).

8. *The Sunderland Study.*

9. Decentralisation developments in these London Boroughs were discussed at workshops held at SAUS in 1982 and early 1983.

10. See P. Lange, 'Crisis and Consent, Change and Compromise: Dilemmas of Italian Communism in the 1970's', *West European Politics*, vol. 2, no. 3, 1979; P. Della Seta, 'Notes on urban struggles in Italy', *International Journal of Urban and Regional Research*, vol. 2, no. 2, 1978; J. Chubb, 'Naples under the Left', *Comparative Politics*, vol. 13, no. 1 1980; R. Seidelman, 'Urban Movements and Community Power in Florence', *Comparative Politics* vol. 13, no. 4, 1981.

11. See R. Hambleton, *Policy Planning and Local Government* (Hutchinson, 1978).

12. The Oslo and Bologna 'models' are compared in K. Kjellberg, 'A Comparative view of Municipal Decentralisation, Neighbourhood democracy in Oslo and Bologna' in J. Sharpe (ed.), *Decentralist Trends in Western Democracies* (Sage, 1979).

13. The Bologna experiment is considered in more detail in R. Narretti and R. Leonardi, 'Participatory Planning: the PCI's new approach to municipal government', *European Journal of Political Research*, 1979 and M. Jäggi *et al.*, *Red Bologna* (Writers and Readers, 1977).

14. See R. Hadley and M. McGrath, *Going Local: Neighbourhood Social Services* (Bedford Square Press, 1981), and Barclay Committee, *Social Workers: Their Role and Tasks* (Bedford Square Press, 1982).

15. Information on Walsall is drawn from B. Powell, 'Walsall's haul to democracy – the Neighbourhood Concept' (1981); D. Nicholas, 'Neighbourhood Offices. The Walsall Experience' (1981) and various internal Walsall papers.

16. *Walsall's Hand to Democracy – the Neighbourhood Concept.*

17. Ibid.
18. Ibid.
19. H. Shannon, 'Walsall: Out of the Civic Centre into the Field', *New Statesman*, 19 March 1982, pp. 10–12.
20. For further discussion of implementing manifestos see J. Gyford, *Local Politics in Britain* (Croom Helm, 1976) and C. Fudge, 'Winning and Election and Gaining Control' in S. Barrett, and C. Fudge (eds), *Policy and Action* (Methuen, 1981).
21. The first draft of the Hackney *Redprint* for decentralisation was published on 15 February 1983.
22. First draft of *Redprint*: introduction pp. 1–2.
23. First draft of *Redprint*.
24. The second draft of *Redprint* was published on 21 April 1983.
25. C. Fudge, P. Hoggett and S. Laurence, *Decentralisation in Local Government: the Hackney Experience,* report to the London Borough of Hackney on its decentralisation process (SAUS, 1983).
26. *Report of the Director of Recreation Services and Officers Working Group to the Decentralisation Sub-Committee,* 22 July 1982, London Borough of Islington.
27. Public consultation took place in 1983. One of the documents available for discussion was the *Brief for Consultation, L. B. Islington,* 7 October 1982. The description of Islington's Scheme is paraphrased from this document.
28. *Brief for Consultation, L. B. Islington.*
29. H. Shannon, 'Walsall: Out of the Civic Centre into the Field'.
30. B. Powell, 'Walsall's Haul to Democracy – the Neighbourhood Concept', p. 17.
31. J. Gyford, 'The New Urban Left: a Local Road to Socialism?', *New Society,* 21 April 1983, pp. 91–3.
32. *London Labour Briefing,* August 1982.
33. Anthony Kendall, *New Statesman*, 18 January 1983.
34. Interview with Ken Livingstone, Chapter 10, p. 27.
35. Quoted in *The Times*, 23 June 1983.

9 Local Councils and the Financial Squeeze

MARTIN BODDY

Attempts to cut back and control council spending have been central to the Thatcher Government's strategy in relation to local government. The financial provisions of the 1980 Local Government, Planning and Land Act and a succession of supplementary measures aimed at enforcing the government squeeze on local council spending culminated, in 1983, in the plan to impose centrally determined limits on rate levels in individual authorities, giving complete control over expenditure levels. It is on these changes which this chapter focusses, changes which, the government has argued, are essential to its overall management of the economy. Here it is argued that these measures do not in fact represent the simple expression of macro-economic objectives. Nor are the issues raised simply 'constitutional', an affront to the historically established place of democratically elected local councils in the British political system, or a question of 'central–local relations' in an administrative sense although both these are important. Financial cuts and controls, it is argued, represent an essentially political and ideological strategy directed in particular against so-called 'high-spending', more radical Labour councils which have been attempting to maintain and expand the scale and scope of service provision. It is a strategy in which macro-economic arguments have been run together with the broader objectives of rolling back the state and the public sector, freeing market forces and individual private enterprise, cutting taxation and privatisation. These moves should be seen, therefore, alongside the measures which the government has taken to privatise local authority provision, force council house sales and push up rents on

public housing, limit fares subsidies on public transport, and
restrict local authority direct labour organisations and council
powers to hold land and property, as well as the 1983 Manifesto
pledge to abolish Metropolitan County Councils and the GLC.

Politically, the financial cuts and controls are crucial. They
constitute an attack on the working class and less well-off, and they
disadvantage women and black people disproportionately. They
directly threaten employment and the growing power of the public
sector unions. They represent an attack on the fundamental
principle of collective provision and financing of goods and
services to meet socially defined needs. And they are a major threat
to the possibility of developing radical initiatives in local government and of building politically from the local level. The struggle
over the introduction of centrally planned local authority finance
is, therefore, crucial not only to the future shape of local government but also the future of labour politics as a whole.

Following a brief sketch of local government finance, the chapter
describes the measures taken by the Thatcher Government since
1979 to cut back and control local government spending and looks
at their impact on patterns of expenditure. It then examines the
macro-economic rationale on which the government has based its
strategy, and offers an alternative interpretation which stresses the
essentially political and ideological character of successive attacks
on the financial basis of local government.

Local government finance

The recent cuts and controls need to be considered in the overall context of local government finance. Distinguishing initially
between revenue and capital expenditure, these are subject to
different regulations and accounting procedures, are funded
differently and are used for different purpose. *Capital* expenditure,
is used to acquire assets such as buildings, land and machinery. It is
funded largely by borrowing, while receipts from the sale of assets,
revenue contributions and government grants account for much of
the rest. Capital expenditure will usually commit an authority to
future revenue-spending, since interest must be paid on borrowed
money and there may be subsequent running costs for a new school
or old people's home, for example. *Revenue* expenditure relates

mainly to the current cost of providing goods and services, including wages and salaries (52 per cent in 1979/80), running costs (37 per cent) and debt charges (10 per cent). Revenue spending is mainly funded from a combination of government grant (49 per cent of spending in 1981/2), rates (34 per cent) and rents (10 per cent). Grant is paid mainly in the form of the general 'Block Grant' (83 per cent of grant support in 1981/2) and the rest as specific grants relating mainly to housing, transport, the police and the urban programme.

Central government funding of locally provided goods and services, which has expanded greatly over this century is, in simple terms, intended to support levels or patterns of provision which central government requires or wishes to encourage local authorities to provide, but which authorities lack the resources to fund. The total grant is set each year as part of the government's overall public expenditure planning exercise. The general grant is distributed, following negotiation with the local authorities, by a complex system of formulae. The aim is to allow all authorities to provide a common level service for the same rate 'poundage' (local tax rate), regardless of variation between authorities in either resources in the form of rateable values, or in needs due, for example, to the age structure or density of the population, the age of the housing stock or infrastructure and other factors affecting the need for expenditure. Rates represent a local property tax levied on the value of domestic and non-domestic property. Non-domestic rates accounted for 55 per cent of total rate revenue in 1980/1. Rate levels are set by individual councils, with political resistance limiting the total revenue that can be raised. Rents and fees, finally, represent charges to users of goods and services with rents on public housing accounting for a major part.

Turning to the pattern of expenditure, revenue expenditure accounts for a much larger share of total spending than capital (90 per cent over the five years up to 1981/2 although this is a lot down on the early 1970s). Education accounts for around half of revenue spending, with law and order and environmental services the next largest. Housing is the largest category of capital spending, with environmental services and education also taking a significant share. Spending patterns vary markedly between categories of authority (metropolitan/non-metropolitan, district/county, and so on) reflecting the services for which each is responsible. Thus, for example, education and social services are a district responsibility in metropolitan areas and a county responsibility in non-metropolitan areas. Beyond this, variations in spending reflect a combination of the duties and standards of provision set by central government, local demands, perceptions of need and political considerations, and an element of historic continuity.

Cuts and controls

This section outlines the attempts by the Conservative Government since 1979 to control and cut back local government expenditure, and their apparent impact, before going on to examine in more detail the rationale underlying the moves.

Capital expenditure

Looking first at capital expenditure, before 1981, local authority borrowing was subject to central control via loan sanction as an element of Keynesian demand management.[3] Authorities were free to finance capital spending from other sources, such as revenue surpluses or receipts from the sale of assets. The 1980 Local Government, Planning and Land Act, however, introduced ceilings on total capital expenditure set annually for individual authorities. There are certain exceptions, designed mainly to encourage councils to sell-off assets such as land and public housing. Although introduced by the Thatcher Government, it should be noted that the new system fits in with the system of cash limits imposed by the Treasury on central government departments in 1976 under Labour. Within these ceilings, authorities have been given greater freedom to determine spending patterns.

In practice, few authorities have been directly constrained by the capital expenditure controls. Spending, in fact, fell short of the total allocation by 21 per cent in 1981/2 and an estimated 36 per cent in 1982/3. This prompted the government to exhort local authorities, in October 1982, to increase capital spending in the remainder of the financial year – largely impracticable on this timescale – and to announce increased ceilings for 1983/4.[4] In fact, the major reason for the massive underspending appeared to be councils' concern for the *revenue implications* of capital expenditure mentioned earlier, at a time when current expenditure was increasingly subject to cuts and controls as described below. This reinforced the longer-term decline of capital spending, from 32 per cent of total expenditure in 1975/6 to 10 per cent in 1982/3.

Current expenditure

Turning to current expenditure, measures have taken two forms. First, the total grant paid by central government to local authorities has been significantly cut. The proportion of total local spending considered relevant by the government in calculating total grant met by central government was progressively reduced, from 61 per cent over the period 1977–80 to 53 per cent in 1983/4.[5] Simultaneously, expenditure totals taken into account by the government in calculating total grant were also reduced, leading to further loss of grant. Simply to maintain levels of provision would thus have necessitated massive rate increases to compensate for loss of grant. Cutting the total grant to local authorities is a simple and effective way of procuring cuts in local spending. It operates essentially on the basis of the political unacceptability in most authorities of substantial rate increases in successive years. Its disadvantage is that it tends to push up rate levels generally and affects all councils fairly uniformly, including those which support the government, have kept their own spending in check or indeed have been pursuing cuts themselves. This probably deterred the government, up to 1983 at least, from even more severe grant reduction across the board.

Second, the Local Government Planning and Land Act and a string of subsequent measures have attempted to increase central control over total current spending by the way that government grant is allocated to individual local authorities. The new Block Grant system which replaced the Rates Support Grant retains the central objective of equalisation between authorities referred to earlier. A second objective was, however, to provide a mechanism to discourage high spending, seen by the Local Authority Associations as 'the government's main reason for the changes in the grant system'.[6]

Outside Scotland at least, where a different system operates, elected councils are still largely free in principle to determine expenditure levels, subject to the level of rates they think are acceptable and to any legal constraints on their powers. The total rate income required for a given expenditure level is obviously heavily influenced by the amount of central government grant received but current expenditure remains, in the sense just described, 'locally determined'. The rules of the game have, however, been substantially changed so as to encourage local authorities to contain spending within government plans. The system itself is complex, confusing and has changed often, but the underlying principle is fairly straightforward. The aim has been to discourage higher levels of spending by ensuring that a greater proportion of the cost falls on local ratepayers. This is in contrast with the old system, whereby the resources element of the Rate Support Grant met a constant proportion of additional spending, regardless of expenditure level. Again therefore, the government has been attempting to harness pressure from ratepayers, real or potential, to keep down rates and expenditure.

In more detail, the system of control as it has evolved has two elements, the one systematic and the other *ad hoc*. Simplifying still, the systematic element operates through the Block Grant. In determining the level of grant to be paid to each authority each year, the Department of the Environment assesses how much each authority would need to spend in order to provide a common standard of services across the country, at a total level of expenditure compatible with overall government expenditure plans. These are termed Grant Related Expenditure (GRE) levels and are different for each authority. A threshold expenditure level was set at GRE, plus 10 per cent. Spending beyond this threshold attracts a lower rate of grant and therefore falls more heavily on the rates.

When, however, by early 1981 it became apparent that total local government spending was, despite the new system, likely to be significantly above government plans, a further set of *ad hoc* spending targets, with associated penalties to discourage 'overspending', was introduced. Unlike the systematic element built into the grant mechanism, the new targets and penalties were based on past expenditure levels and were totally extraneous to the grant system. Thus targets for 1981/2 were set at 1978/9 expenditure, less 5.6 per cent in real terms for each authority. Initially, any authority exceeding this *ad hoc* target was to have been penalised. Many Conservative councils, particularly non-metropolitan counties would have been caught in this net. Traditionally low spenders, many had been cutting expenditure on their own initiative in the recent past, so that targets based on past spending were significantly below GRE levels. It became apparent during the year, however, that the government wanted to direct penalties at a minority of high-spending, Labour-controlled councils. So for 1981/2 and 1982/3 additional penalties were incurred only by authorities which exceeded *both* their GRE level and target, largely Labour-controlled metropolitan authorities, London Boroughs and the GLC.[7] Penalties were tightened in 1982/3 and again, more severely in 1983/4. And from 1983/4 penalties were incurred for spending beyond targets, regardless of how this related to GRE levels. This caught in the net more non-metropolitan authorities, which had previously been let off. Expenditure plans for 1983/4 showed 25 out of 39 non-metropolitan counties and 75 of the 297 districts in England incurring penalties, to the tune of £110 million. A sharp contrast was, however, evident on political lines, with Conservative-controlled councils planning to spend 0.3 per cent above target, incurring penalties of £24 million, and Labour councils budgetting to spend 7.7 per cent over target, incurring penalties totalling £217 million.[8] The severe penalties introduced in 1983/4 were such that many authorities were in the position of receiving less grant in *absolute* terms, at higher spending levels.

The system as it evolved up to 1983/4 did not represent absolute control. It was essentially indirect. It did, however, constitute a strong disincentive to 'overspending' as centrally defined. The introduction of centrally defined spending levels in the form of norms or targets for individual authorities was politically very significant. It served to increase the leverage of ratepayers and particularly local media pressure on local authorities to conform and to keep down the rates. 'High spenders', overstepping targets in order to maintain and expand effective service provision could be labelled profligate 'over-spenders' with connotations of bureaucratic waste and inefficiency. Attention is, moreover, focussed on money rather than on the level and quality of local service provision.

Alongside the major changes in the grant system, the 1980 Act also required local authorities to publish additional information to encourage their accountability to ratepayers. The 1982 Local Government Finance Act removed local authority powers to levy supplementary rates – this came after earlier proposals to require supplementary rate increases to be approved by a local referendum ran into opposition which included Conservative authorities and the Tory backbench, who saw in this an infringement of the 'constitutional' position of local government. And there were developments in the legal front, with Bromley London Borough's successful case against the GLC, upheld in the House of Lords. This outlawed the GLC's cheap fares and challenged the legality of transport subsidies. It also, however, raised the more general possibility of authorities facing a legal challenge for failing in their fiduciary duty towards their ratepayers, by setting unreasonably high rate levels and thus, under the new grant system, losing grant. This could leave councillors open to personal surcharge and disqualification. Although no such action has subsequently been brought, and it is unclear what the outcome would be, councillors have been operating increasingly in the shadow of the courts. This became more explicit with the 1983 Transport Act, in the wake of the GLC case. This legalised public transport subsidies in metropolitan areas up to levels prescribed annually by the Transport Secretary, in effect inviting a legal challenge to councils which went above this. The way in which the government has sought to control spending and limit transport subsidies has thus tended to shift the conflict away from the overt political arena, into the more 'neutral' arena of the law courts.

Finally, it is important to remember that the situation in England and Wales was developing against the background of the Scottish system. Legislation here gave the Secretary of State for Scotland powers to enforce centrally determined rate and expenditure levels directly. Thus Lothian Regional Council were forced to capitulate to demands for cuts under threat of the appointment of commissioners in place of the elected council. The system is already routine, with Parliament in July 1983, for example, approving the Scottish Secretary's decision to reduce the rates in four authorities. This included a cut in Lothian's rate from 92p in the pound to 86p. The spectre of direct action in England and Wales was thus lurking in the background throughout this period.

Changing spending patterns

Before going on to consider the latest phase in the evolution of central financial control of local government, it is worth looking at what happened to spending over the period up to 1983–4.

TABLE 9.1 Local government expenditure and government spending plans, 1974–81*

Year	Over/under spend
1974/5	+ 5.4%
1975/6	+ 0.7%
1976/7	− 1.8%
1977/8	− 1.5%
1978/9	− 1.0%
1979/80	− 3.2%
1980/1	+ 0.1%
1981/2	+ 8.7%
1982/3	+ 7.7%
1983/4	+ 3.3%

*Shows local government expenditure minus Rate Support Grant. Relevant expenditure for England and Wales. Outurn data to 1982–3, estimate for 1983/4.
Source: *Financial, General and Rating Statistics*, CIPFA.

Initially at least, it seems that the Thatcher Government failed to keep local spending in line with its expenditure plans (Table 9.1). Whereas from 1975/6 to 1980/1 spending was roughly on or below the level planned for by central government, it overshot by 8.7 per cent in 1981/2 and an estimated 7.7 per cent in 1982/3. Recognising, presumably, the need for more realistic targets, government plans for local spending were increased by £1000 million in 1982/3 and again in 1983/4. In 1983/4, however, authorities budgetted to spend only 3.3 per cent above the government's (revised) planned level, suggesting that control was starting to become more effective. Current spending in *real* terms has moreover shown no great increase. In fact it fell 2.6 per cent in 1981/2, rose by 0.5 per cent in 1982/3 and an estimated 1.6 per cent in 1983/4.[9]

For the government's overall spending plans to have been met, either all authorities would have to roughly conform to their individual targets or 'overspending' would need to be offset by 'underspending'.[8] In practice, a significant number of authorities have persisted in overspending. In 1981/2, when the government called for revised budgets, 156 authorities increased their planned expenditure to a total of £211 million, £167 million of this accounted for by the GLC, West Midlands and Merseyside County Councils where Labour took control in May 1981. High spending, Labour-controlled authorities were willing to risk the rate increase implied by these spending levels and felt able to sustain them politically. The problem of non-compliance was not, however, entirely confined to a handful of profligate 'left-wing' authorities, as the government frequently maintained. In 1982/3, whereas the Inner London Boroughs budgeted to spend 4.5 per cent more in cash terms than the previous year, the mainly Tory non-metropolitan counties (which accounted for 45 per cent of total expenditure) budgeted for an 8.8 per cent increase.[10] This suggests considerable unwillingness, even among Tory authorities, to cut back on services. Low spending authorities, because they faced no penalties for exceeding targets based on past expenditure provided they were spending below their GRE, had no disincentive to increase spending up towards GRE levels. Underspending, therefore, did little to offset overspending. By 1983/4, however, with tougher penalties, the non-metropolitan counties had cut back their proposed increase to 3.7 per cent and the metropolitan districts to 3.5 per cent whereas the Inner London Boroughs were budgetting for an increase of 7.4 per cent.[11]

Cuts in grant and changes to the grant system were thus unable to force complete compliance with government spending plans. There was, nevertheless, evidence of more effective control by 1983/4, and growth in local spending in real terms does appear to have been contained. What the cuts and controls have done, however, is shifted the burden of local spending much more heavily on to the rates, particularly in some high spending, high resource authorities – the GLC as an extreme case, received no central government grant, in 1983/4. The average rate increase of 6 per cent in 1983/4 could be attributed entirely to cuts in central government grant, which switched a total of £1800 million from central taxation to the rates, representing an increase of 90p a week for the average domestic ratepayer.[12] Industrial and commercial ratepayers have obviously been heavily hit as well. While some authorities have effectively absorbed the cuts through rate increases, passing them

TABLE 9.2 Expenditure and grant for selected Local Authorities 1980/1 to 1982/3*

	Percentage change 1980/1 to 1982/3 in real terms		Grant as percentage of expenditure	
	Expenditure	Grant	1980/1	1982/3
GLC	40.5	−50.8	51.3	18.0
Camden	−3.7	171.6	4.5	12.7
Lambeth	−3.0	13.2	48.6	56.8
Brent	5.0	−2.2	49.3	45.9
S. Yorkshire	10.4	−14.2	68.8	53.5
Sheffield	8.3	−10.9	55.9	45.9
Manchester	−2.9	−13.5	55.3	49.2
Solihull	6.8	4.6	48.6	47.6
Avon	5.9	−14.4	56.5	45.6
Bristol	−1.6		38.7	34.8
Bath	−15.3	11.8	53.2	70.2

*Expenditure includes all rate- and grant-borne expenditure. Grant includes needs and resources element of Block Grant, plus specific and supplementary grants, after London equalisation payments. In 1980/1, needs and resources elements have been apportioned to all tiers so as to allow comparisons with the new Block Grant system. For each county area, needs element is allocated between tiers in proportion to net expenditure. Within each area, district shares of re-apportioned needs element are distributed in proportion to rateable value to reflect precepting. Resources element entitlements are then re-calculated for each authority.
Source: *Financial, General and Rating Statistics* 1980/1 and 1982/3, CIPFA, calculated by G. Bramley.

on to ratepayers at large, others have been forced to accept significant cuts in real terms (see Table 9.2).

In aggregate terms, central government grant as a proportion of local spending fell from 63 per cent in 1975/6 to 54 per cent by 1981/2, a 13 per cent cut in grant in real terms, and the downward trend has continued since (see table 9.3). The impact can also be seen in terms of local government employment, which grew 0.4 per cent per year in England and Wales from 1975 but fell 1.3 per cent per year from 1979 to 1982.[13]

Rate limitation

While the evidence suggests that real growth in local spending had been largely contained by 1983/4, the government continued to argue that expenditure and rate levels were excessive. According to the 1983 *Rates* White Paper, 'local government as a whole continues to spend more than the Government believe the country can afford' and 'the problem has been greatly aggravated by the behaviour of a small number of large authorities'.[14] The long running issue of local authorities' limited accountability to those whom they tax via the rates was also raised. Abolition of the rates, to which the Conservatives were pledged in 1979 was, however, rejected and with it the Layfield Committee's 1976 recommendation in favour of the introduction of local income tax. Instead, the White Paper indicated the government's intention to introduce legislation 'to curb excessive rate increases by individual local authorities, and providing a general power, to be used if necessary, for the limitation of rate increases in all authorities ... The purpose will be to restrain both the expenditure and the rates of these authorities.[15]

The proposals included both a selective scheme intended to apply to a small number of authorities, and a general scheme applying to all. The selective scheme would apply to authorities identified by criteria relating to recent spending levels and their variation from GRE's, although other factors might be taken into account. During the 1983 election campaign, it was suggested that councils exceeding government spending targets by more than 25 per cent and raising their rates by more than 8 per cent would be liable to rate limitation – fifteen Labour authorities on this definition. Offending authorities would be identified in 1984 and maximum rate levels specified for 1985/6. Authorities spending below a minimum level will not be liable to selection. The White Paper talks about £10 million which would remove 275 of the 296 non-metropolitan districts from the net. Targets and penalties under the Block Grant system continue, however, for the time being.

Authorities which reckon they cannot contain spending within the limits specified can make a case for an exemption or 'derogation'. Normally, however, expenditure levels would then be translated into maximum rate levels set by the Secretary of State. Where an authority failed to agree to its maximum rate level the government would fix the level by an order approved by Parliament. A local authority would have no power to impose a rate higher than the maximum determined by the Secretary of State or set by Order. The consequences of non-compliance are not spelled out. It is clear however that an authority failing to comply would be acting beyond its legal power, *ultra vires*. The appointment of commissioners in the short term, coupled with the disqualification and possible surcharge of the existing councillors, would therefore be the likely outcome. Powers for the general scheme would allow it to be introduced 'if necessary'. Since all authorities would be affected, there would be no need for selection criteria. Otherwise, it would operate like the selective scheme.

The proposals give the government complete control over expenditure and rate levels in individual authorities. In this respect, they break with the earlier attempts to control spending via grant levels and distribution, which were essentially indirect. The latter could not control spending or rate levels where councils felt politically able to push up rate levels to compensate for lost grant. In principle then, although not in detail, the new control system is the same as the Scottish scheme.

The intention to direct the attack against 'the minority of authorities whose spending and rating is clearly excessive'[16] is clear. Discretion to determine the criteria defining 'the minority' and, in particular, provision for a general scheme applicable to all authorities, represent a much more fundamental shift in the relationship of local to central government. From an essentially arm's length system of guidance and influence in the mid-1970s with the overall rate of government grant the only real lever, the government has moved to absolute central control over local expenditure levels. Particularly significant in this is the fact that the government has increasingly sought to control the spending of *individual* authorities, rather than simply aggregate expenditure. Rate limits are merely the logical end-point of the government's strategy as it has evolved since 1979.

The Thatcher government's rationale

The apparent rationale for controlling local authority expenditure is located in the government's overall concern with economic management. Its roots lie in the shift in Treasury strategy under the last Labour government. This moved policy away from conventional demand management towards a form of monetarism involving, particularly after the IMF intervention in 1976, reductions in the Public Sector Borrowing Requirement (PSBR).

This was reflected in a growing concern to limit the expansion of local government. There is a strong element of continunity, therefore, the Thatcher Government making more explicit and single-minded strategies which evolved in the 1970s under Labour. Nearly a decade ago, the Treasury is reported to have described local authorities as the 'Achilles Heel' of public expenditure control,[17] while the 1977 Green Paper on Local Government Finance argued that: 'Because of their responsibilities for the management of the economy, central government must concern themselves with total local government expenditure and taxation ... Central government's role is therefore: (*inter alia*) to ensure that, in aggregate, local government's spending plans are compatible with the Government's economic objectives.'[18] Statements and circulars under the present government have re-emphasised this. Leon Brittan, when Chief Secretary of State to the Treasury, setting out the government's case argued that: 'most importantly, we are concerned to ensure that our policies designed to improve the health of the national economy are not frustrated by the actions of local authorities. This necessarily means that we are concerned to influence their decisions about spending and the level of rates which they set'[19] and, in a specific challenge to local autonomy worth quoting at length, the Treasury line on the consequences of continued 'overspending' were set out:

My main message to you today is that it is in the interests of the national economy and of the health and viability of local government to seek to overcome the real problems which repeated overspending brings with it. Local government spending plays such an important part in our economy that a failure to overcome the problem of overspending is bound to lead ultimately to developments which the friends of local government will find extremely unwelcome. It is bound to cause central government to intervene ever-more obtrusively and seek ever greater powers over local authority finances.

The political strength of local government may for a period check the growth of such an assumption of power. But any such check will only be shortlived if overspending continues, whichever government is in power, because its damaging effect on the national economy and on industry will soon force any government to take further steps in the direction of central control. The only way in which this process can be avoided is for the old and valuable consensus to be restored, and for local authority spending to be contained within limits set by what the nation can afford.

The case for control has tended to draw together three rather disparate lines of argument. First, the need to cut local spending is related to monetarist policy: inflation is the main target of economic policy, with money supply the only important variable to be controlled. Public sector borrowing, to which local authorities contribute, must be cut in order – following monetarist logic – to cut the money supply and, in turn, inflation. Second, it is argued that in the longer term local authority spending, borrowing and taxation is 'crowding out' the private market sector, starving it of resources and funds and pushing up interest rates.[20] Local taxation is argued to eat into the taxable capacity of ratepayers which central government can tap. Underpinning this thesis is a view of public spending as somehow necessarily unproductive. If people have to pay more in rates 'they cannot invest it in something productive. Or use it to buy goods produced somewhere else in the economy.'[21] Finally, at a more general level, it has been argued that excessive rate levels have damaged industry and commerce, and in the Treasury statement quoted above, Brittan noted the rise in the ratio of industrial and commercial rates to profits from 24 per cent in 1979/80 to 52 per cent in 1981/2.

These arguments were reiterated in the *Rates* White Paper. It argued first, that in the interests of the 'broad conduct of the economy' it is necessary 'to reduce public expenditure as a proportion of Gross Domestic Product, so permitting a reduction both of public borrowing and of the burden of taxes'.[22] This, it argued, is needed in order to control inflation and interest rates, increase incentives to create wealth and avoid competition with other taxation and expenditure programmes. In a nutshell, 'the economic regeneration of the country cannot be secured if the cost of local government is too great a burden for the private sector to carry.'[23] Second, the burden of rates on business and commerce was seen as excessive. Third, it was argued that rate increase push up prices and pay demands, fuelling inflation. Finally, the legitimacy of central government's concern with the costs and standards of local services which are national in character or of national importance was claimed. The limited accountability of local government to those whom it taxes via the rates was also criticised, on the grounds that 'many of those who vote for local spending do not have to make a contribution through rates' while non-domestic rate payers 'have no votes and only a limited influence on local policies'.[24]

Looking at the arguments in turn, monetarist policy offers little support for the measures taken to control local authority expenditure.[25] In particular, current expenditure contributes neither to the PSBR, the money supply, or aggregate demand. With central government grant subject to an overall cash limit since 1976/7, spending above government plans must be funded largely from the rates. There is no rationale, therefore, in monetarist (or indeed Keynesian) theory for the system of current expenditure control introduced since 1979. Borrowing to fund capital expenditure will increase the PSBR and aggregate demand, but there is, however, no reason on grounds of monetarist policy to control capital spending as a whole. It would be more logical therefore from a monetarist perspective to retain the pre-1981 system of loan sanction to control borrowing, than to bring in capital expenditure ceilings as in the 1980 Act. In any case, local authority borrowing represents a negligible share of total PSBR, a mere 4.1 per cent in 1982/3 compared with 79 per cent for central government and 17 per cent for public corporations.[26] Therefore, tight control even over local authority borrowing is hardly crucial.

Arguments that local authority spending 'crowds out' the market sector with adverse economic effects are also unconvincing, in part because the recent context has been of spare capacity and high unemployment. More specifically, much capital spending is complementary to, rather than competitive with, private investment, providing roads, infrastructure, community facilities, and so on – indeed much of this spending results in contracts to the private sector, particularly construction. The impact of current expenditure is more complex, but again yields no strong case for control. The simple 'crowding out' thesis has to argue that public spending is inherently less 'productive', less necessary than the use of resources in the private sector and is grounded more in political and ideological commitment to the private sector than economics. Again, the specific argment that rates crowd out central government taxation rests on an assumption that central government spending is more necessary or productive than local spending and, in any case, as Jackman has argued we are in Britain nowhere near the limit of taxable capacity, which this argument assumes. To portray the cost of local government and local expenditure simply as a 'burden' on the private sector, as in fact the *Rates* White Paper does, is naive in the extreme, for it disregards the impacts of and benefits derived from such 'costs'.

Turning to the impact of rates on business and commerce, national figures relating rates to profits as quoted by Brittan (see above) reflect declining profits much more than rising rates. There have been large rate rises in some areas, particularly where authorities have suffered grant penalties. This coincided with the general profit squeeze and some businesses will undoubtedly have suffered to some extent. It is likely, however, that rate rises are largely passed on by businesses, in prices charged to consumers or reduced payments for premises, and so on. Nor is there any simple relationship between rates and inflation as the White Paper would suggest. Higher rates represent, in part, payment for a larger volume of goods and services rather than a simple price increase. And it would be very difficult to argue that any impact on inflation was significant relative to other factors. Rates, moreover, represent a very small proportion of total costs (as opposed to profits) in most businesses (under 3 per cent for the most part) while the non-domestic contribution to total rate revenue has declined since the mid-1970s. In any case, the average rate levied in England and Wales was the same in 1983/4 in real terms as it was in 1974/5.[27] Again, rates may be a cost, but they contribute to the provision of the wide range of local authority goods and service which benefit business and commerce directly or indirectly.

Finally, it is worth looking more closely at the underlying assumption that local spending is out of control. Local government's share of public expenditure in fact *fell* from 32 per cent in 1974/5 to 26 per cent in 1981/82, and from 16 per cent to 13 per cent as a share of Gross Domestic Product. In contrast to this, central government spending increased its share of public expenditure from 68 per cent to 74 per cent, and increased as a proportion of GDP from 33 per cent to 37 per cent over the same period. And whereas local spending fell by 15 per cent in real terms from 1974/5 to 1981/2, central spending *grew* by 14 per cent (see Table 9.3). If anything, therefore, it is central rather than local

TABLE 9.3 Central and local government expenditure, GDP and government grant to local authorities, 1975/6 to 1981/2, UK

		1975/6	1976/7	1977/8	1978/9	1979/80	1980/1	1981/2
Central government expenditure*†								
at current prices	£m	33,932	37,367	40,014	47,880	56,734	69,593	78,299
at 1975 prices	£m	32,705	31,937	30,559	33,056	34,245	35,276	36,018
percentage of GDP	%	34.3	32.6	30.6	32.5	33.3	35.3	36.9
percentage of public sector	%	68.9	69.6	70.1	71.8	71.7	72.3	73.7
Local authority expenditure‡								
at current prices	£m	15,345	16,360	17,050	18,823	22,425	26,613	27,885
at 1975 prices	£m	14,790	13,979	13,021	12,995	13,536	13,490	12,827
percentage of GDP	%	15.5	14.3	13.1	12.8	13.2	13.5	13.2
percentage of public sector	%	31.1	30.4	29.9	28.2	28.3	27.7	26.3
Central government grant§								
at current prices	£m	8,360	9,041	9,524	10,386	11,845	14,634	15,744
at 1975 prices	£m	8,360	7,775	7,048	7,063	7,107	7,463	7,242
percentage of LA expenditure	%	63.1	59.9	58.4	56.9	54.0	55.0	54.2

*Capital and current expenditure less debt interest, and loans, grants and transfers to local authorities.
†Public expenditure defined as central government and local authority expenditure.
‡Capital and current expenditure, less debt interest.
§Current grant only, and current grant as a percentage of current expenditure.

Note also that, more recently, current grant as a percentage of rate and grant borne expenditure in England and Wales fell from an estimated 53.2 per cent in 1981/2 to 49.6 per cent in 1982/3 and 48.1 per cent in 1983/4, falling 12.4 per cent in real terms over this period. Local rate and grant borne expenditure increased by an estimated 0.5 per cent in 1982/3 and 1.6 per cent in 1983/4, taking account of pay and price changes specific to local government ('volume' terms). Figures in main table refer to the UK.

Sources: *Local Government Trends, Financial and General Statistics* (CIPFA) and *Financial Statistics* (CSO).

spending that seems to be out of control. Indeed, as we saw earlier, there is little evidence of major overspending, even in relation to the government's own plans.

On the issue of accountability, which the White Paper raises alongside the government's concern for economic management, suffice it to note that removing local autonomy over expenditure and rates is hardly a logical response to concern for lack of local influence over council decision-making. Accountability does raise important questions. The government however, particularly in rejecting the argument for a local income tax, turned its back on them.

To summarise, the government's macro-economic policy objectives offer little justification for the measures it has taken to control and cut back local authority spending. There may be an argument (from a Keynesian as much as a monetarist perspective) for controlling borrowing via loan sanction. There is however little justification for control over capital or current spending in aggregate which would be inconsistent with monetarist strategy as such. Crucially, macro-economic arguments by no means require the sort of detailed control over the budgets of individual local authorities which has evolved, nor the detailed footwork of adjusting targets to isolate major 'overspending', Labour-controlled authorities which we have seen in the past.

Discussion

In practice, macro-economic arguments have been run together with central government's broader political and ideological objectives revolving around rolling back the public sector, freeing market forces and private enterprise, privatisation and tax cuts. This has fed off the populist appeal of the portrayal of local government as profligate and inefficient bureaucracy, and the unpopularity of rates as a form of taxation. Hence the loose interpretation of monetarist strategy, the appeal of the 'crowding out' thesis and the attack on rates. Failure to understand or at least acknowledge the shortcomings of the economic rationale seems to reflect, on the part of ministers if not the Treasury and government advisers, the triumph of political and ideological expediency and belief over reason.

Compared with local government spending, public expenditure as a whole has of course been far from contained. Attempts to cut local spending and taxation may, to some extent, represent compensatory or diversionary action, reflecting the central government's failure to deliver significant tax cuts or contain its own expenditure. Significantly, the government's overall economic strategy seems to have focussed more on privatisation than direct cuts in spending and taxation. The relative lack of concern at this failure, particularly when set against the enthusiasm with which cuts in *local* spending and taxation have been pursued, makes it hard to see central government's attack on town-hall spending as simply part of an overall plan to cut public spending and taxation. Particularly since what has evolved is a system of control directed at individual high-spending authorities, above all Labour-controlled metropolitan authorities, inner London boroughs and the GLC.

Nor are the issues raised simply constitutional or a question of central–local relations, even though much of the debate has been conducted on this terrain. Supporters of local government have put the constitutional case for local government autonomy and the more open, democratic, accountable and responsive character of local as against central government.[28] But what has developed over and above the general conflict between central control and local autonomy is conflict on a narrower front, between high-spending Labour councils intent on maintaining and expanding services, in some cases developing the sort of radical strategies described elsewhere in the book, and the political strategies of the Thatcher government. Most Tory councils will, of course, tend to go along with the government's policy of cuts and support for privatisation, provided it does not go too far – how far is too far remains to be seen. The central–local debate obviously intersects with the basically political conflict that has been generated around cuts and controls, and the force of 'localist' arguments and campaigns is of great importance politically in terms of resistance to central government. To frame the issue solely in terms of central–local relations or constitutional questions is, however, to obscure the essentially political nature of the conflict.

What the government's strategy of cuts and controls represents is not the logical outcome of macro-economic policy leading to constitutional questions and issues of central–local relations, but a political and ideological strategy to restructure collective social provision, the bases of political power within the structure of the state and, ultimately, relations between labour and capital. This is not so much a coherent, conscious strategy, worked through and systematically applied across the board. It is, rather, the uneven translation into specific and in some respects inconsistent measures which reflect the government's over-riding political and ideological objectives.

In an immediate sense, attacks on local authority provision of goods and services, public housing, cheap public transport, personal social services, care for the elderly, nurseries, leisure facilities, and education, represent on balance an attack on the living standards, real wages and quality of life of the working class and least well-off. These groups are disproportionately reliant on local authority provision of goods and services, funded collectively by ratepayers at large, plus central government grant, and less able to afford substitutes such as private cars, home ownership, commercial, cultural and leisure facilities or private care for children, the elderly and other dependants. Women, in particular, are adversely affected (see Chapter 5). Cuts in local authority provision reduce their ability to compete effectively in the labour market, and increase demands for service provision and support in the domestic sphere which fall disproportionately on women's shoulders.

More generally, cuts, controls and privatisation represent an attack on the political and ideological principles of collective provision of goods and services to meet social need, funded by the community at large. This is not to argue that local spending is in any simple sense necessarily orientated to social need. The nature and forms of expenditure are crucial. Local government does, however, provide a powerful base from which to pursue these principles in practice, given its political and organisational structure, its powers and responsibilities in terms of functions and, last if (not yet) least, its financial resources – this indeed is why all three have been under attack. This involves a fundamentally different view of public expenditure than that of the present government, which has sought to equate the market sector with 'productive' expenditure and the non-market sector with 'unproductive' spending. It implies, among other things, equating effective use of resources with the extent to which socially defined needs and distributional goals (who gets what) are met rather than with cost cutting, profitability or the operation of market forces; aiming to eliminate any waste in the use of scarce resources; and improving the wages, benefits and conditions of those working in the public sector.

It is these principles of collective provision for social need which,more explicitly in some cases than others Labour councils have been exploring, through their efforts to maintain or expand levels of service provision, defend local authority employment and pursue the sort of radical strategies relating to employment, women, blacks and the decentralisation of town-hall power described in earlier chapters. The political and ideological nature of the government's frontal attack on local government finance seems therefore evident and well chosen, particularly the extent to which it is targetted so as to isolate individual, high-spending councils.

The last act?

This leaves, then, the question of how far effective opposition to the government's ultimate solution will be possible, which is inevitably somewhat speculative. So far, local authorities have either implemented cuts, increased the rates to maintain service provision and employment, or some combination of the two, while trying to pin as much blame on central government as possible and mobilise support for the maintenance of service and jobs. More extreme proposals have not, as Keith Basset has argued, offered any real alternative. In a sense the cuts have been transferred to the locality either way, as rate increases or service cuts, although the pattern of cuts and/or the incidence of rate increases, falling more heavily on high-value housing and non-domestic property, has to be taken into account. Nevertheless, a number of councils, partly those with a strong political base, have been able to maintain spending well beyond government targets on the basis of large rate increases which have allowed, in a number of cases, the development of radical initiatives as well as defense of services and jobs. Government effectively lost control of councils which were prepared to push up the rates, despite consequent loss of grant.

This avenue would be finally blocked by the introduction of rate limits. Faced with approved spending limits and rate levels and tightly drawn legislation, as with the right to buy provisions of the 1980 Housing Act or the financial controls applicable in Scotland, councillors would have few alternatives. The proposals provide for some negotiation over individual expenditure levels, and protracted wrangling over details seems inevitable. Authorities would undoubtedly try to exploit this to the limit. Some concessions might, in fact, be secured on technical issues to do with GRE formulae and the particular situation of individual councils. This, however, would not challenge the basic structure of control. The main choices then would be to implement the cuts, resign (and let someone else implement them), or suffer the legal consequences if, for example, councillors failed to approve a budget incorporating recommended expenditure and rate levels. The consequences would potentially include personal surcharge and disqualification, with the appointment of commissioners or the formation of an alternative council prepared to operate within the government's expenditure ceiling. Again therefore, overtly political conflict over spending levels will be shifted into the courts and translated into points of law. Other forms of oppositional strategy might be possible. An authority might, for example, aim to target any cuts it is forced to make on areas from which the Tory Party draws its support, although precise targetting would present practical problems and might also be open to legal challenge.

Any effective opposition is bound to involve more concerted joint action by local authorities than has been achieved in the past. In this respect, the coming together of those Labour authorities most immediately at risk, with an initial meeting in Sheffield in June 1983 and moves to establish a broadly based 'Campaign for Local Democracy' were significant first steps. Those Labour councils faced with the more immediate threat of rate capping under the selective scheme, together with the metropolitan counties and the GLC which face abolition, will inevitably be in the front line. Effective opposition will, however, almost certainly require a much broader alliance of interests behind the principle of local democracy, autonomy and the 'constitutional' role of local government.

This implies the need for cross-party support at local government level, coupled with and reflected in back bench Tory support at Westminster. In this sense, the united opposition of the local authority associations to the White Paper proposals, including the

Conservative-controlled Association of District Councils and Association of County Councils was vital. Commenting on the Queen's Speech, the leader of the ADC argued that the government's proposals had 'grave constitutional implications. Such powers would directly undermine a local authority's responsibilities and accountability to its electorate and substitute the judgement of Whitehall for that of the town hall',[29] while the leader of the ACC confirmed that his Association would be campaigning 'hell for leather' against the Bill.[30] The question is, whether this united front can be maintained and what it might achieve. At the time of uniting, not very much.

Opposition to the 1980 legislation broke down in the end, when the ACC finally broke ranks following what had been similarly a common stand.[31] Opposition in 1982 did induce the government to drop plans for referenda on supplementary rates, but this represents a fairly minor concession. Particularly as subsequent legislation simply banned supplementary rates altogether. Given the size of the government's majority they are, in any case, unlikely to be seriously embarrassed by any back bench revolt this time around. The exclusion from the proposed controls of councils with relatively low budgets may well mute the opposition from many Conservative authorities. And even such a major concession as dropping the general scheme, which would (if the Treasury allowed) buy off much of the 'localist' opposition within the Party, would leave the selective scheme. The latter would be perfectly adequate to control the high-spending Labour councils which have been the government's main target throughout. The problem for these authorities will be to develop their own campaigns without alienating broader based support, particularly from the Associations which necessarily reflect a broad range of opinion.

One possible problem for the government is the fact that they are unlikely to secure real spending cuts without some impact on educational provision and standards, which could prove unpopular with the mass of middle-class Tory support. There is already official evidence that cuts are being reflected in standards.[32] If this did prove a major problem, a solution for the government, talked about in the past but shelved, would be to remove education from local authority control. Boards might be set up, responsible to and funded via the Department of Education and Science. This would give firmer control and insulate education budgets from the impact of local government expenditure cuts.

Tightly drawn legislation would inevitably throw the emphasis of opposition beyond the arena of formal politics and on to industrial and popular action. This will be a key element, if opposition to the introduction of rate capping is to have any hope of pursuading the government to drop or significantly water down its proposals. It would, however, be particularly significant once such measures had been put into effect and were starting to bite. Since well over half of local authority expenditure goes on wages and salaries, the scope for real spending cuts without significant cutbacks in local authority employment, which would probably involve compulsory redundancy, is very limited. The extent of union action provoked, and the extent to which this would be linked in to more general opposition to centrally planned local spending and cuts, would therefore be a crucial factor. The mobilisation of support for the principle of local authority provision as well as defense of jobs would strengthen this action.

Similarly, the extent to which popular reaction to the impact of the cuts could be mobilised among groups in the community and among consumers of local authority goods and services would be vitally important. As Keith Bassett has argued in Chapter 4, action by individual councils is unlikely to succeed, unless backed by union action and popular support in a concerted campaign, drawing together different localities and backed by the Labour leadership. Orchestrated action on this scale has failed to materialise in the past. Minor concessions wrung from the government during the legislation's parliamentary passage may look like a more likely scenario. The stakes now, however, are much higher. And given the all-pervasive importance of local government's financial framework, should such legislation be sucessfully brought in it would bring about massive shift in political power. On one level, it is a fundamental threat to the principle of democratically elected local government. But it threatens also to stop in its tracks the development of collective provision, the pursuit of radical initiatives in the local arena and the potential for building politically from the local level which it seemed possible to explore in the early 1980s. This is the challenge which Labour councils, the Left and the labour movement have to meet.

Acknowledgement. I would like to thank Glen Bramley at the School for Advanced Urban Studies for contributing to my understanding of some of the complexities of local government finance and to the production of this chapter without, of course, holding him responsible for the result.

Notes and References

1. Figures in this paragraph are from *Local Government Financial Statistics* (Department of the Environment and Welsh Office, HMSO).
2. *The Government's Expenditure Plans 1983/84 to 1985/86*, Cmnd. 8789 (HMSO, 1983).
3. On capital expenditure, see: P. A. Watt, 'The Control of Local Authority Capital Expenditure', *Local Government Studies* May–June 1982, pp. 91–5; see also J. Barlow, 'The Rationale for the control of Local Government Spending for the Purposes of Macroeconomic Management', *Local Government Studies* May–June 1981, pp. 3–13, and R. Jackman, 'Does Central Government Need to Control the Total of Local Government Spending?', *Local Government Studies* May–June 1982, pp. 75–90.
4. *The Government's Expenditure Plans 1982/83 to 1984/85* Cmnd. 8494 (HMSO, 1982) and *The Times*, 16 November 1982.
5. Public expenditure White Papers.
6. Association of County Councils, Association of Metropolitan Authorities, Association of District Councils, London Boroughs Association, Greater London Council, *Rate Support Grant (England) 1981/82* (1981) p. 25.
7. Note also that central government grant to local authorities in aggregate is subject to a Treasury cash limit. Should total grant in any one year be overshooting this limit, the DoE is empowered to 'claw back' grant from authorities part-way through the year.
8. P. Smith and J. Stewart, 'Local Authority Spending 1983/84', *Public Finance and Accountancy*, June 1983, p. 35.
9. Chartered Institute of Public Finance and Accountancy, *Finance and General Statistics 1983–84* (CIPFA, 1983).
10. P. Smith and J. Stewart, 'Local Authority Spending 1983/84', p. 39.
11. Ibid. p. 37.
12. Ibid. p. 38.
13. *Local Government Trends 1982* (CIPFA, 1983) p. 22.
14. *Rates*, Cmnd. 9008, (HMSO, 1983) p. 8.
15. Ibid. p. 1 and p. 15.
16. Ibid. p. 10.
17. S. Lewis and A. Harrison, 'Local spending: striving for control', *Public Money*, September 1982, p. 56.
18. In R. Jackman, 'Does Central Government Need to Control the Total?', p. 75.
19. L. Brittan, 'Why Control: the Treasury Case', *Public Money*, September 1982, p. 60.

20. R. Bacon and W. Eltis, *Britain's Economic Problem: Too Few Producers* (Macmillan, 1976).
21. L. Brittan, 'Why Control: the Treasury Case', p. 60.
22. *Rates* Cmnd. 9008, p. 3.
23. Ibid. p. 2.
24. Ibid. p. 11.
25. See R. Jackman, 'Does Central Government Need to Control the Total?', and J. Barlow,'The Rationale for the Control of Local Government Spending'.
26. *Financial Statistics*, Central Statistical Office (HMSO, 1983).
27. *Financial and General Statistics* Chartered Institute of Public Finance and Accountancy, deflated by 'purchasing power of the pound', *Economic Trends* (Central Statistical Office, HMSO, 1983) table 42.
28. G. Jones and J. D. Stewart 'The value of local autonomy – a rejoinder' *Local Government Studies* September–October 1982, pp. 10–14. J. D. Stewart, G. Jones, R. Greenwood and J. Raine, *In Defence of Local Government* (Institute of Local Government Studies, Universtiy of Birmingham, 1981).
29. *Guardian*, 30 June 1983.
30. *Guardian*, 3 June 1983.
31. See the excellent account of this earlier period in J. Gyford and M. James, *National Parties and Local Politics* (George Allen and Unwin, 1983).
32. *Report by Her Majesty's Inspectors on the Effects of Local Authority Expenditure Policies on The Education Service in England in 1982* (Department of Education and Science, 1983).

10 Local Socialism: The Way Ahead

*   *   *

**Interview with DAVID BLUNKETT,
Leader of Sheffield City Council**

Interviewed by Martin Boddy and Colin Fudge

DAVID BLUNKETT became leader of Sheffield City Council in
1980. He was born in Sheffield in 1947, on a council estate in the
area he now represents. Blind since birth, he attended a special
boarding school near Shrewsbury between the ages of four and
sixteen, but has lived in Sheffield since then. He took a commercial
course, learned shorthand and typing and had a clerical job in the
gas industry for two years. He passed O and A levels through day-
release and night classes, and was later accepted by Sheffield
University to read politics. After postgraduate studies, he became a
lecturer in politics and industrial relations at Barnsley College of
Technology – he is currently on leave of absence. He joined the
Labour Party in 1963 aged sixteen, and was elected to the City
Council in 1970 while still at university. He was also a member of
South Yorkshire County Council, 1973–4. He was elected leader of
the Labour Group and the Council in 1980, before which, he
chaired the Family and Social Services Committee. He also chairs
the Association of Metropolitan Authorities Social Services
Committee. In 1978, he failed to secure the Labour nomination as
parliamentary candidate for the City's Penistone constituency by
one vote, but has not put himself forward as a parliamentary
candidate since. He was elected to the Labour Party National
Executive Committee in October 1983.

242

Sheffield City Council itself, is a metropolitan district within South Yorkshire County. As such, its main functions include education, planning, social services and housing. With a population of 531,000 (mid–1981) it is the third largest administrative district in England and Wales. In 1926, it became the first municipal borough in the provinces to return a Labour majority and except for two brief periods, in 1932 and 1968, it has been Labour-controlled since. There are 87 members, and after the 1982 election there were sixty Labour Councillors, eighteen Conservative and nine Liberal. Sheffield has traditionally specialised in steel, engineering and cutlery, which have suffered massive job losses in recent years. This contributed to an unemployment level of 13.7 per cent by mid–1983, compared with 12.3 per cent nationally, in contrast to the 1970s when the City compared favourably with national picture. In 1982, the Council became the first in the country to set up an Employment Department. Faced with central government cuts and controls, the Council has pursued a policy of no cuts and no redundancies. This helped push up the rates by 40 per cent in 1980/1 and 37 per cent in 1981/2, although by 1983–4 the increase had been pulled down to 9 per cent. Sheffield's expenditure for 1983/4 was budgetted at £220 million and the rate was 199p in the pound.

The succession of cuts and controls imposed by central government over the last few years, culminating in 1983 in proposals to cap rate increases and abolish the GLC and metropolitan counties, has led many people to proclaim the end of local government. Yet we have seen recently the development in a number of local authorities of radical inititiatives relating in particular to employment, women and race, and moves in some authorities to decentralise town-hall power. Do you think that on balance the Left has achieved gains at the local level?

DB Demoralisation and retrenchment has been one response, but there has also been a total reappraisal of the role of local government in the 1980s. This is not an entirely new approach, but a return in a sense to earlier years, when people saw local government as a very positive tool for making progress, for establishing democracy in its truest sense with people actually participating in decisions as to how their resources were to be used.

There has been a shift away from seeing local councils as local administration, to seeing them again as local *government,* with the opportunity for people with different political perspectives to see what role local government can play. Birmingham, for example, are reappraising the role of the local council from a right-wing stance whereas the GLC, Sheffield and elsewhere are doing so from a socialist perspective. We are saying it isn't good enough simply to run services in their present form, reduced to fit parameters set by central government. We really have to decide what we are doing in the local community and how we can build on this.

How temporary do you think this is? Are Labour councils taking these measures because there is no opportunity to pursue radical initiatives at the centre?

DB   There is some truth in the view that if you are not achieving change at one level, you obviously look at how you can get round the problem and bring about change elsewhere. What the situation has, of course, done is highlight the fact that local government can be a tool for achieving socialist change. This has been submerged in parliamentary, centralist views of progress. Local government is now seen by Mrs Thatcher as a threat. There has also been a reaction within the Labour Party. People have recognised that local government is a far more important vehicle than they had ever believed. The belief in paternalistic, parliamentary change is still, however, strong within the Party, and there is also the worry, which we have to acknowledge, that people may believe that things can be done at the local level alone, without changes at national government level and without the necessary control of the economy requiring parliamentary and international action. We have to pursuade those who are still living in the 1950s and 1960s that the way forward is to commit people from the bottom up in a jigsaw – a jigsaw that doesn't ignore national and international parameters, but relates to them. This can make it possible to mobilise people in every sense of the word at the local level, in their work, their community activity, and their commitment to the collective approach. What we are trying to do is to change a climate of opinion that Mrs Thatcher has very successfully fashioned, to the benefit of her own government. This can only be done from the local level, because you do have to fire people's imagination and commitment. They do have to have an alternative vision of the world, if you are to overcome the obstacles. The idea that legislative paternalism is going to be successful has been discredited so many times that it is amazing that anyone in Parliament still believes it. I think that the parliamentry process should be more concerned with the multi-nationals and international finance, than with the details of local action. The national public corporations and nationally oriented planning processes that work from the top down frighten people, they are anti-socialist, and they can be discredited very easily by the opposition. The only way to suceed is to build a different sort of perspective, in which local government acts as a catalyst, providing examples and motivation and defending alternative strategies in the face of considerable opposition.

You are emphasising the important of struggles around local services – housing, fares, education – as opposed to struggles in the workplace, which are more directly rooted in the basic labour–capital conflict. Do you think, however, that such struggles over local services are more marginal, less of a threat to capital and the capitalist state?

DB   If we see local action on its own, then there is a danger that gains can be picked off. We have to link action at the local level to people's awareness of their own situation, and how this relates to national and international processes. We have to avoid isolating people, or pretending there are solutions at the local level alone. Instead, we have to use examples and the experiences people are having to illustrate what is necessary in terms of national policy. If, for example, we are helping workers in the face of redundancy we have to help them understand what is happening to them and why. We can make marginal changes, we can put resources at their disposal to fight the battle, but this has to fit into the overall political framework. Equally, when we help people in a more positive sense, for example to establish new forms of democratic control in the workplace, we are also helping to broaden their perspective on the political scene. It enables people to relate to economic strategy at the national level and understand it through their experience of sector working parties and planning agreements at the local level. Through the Employment Department and Committee in Sheffield or local Enterprise Boards elsewhere, people can become involved through their local experience in national and international issues. For the Labour Party, of course, this is crucial because its survival depends on its reconstitution as a mass party.

It is sometimes suggested that local government is the 'Achilles heel' of the capitalist state. Is it possible, however, to get beyond the idea of socialist islands, beyond the Socialist Republic of South Yorkshire?

DB   This again is the process of changing people's consciousness and the climate of opinion. I'm sorry to keep repeating it but I do think it's very important. There is a terrible belief that there are so many Labour voters and so many Tory voters and that all we have to do is win the margins. What Thatcher has set out to do, and superficially, at least, has done very successfully, is to win people's hearts and minds. We can do the same, but in a more fundamental way. I believe it really is possible to change the perspective not only of those who vote Labour, but also of those who see themselves as anti-socialist. You can actually pull them across the boundaries. That's how we got a welfare state. We actually shifted opinion. Now the government is rolling it back again. Our job is not to try and get back to where we were before. Instead we have to pick up on what people are thinking now, and be able to articulate and develop strategies that make the current situation relevant to them. People *are* concerned about freedoms, they *are* concerned about open government and reducing bureaucratic procedures. At first our achievements can only be beacons. They are examples, and their credibility is often dangerously at stake. So the quicker we can enthuse people with the battle and spread the vision across the country the better. But I think that we can change the climate of opinion across the country, we can avoid there being only isolated islands.

Places like Sheffield, West Midlands County and the Greater London Council are very much in the forefront as radical authorities. Is this always a good thing? Can it always be used positively, or are there dangers of a gap opening up between the necessary political rhetoric and concrete achievements on the ground?

DB   In building up people's confidence and winning them over to the cause, in providing the evangelical movement actually to give them the fire in the belly, you do often run the risk of carrying what you are saying and carrying people's hopes and expectations beyond what can be achieved in time-scale necessary to retain credibility. You also risk reactions from elsewhere. These include normal human jealousy at the limelight which you attract, through to sheer scepticism that anything can be achieved, plus fear that you are endangering what others think they are already achieving. It may be argued that to make a stand against the cuts, or to push ahead with economic and industrial strategy at the local level is so much of a challenge to central government that it will smash all local authorities in smashing the radical councils; that we would do better to draw in our horns, because eventually Labour will get back into power and everything will be all right. I reject that absolutely. I believe the subservient approach feeds central government powers and makes it possible for them to go even further. Only by challenging the government head-on is it possible to push them back.

This is central to our strategy on cuts. The question of whether to make cuts or to increase the rates to protect people from the cuts is not an esoteric argument about Labour politics. It's about the whole perspective on where we're going and how we challenge the government. It's about the public profile. We have had to adopt a much higher profile than Sheffield is used to, in order to provide that beacon I mentioned, to provide hope for people elsewhere who are struggling and indicate to central government that if they want a fight they've got one. We may lose, but we'll lose honourably and lose in the traditions of the labour movement that fought and struggled and didn't keep its head down, a labour movement without which we would never be where we are today.

You emphasise the importance of political education and consciousness-raising at the local level as a part of the 'bottom up' approach. What are the practical steps that local authorities can be involved in?

DB   We are keen on a number of things. Firstly, we are aware that most people read local rather than national newspaper, they listen to local radio, they watch regional television at peak times. We are fortunate in Sheffield that our media are not paranoically against us, like they are in London. They have not gone in yet for total character assassination and gutter politics. There is an opportunity, therefore, to use the platform which local government gives us. So first of all, you use the public media that's available. That's number one, it's important. That's how you get to the mass audience. It's why it sometimes seems that personality cults are coming into it. They aren't. You are using your position and the media will respond to it. They'll cover a news conference called by the leader of the council, they won't cover one called by a ward secretary or constituency chair. Therefore, we must use this public platform to articulate and develop what we believe in. This goes back to seeing local government in more than purely administrative terms.

Secondly, we must develop within our own employees some perspective on what it is we are trying to achieve. We are not setting out to indoctrinate people, but they should at least understand what we're trying to do, even if they don't agree with it. Finally, we have to remember that the ordinary person's experience of the council is the officer on the desk in the housing department, the home help or the social worker, the school their kids go to or leisure facilities. There are therefore all sorts of ways in which, without bringing politics into it in the normal sense of the word, we can raise people's awareness.

How do you, as the political leadership, go about this within the authority? Obviously its not a matter of simply working through chief officers in the departments and down the hierarchy.

DB That's the danger because the traditional way of communicating is from the top, down through the hierachy. The problem is that people are sceptical about change – changing management structures, changing internal methods of decison-making, even though these may be changes which can make their contribution relevant. We have an enormous task to shift the ethos in different departments. We tried to ensure that people could debate things openly by removing the threat of redundancy. We have also tried to ensure that councillors and council processes are open to officers in different tiers. This has led to clashes with senior officers, who clearly suspect that their traditional management prerogatives are being undermined and are very worried. They fear this, instead of seeing it as an opportunity for everybody at the coalface to make a major contribution. We are also going through a major review of the personnel function, including looking at how all departments function.

There are a number of other problems. One is that traditional trades union practice as interpreted by those unions that have just emerged into the trades union arena sees things in defensive terms, in terms of regrading for additional responsibilites. This makes delegation difficult. Changing hierachical patterns of management becomes more difficult if you're immediately into a petty grading arguments, if I can use that term, rather than discussing how people are really involved in decision-making. There are also problems in trying to do everything at once. Changing people's awareness, changing structures to make things possible, opening up the political process to people down the ladder, all those things are taking place. And at the same time we are trying to delegate, to decentralise services into the community, to bring the community into the process with tenants, works department shop stewards and councillors, for example, meeting together and forming working groups, trying to get people involved in the running of social services at local level. All this is happening at once and that is a very difficult process to manage. There is the danger of it collapsing under its own momentum. But it has its benefits. If you are challenging people then you bring them alive. You are increasing the potential for dynamic change, and people will begin to respond.

There is, however, the problem that if you increase people's expectations of change, then they are more disillusioned by failure than if you hadn't raised expectations in the first place. We can't however change things without people struggling themselves. This is what the bottom up approach is about. People will get disillusioned if they expect what they have always had, change from the top, if they expect us to do it for them. They have to stop sitting back and expecting committee chairs and leaders of councils to do things for them.

Do you see any tension in this? You are trying to build from the bottom up, trying to build awareness both in the community and within the Town Hall, but you have fairly definite political ideas as to where you would like this political consciousness to lead. Isn't there a tension here?

DB That is spot on. There is a danger of only wanting community involvement when it backs up things we have already decided. Tenants' groups and action groups in the community won't always love us. We're the establishment. They'll fight us, but something good will come out of the fight. People will be politicised, although there is the possibility that some of us may suffer and things we want may suffer setbacks. We've got to learn to accept this.

There is, however, a real difficulty in establishing what we are asking of people. I'll give you two examples: our decision, set out in the 1980 Manifesto to abolish corporal punishment, and our decision to abolish school uniforms. Both were seen in political and democratic terms. We don't believe that people should have physical violence inflicted on them. We believe it ingrains in people the philosophy that violence is necessary to keep order. Similarly with the issue of uniforms, we don't believe people should be forced to conform.

The issues were, however, put to the schools very clumsily, as though we were having a referendum instead of simply asking how best to put into practice what had been decided. And, taking parents, teachers and pupils as a whole, we lost. So we were left with a policy for which we had a mandate but which people on the whole had rejected. This damaged the credibility of the democratic process, and also made us wary about consultation next time. We have, as it happens, abolished both corporal punishment and school uniforms amicably, without the education system or the local state falling apart, but it was all mixed up with the politics of the 1982 elections and could have been very nasty. These are small examples perhaps, but the danger must be recognised. We must be absolutely clear in communicating with people what we are asking for and what we are offering a lead on. There is room for leadership, as Mrs Thatcher has rightly shown, but you also have to be involved in a process of persuasion and taking people with you.

Looking back at the period since 1979, it might be argued that local councils have made ground in terms of politicisation and raising awareness, but that they haven't been able to mount effective opposition in a more immediate sense to central government cuts and controls. How do you think more effective opposition could have been mounted?

DB I don't think we should be too demoralised. There have been defeats. There always will be when Davids are facing Goliaths. Personally I would like to believe that Davids always beat Goliaths! But they don't. We mustn't believe things are a great success when they are not, but we mustn't on the other hand be depressed by it. You have to create the right ethos, the common philosophy. If Labour councils half accept monetarist doctrines and believe that public spending must be cut in order to restore the economy, then it's quite logical that they'll cut. They won't put up a strong fight.

You also have to accept that local government can only play a part in bringing the government down. The view of the factional Left who suddenly thought in 1980 or 1981 that if all else fails we'll push local government over the barbed wire was nonsense. We have to accept the limits of our own strength and ability to lead. We have to work with all those who are with us in challenging existing doctrines and building up alternatives. The reason, for instance, that we accepted large rate increases were firstly to defend services, but also as a crucial part of the philosophy that we don't inflict government policy on the most vulnerable and least articulate. We said the community as a whole is going to bear the burden of Thatcherism in this city.

Can we turn to some more specific initiatives? Thinking first about employment policy, most local authorities are involved in industrial development of one kind or another, but the initiatives being taken by Sheffield along with West Midlands County Council and the GLC are a new and more radical departure. How do you see Sheffield's long-term involvement in this area?

DB It is very important to see whatever we do as relating to an alternative strategy at national level. We see it also, however, linking in with an alternative social strategy as well, which is not yet accepted by the leadership at national level. Firstly, it's an obvious response to the critical unemployment situation. Traditionally, however, local government has been a facilitator for private enterprise. It has made public resources available for people to exploit as they will, in terms of land, property, factories and cash handouts. We would like to see a whole range of developments at local level making it possible to extend democracy into the economy and into local industry, at the same time linking this to the development and protection of services. We see the provision of traditional local authority services as part of the economic and industrial development of the city, rather than simply delivery of welfarism. The various parts of this strategy would make it possible to have a really responsive alternative at national level that reflected local potential and local needs.

The development, therefore, of sector working parties – in this city steel and engineering are the obvious ones – are important. Provisions for investigating and developing new technology, including information technology, with the community playing a part are exciting and worthwhile developments. Putting research at the disposal of people; the Labour Research approach is important because people can then understand their own local economy and community.

The purchasing policy of the local authority as a market, and the provision of back-up for developing new and alternative products are both significant. We employ a couple of people who were involved in the Lucas Aerospace combine and so do the GLC. Product development and employment policy go together, because the development of alternative products develops jobs and manufacturing potential from the bottom up again. It's a direct challenge to the Tory Enterprise Zone approach – attract people, give away public assets and resources and hope eventually they may create some jobs for you.

The development of people's belief that they can do something themselves, developing democratic structures is crucial. One approach is helping people save their industries, genuinely having the back-up resources. It's a politicising process as well. People understand a lot more, even if they lose. We have to work with those that are made redundant, using whatever money we can get, including, say, MSC and EEC cash for re-training. We see re-training a trying to give people something worthwhile, not just another exercise in keeping them off the dole queue for a year.

Another approach is resourcing what workers want to do with their industry, if it can't be saved in the normal form. If a multinational pulls out, is there a market for that product or the skills those people have? Can we save the plant ourselves with the workers, all the time using resources to back *them* rather than trying to do it *for* them. This means that sometimes people won't have the courage to go through with it, or the market may not be there or whatever. It may mean finding it possible to work with capitalist institutions like ICFC and the banking system, part of which is willing to work with us on saving industry.

These strands link in to aspects of an alternative economic strategy. The strategy would put the bits together from different parts of the country, different industries, different sectors of the economy and make it a living strategy, regionally and nationally. We'd like to see national strategy based on regions whose component parts already exist, rather than new constituencies. This would mean drawing on the component local authorities and on trades unions.

We'd also like to see the social strategy linked in. Developing social provision, whether in an immediate sense to prevent the total collapse of our society because of mass unemployment or, in the longer term, to provide services because of their own worth – community health services, social services, decent education for the kids – this all generates demand. It all needs products, all links in to the economy. We need to see that interdependence as crucial. Social service spending, education spending don't come *after* we've regenerated the economy, they're a part of it. It is nonsense that you can buy space invader machines, because that represents productive activity in the private sector, but can't produce wheel chairs or other equipment to make peoples' lives more acceptable, in the public sector. The separation of public and private spending, the balancing and percentaging of public and private spending has to be challenged.

We see this very clearly in public capital spending. When, for example, the water authority cuts back, the people who make the piping and equipment are made redundant. If we invested in rail electrification we'd put not only those working on it but all the related industries to work. They would be manufacturing for and selling to the community. We've got to get over to people the value of this sort of public expenditure, so they can contrast it with a lot of the junk which is produced in the private sector without any debate on how resources as a whole should be used.

Can we turn to the issue of women in relation to local govern-

ment? A number of councils, so far only in London, have set up
women's committees. In part, these initiatives are a response to the
fact that most councillors are men, career opportunities for women
within the local government have not been advanced that much,
and facilities such as nursery provision are very poor. What pres-
sure for change do you see in Sheffield in this area or is the issue
not really on the agenda?

DB It is on the agenda, but we're doing it in a non-adventurist
way. People have accused us of sneering at middle-class feminists,
but I don't think that's true. What we've said is we want to give
opportunities to all women not just a few. We've set up a section in
the Employment Department to promote opportunities for women.
We've had to expand that because we only employed one person
and she got overloaded rather rapidly. One important area involves
looking at our employment practices as an authority. We also have
to look to the economy at large, where women are being hit harder
than men on the whole because part-time work, which is often
crucial to family budgets in a working-class city like ours, has been
particularly hard hit. It's not therefore just an argument about
allowing women to get to the top of the professions, although this
is important. We've taken the view so far that separating women
out in the struggle is not a good idea apart, that is, from the work
of the Employment Department. So we haven't set up a separate
women's committee. We have tried to give support in a non-
patronising way to the women who are on the Council, not only to
develop their own potential but to give others confidence as well.
The Chair of the General Purposes Committee which deals with the
legal side, transport and catering, a variety of things that don't
often excite people, is a woman. The Chair of the new Employment
Committee is now a woman, as are the deputy Chairs of Education
and of Planning. We think that if we can encourage people to
develop their capacities, capabilities and confidence it'll help others
to have confidence, as people, and that they won't be discriminated
against, put down or face obstacles as women. It's a long, difficult
process.

We will, certainly, give grants to groups working in the
community, but we'd rather not separate out grants to women
from the overall struggle because we believe it's a struggle of
working people for control over their lives and resources, not a

separate struggle for women. In a sense it's not wanting the women's issue to sap the energy of the class struggle generally. We think there's a danger that it can come to be seen not only as more important than but separate from that battle. We're not antagonistic to the developments that have taken place in the GLC and Camden and so on. It'll be interesting to see how it goes, but we've got our own job to do. You need the people who are at the focal point of it all to want things to happen. The women on this Council and in the Party have said they are behind the things that have been done here. We're not going to do it 'for' them.

Can we switch to the question of political appointments? A number of large authorities have had political appointments for a number of years. Recently however they've developed and become more widespread and acceptable. How important are political appointments in pursuing radical strategies?

DB You've got to define exactly what this means. We've had secretarial support which gives us confidentiality and facilities of our own for a long time. The strategy appointments we have made have not simply involved appointing people whose views accord directly with ours, or who are members of the Labour Party. We have appointed people who have a perspective on what we're trying to achieve which goes beyond normal local government thinking, but who can help us to achieve our aims within the ordinary structures of the local authority. There is a danger that by appointing people to strategy groups you actually place them outside normal structures and reduce their influence. We haven't appointed political advisors. We have been very careful not to refer to them as such. Our political advisors are the District Labour Party and the labour movement in Sheffield. It's they that determine policy with us, monitor it and help us carry it out. They advise us what's acceptable.

The strategy officers are not straight political party appointments linked only to the controlling group. They are officers whose jobs is to help change the direction of the authority and open it up to all the influences in the community. The local authority has traditionally been open to establishment pressures. Chief officers have lunch with the Chamber of Commerce and the Rotary Club. We're involved in the difficult process of opening up channels to community groups, tenants and unions. Our appointments have been to enable that process to take place, to develop alternative economic and social strategies and do this in a flexible way. There is a tendency, however, to involve strategy officers in crisis work, fighting off the latest attacks from central government or working out how to save public transport. I'm in favour of this provided it's seen as part of the total process, as part of this opening-up process, helping the debate, helping us democratise and challenging existing attitudes.

Assuming we get a Labour government returned at some point, what changes would you want to see in terms of financial controls and legislation?

DB I think they could very quickly lift some legislative regulations to make it easier to experiment. They wouldn't be able to make major legislative changes immediately, so what we'd want is relaxation. We'd obviously be able to do a lot more if they relaxed the financial controls and put resources back, which they'd have to do as part of the reflation of the economy. Part of our task is to plan for that. If you're going to build houses you've got to start planning now – most people haven't cottoned on to this. It could take two or three years to get programmes off the ground unless Labour authorities planned in advance.

I'd want the regulations that prevent our involvement in direct municipal enterprise relaxed immediately, so that we could extend the work we are doing in the local economy, whether through the Direct Works Department or new forms of municipal enterprise, without fear of central government challenge. We could then develop examples, illustrating the possibilities – it has to be remembered that the health services, gas, water, electricity, telephones, sewerage were all started by local government in the urban areas. We want to do something similar with modern enterprises. Above all, we would want central government to accept the role of local authorities in this overall planning process. Local government should be involved in an experimental sense. The government should allow this exploratory work to take place and be prepared to risk funds to support it.

They should also be prepared to introduce fairly major legislation to allow local authorities to get much more involved in finance and banking, as part of a general change in the commercial and merchant banking system. Then we would have real partnership between national and local government, not only in restoring the economy but also in extending democracy. In the longer term, it would be important that the government didn't retrench or retire into the parliamentary committee system, thinking that what is said in Parliament changes the world or brings about socialism.

You obviously see a very important role for local government and have spelled out some of the ways this might be played out in practice. But what about the missing bits of the jigsaw? Anything like complete Labour control at the local level, certainly beyond the metropolitan authorities, is surely impossible in the forseeable future?

DB That's correct. So we need a very open and flexible approach. We've got to let those local authorities that are forging ahead carry on. In other places there will be slightly more involvement from the centre. There will need to be a different set-up in some areas, in terms of enterprise boards and so on. We'll invite the local authority to take the lead. If it declines, an alternative structure will be set up, in which the authority is constantly asked to participate. We'll challenge the electorate to say whether they want to be democratically involved in developing economic and social strategy and whether they want their local authority, Labour, Tory or whatever, to take part. The model of Transport Plans or Structure Plans might be applied to the economic field, for example. After all, Tory councils accept their role in providing public education and social services. So where the local authority was willing, it would be the catalyst and central government's role would be low profile. Central government should be left free to concentrate on more fundamental restructuring. Indeed if central government tried to interfere and obstruct local initiatives, then the weight of the nation and the legitimacy of Parliament would once again be thrown against radical change, against socialist democracy and against ordinary people rather than for them.

Coming finally to the more immediate problems posed by the Thatcher Government's second term of office and the latest proposals, what first of all do you think can be done to resist the financial controls and rate capping?

DB   The Tory Government's proposals to take selective powers to tackle individual local authorities, and a general power against all local authorities to 'prevent the local community deciding its own level of spending, the quality of services and local rate level to cover that expenditure, is a logical extension of previous legislation. The ability to use penalties against the local community and withdraw grant over and above the general withdrawal of government grant from local authorities, all authorities, enables the government to force up rates in those areas of the country where local authorities have refused to implement cuts in essential services. When the rates are increased to cover the lost grant and subsidies, the government can trot out the spurious argument of large rate increases, without tacking the real issue.

The obvious problem in tackling this is that people are very happy to see their rates frozen or reduced, whereas the impact on services only comes afterwards. There is very wide opposition to the measures from local councils including Conservative authorities. The need, however, to get local councils to work together in a coherent manner and not simply to be restricted to the pace of the most reluctant Conservative authority was recognised in the summer of 1983, when those councils most at risk got together in Sheffield only three weeks after the general election. Practical steps to counter the legislation are starting, although the actual outcome cannot as yet be determined.

One thing is absolutely clear. As well as the normal lobbying activity, a great deal of imaginative thought has to go into ways of presenting local government's case and mobilising the strength of both the workforce and the local community. Sharing ideas, and councils pulling together, in a way that avoids 'one upmanship' and the danger of people trying to retain their own 'purity' at the expense of others, has to be fully recognised this time round. Unfortunately the local authority associations, including the Association of Metropolitan Authorities, are not in a position to mobilise imaginative schemes. They are geared up to a totally different era. The need to maintain the maximum unity and draw in the widest possible support is, however, paramount if the legislation is to be significantly altered. Tactics have to be considered which will evoke the same spirit in defence of our democracy and freedom as that which the opposition have so often initiated.

This is not simply a constitutional matter. At issue is the fundamental right to raise and spend local money, as determined by the local electorate. Sheffield has had £127 million in grants and subsidies removed from it in the last four years, amounting to a staggering £258 for each family in the City. Despite that, the popular vote in May 1983 went up to over 50 per cent and we won additional seats. There is a level of public support. It is important that demoralisation and despair do not blind people to the fact that Mrs Thatcher is not invincible.

What is your view on the proposed scrapping of the metropolitan counties and the GLC?

DB Labour Party policy on the question of metropolitan counties is clear. Reorganisation of local government should not be done piecemeal. An overall review is needed with the intention of providing unitary authorities. The retention of the GLC is a different matter. The main argument against abolition is that the government are unlikely to allow services run by the counties and the GLC to be transferred to the districts and boroughs. Dismemberment will most likely bring a shift away from local democracy, with the government taking over the most politically sensitive and important areas of activity, in particular the running of public transport, through departmental edict and Regional Office, or some form of quango. Since the government clearly see the true road to democracy in privatisation and the operation of market forces, the interface between consumers and capital, they can easily sacrifice accountable, representative democracy and participation. This is the battleground. It is part of the overall threat to local democracy and freedom.

What finally, in the light of the government's plans, are the possibilities for the continued development of radical initiatives at the local level?

DB Radical, innovatory developments by local government do not depend on the structure of the local government system. They do, however, depend on the freedom to determine local policy and the freedom to raise money to implement it. Thatcher's obssession with destroying local democracy is based on the clear belief that socialist local government provides not simply a bulwark against Tory policy, but fertile ground for developing genuine alternatives to the market economy, in a way which will appeal to people who are sick and tired of the old fraternalistic bureaucratic structures.

Just as the early socialist pioneers used local government to develop collective and community consciousness, so the Labour Party has no option but to use local government to develop sensitive policies that relate to people in the community; to rebuild from the grassroots in a way which is reminiscent of the original creation of the political electorate. Thatcher has been able to adopt that policy in reverse. Now, local government offers the only major area where the Labour Party has any real influence or base for reconstruction. The Tories see the smashing of collective, community provision as part of their overall strategy for reshaping the economic and social life of the country in their own image. The threat to remove the fundamental right to raise and spend revenue is, therefore, much more significant than the restructuring of metropolitan authorities, which will in any case take a considerable time and is possibly an example where local government's refusal to cooperate in its own execution could actually be a major example of the real strength that lies in the hands of local councils, if they choose to use it. The battle over the next five years to save local democracy is, therefore as much a part of the struggle to save the collective approach in politics as it is about protecting the wellbeing of millions of people.

*   *   *

Interview with KEN LIVINGSTONE, Leader of the Greater London Council

Interviewed by Martin Boddy and Colin Fudge

KEN LIVINGSTONE became leader of the Greater London Council after Labour took control in the May 1981 election. Born in 1945, he went to Tulse Hill Comprehensive School, Brixton, worked for eight years as a medical technician, and then did a three-year teacher training course at Phillippa Fawcett College. He now works full-time as a GLC councillor. He joined the Labour Party in 1968 at the age of twenty-three and is a member of the Transport and General Workers Union. He was a Councillor for the London Borough of Lambeth, between 1971–8, being Vice-Chair of the Housing Committee 1971–3, and was Councillor for the London Borough of Camden, 1978–82, where he served as Chair of Housing, 1978–80. He was elected to the GLC in 1973 and elected Leader of the Labour Group and Leader of the Council in May 1981. He stood for Parliament, unsuccessfully, as Labour candidate for Hampstead in the 1981 election.

The GLC was set up in 1965. It is an 'upper tier' authority, unique to the capital but equivalent in this sense to the county level outside London. Within the GLC boundary, there are thirty-two Borough Councils plus the City of London Corporation. The GLC's main functions include strategic planning, broad policy and financial control of bus and underground services operated by the London Transport Executive, highways and traffic, parks, and waste disposal. Local planning, along with housing and social services are Borough functions. Education is the responsibility of the Inner London Education Authority in Inner London and the Boroughs in outer London – thirty-five of ILEA's forty-eight members are GLC members from Inner London Boroughs. The GLC has ninety-two members and after the May 1981 election there were forty-eight Labour members, forty-one Conservative, two Social Democrat and one Liberal. GLC was controlled by Labour 1965–7 and 1973–7, and by the Conservatives 1967–73 and 1977–81. Greater London's population is 6.6 million (mid–1981) and GLC expenditure for 1983/4 was budgetted at £824 million. The rate levied in 1983/4 was 37.7p in the pound, excluding the ILEA rate – this was on top of Borough rates. In 1983/4 GLC's budgetted spending level was such that the Block Grant system provided no central government grant to fund spending. Following the 1981 election, several new committees were set up including Industry and Employment, Women, the Police, and Ethnic Minorities.

The succession of cuts and controls introduced by central government over the last few years, culminating most recently in proposals to cap rate increases and abolish the GLC and metropolitan counties, has led many people to proclaim the end of local government. Yet we have seen the development, by many councils, of radical initiatives related in particular to employment, race, women, and moves to decentralise town-hall power. Do you think that on balance the Left has achieved gains at the local level?

KL Yes, certainly, because until some years ago, the Left bypassed local government completely. If you compare the Labour-controlled London Boroughs with the situation in the 1960s, virtually all the old guard, the sort of people you still see around in the North East, have been replaced over successive elections, with a most incredible shift in personnel, style and policies. The incoming members have been very keen to use local government to try to expand public involvement and the ability of people to control their own lives, as well as trying to take a particular service and push back the frontiers. Different councils have done different things. From 1970 on, councils did a lot simply in terms of extra spending on social services; then the attempt to use the Housing Finance Act [1972] to municipalise the private rented sector was very dramatic in boroughs like Lambeth and Camden. In London we've gone through a long period, from the mid–1970s until 1981, when there was a retrenchment and in most places we had centrist councillors resisting the demands of the constituencies and of the radical wing. I think what we've seen is a complete breakthrough. With the exception of, say, Newham, Tower Hamets and Barking all the Labour authorities in London are now very much along the lines of the GLC.

How do you make sense of that change, what is the background?

KL There was a long period during which the potential of local government wasn't seen. In the Labour Party in the 1950s and 1960s, people were concerned with human rights and foreign affairs. Issues like housing and transport didn't seem good things to get involved in, and it wasn't until Britain completely shed its imperialist role that people no longer thought of the Labour party in terms of liberating this colony or that, or of introducing homosexual law reform. The removal of empire, plus great achievements in the liberalisation of censorship, divorce and gay rights, meant that 'the issues that dominated the 1950s tended largely to be resolved in the 1960s. It then became a question of looking at the problems that had arisen out of the 1945 Labour Government, Morrisonian nationalisation and the growth of local state – how to make it more accountable and more responsive. With the initial response in the 1960s, this nonsense about managerial efficiency, the Bains Report and so on, it took the Labour Party, certainly the radical Left of the Labour Party, a long time to recognise the importance of local government. It didn't seem to be much more than old white men coming along to general management committees and talking about rubbish collection. Most of the radical activists who were concerned particularly with housing issues, transport and other things were outside the Labour Party. It was only following the nadir of the Labour Party in the late 1960s under the Wilson Government, that you had this gradual drift of radicals back into the Party, who started to think about local government. After the setbacks of the last decade, or at least since the IMF cuts, the Left have been forced to consider what they want to do with local government. The radical Left has also been won over to the idea of strong local government as a policy objective in itself, rejecting the idea of using it simply to attack the government. I think that the effect of the IMF, followed by Heseltine, was to convince the Party of the importance of strong local government as a counterbalance to central government.

Do you think the fact that central government has been blocked since 1979 has advanced local radicalism? Has this energy been diverted to the local level by the fact that the Labour Party at least has been unable to pursue radical strategies at central government level?

KL I think the problem is that not only is Labour out of government but also that this has been the most dismal period of opposition the Labour Party has ever had. It hasn't done anything. I think the dramatic attention on places like Sheffield, London and elsewhere has reflected the weakness of the national Labour leadership, whether Right or Left. No-one in Parliament seems to make an impact on anything. They've spent so long attacking other members of the Labour Party that they can't see how this platform can be used for other things.

Do you think this focus on the local level is temporary? How might it change over time?

KL Well, with Mrs Thatcher now re-elected, there will be a lot more in the way of centralising measures. I think you're going to have to wait for a Labour Government before you can get a real shift in power on a fundamental basis in local government. I cannot see the Tories doing it. If you look at the surveys of Tory councillor opinion, only about twenty per cent are critical of measures the government has taken. The Tory Party is at heart a very centralised party, so I think it *will* take the election of a Labour government to change things significantly. The commitment within the Labour Party will only grow if there is a period of time when a lot can be done locally. Once you actually give a lot of independence to local government, it'll be very difficult for a Tory government to take it away. It's been very easy for the Tories to contain the powers of local government, given the track record of the last Labour Government. The Tories have continued what was begun under Crosland and Shore.

A final point on this. How far do you think the focus on local government and the shift in emphasis, perhaps, away from the workplace reflects the demise of trades union power in workplace struggles, particularly under the present government, so that local government is a new arena for struggle?

KL I don't think there's ever been a great shift in activists between the trades unions and the constituency parties. They've tended to be in one or the other. It's just that local government has achieved the full prominence it should have on the constituency Labour Party side. Indeed, unions have got better at and more used to using Labour councils now. I would have thought, particularly in London, that it's more a result of the weakness of industrial trades unions, the fact that for twenty years or more there was a policy of driving industry out of London so that two thirds of redundancies have been in manufacturing industry. If you look at the London Labour Party Conference, the two largest block votes are the Transport and General Workers Union and NUPE. Between them they've got a quarter of the votes. The industrial trades unions are small, and absolutely splintered. In London at least, therefore, the absence of solid trades union vote dominated by the Right, which is still a problem at the national conference, has allowed the Left to advance. And given that the percentage of the workforce in industry is not much more than a third, and going down, that dominance is never again going to be what it was in the 1950s. So I think this is a permanent shift, and local government will be seen as a much more powerful component of the labour movement and society generally in the future.

Do you think that the sort of issues that are of major importance to local government, like housing, fares and education, are in any sense more marginal, in that they don't so directly challenge the basic relationship between labour and capital in the workplace?

KL The way that housing, transport or education are funded by local government does directly challenge capital. The rating mechanism is the best method of redistributing wealth that the labour movement has ever had its hands on. It beats hell out of any policy which government has for financing central programmes. To be able to spread the burden of financing services in such a way that the greater part is paid by industry and commerce is incredibly advantageous to the labour movement. That's why the Tories have woken up to the importance of centralising the state. If you have radical socialist administrations prepared actually to fund services, you are redistributing wealth in a big way, as for example with fares policies. If you look at it, a third of all we spend is financed by the City of London and Westminster, which means mainly the office blocks in those two areas. Out of a current rate product of £19 million per penny rate, £3 million comes from Westminster and £2.7 million from the City of London. That's fantastic redistribution of wealth, it makes the GLC the best redistributor of wealth we've ever been able to take control of, much better than any other council in the country. That's why I think the government is moving to abolish the GLC.

Can we look at how strategies at the local level relate to the wider labour movement? It has sometimes been suggested that local government could be the 'Achilles heel' of the capitalist state. But how do you think you can get beyond the idea of socialist islands?

Taking the GLC, for example, can one part of the state be colonised or subverted?

KL That's the way the labour movement has always proceeded, making advances where it can and learning from success and failure. That's what we've been doing here. A lot of very valuable lessons about, say, industrial policy for a future Labour government have been learnt. We've also completely shifted the policy of the national party in favour of public transport in the last eighteen months. If you actually look at it, the policy of the last Labour government was no different from the Law Lords. Bill Rodgers actually used to insist that we run London Transport without subsidy, and used to haul Jim Daley over there to tell him so when Jim Daley was Transport Chair here. So we've been able to use the GLC in a way that's swung party and trades union opinion. If you look at the TUC annual report, it's peppered with references to the GLC. So we are finding out and learning from this. As to the actual possibility of socialist islands, no, I don't believe that at all. We did always maintain that we would use the GLC as a shield to protect people from the worst effects of this government and do the best we could to improve conditions, but what can be achieved is always going to be marginal without a shift in the balance of power between central and local government. But then I don't think people actually expected more. Labour voters, when you talk to them, are quite realistic about the allocation of power in society. They've grown up being told there's one law for the rich and one for the poor, they don't really expect a Labour council to be some sort of socialist haven. But leading by example gradually builds up a stronger commitment among working-class people to the Labour Party. A lot of people are very pleased to have seen a Labour council elected which has at least consistently fought on these issues, even if it has been defeated. It's an improvement! If we really restructured powers between central and local government, I think we could have very strong independent local government introducing radical socialist measures which would shift power to the local area. It will always be easier for people to get their hands on the local council than on the neck of a government minister. In that sense the more services that are provided by the local council the better and the more accessible they will be, allowing people to control and change them.

Although there have, on the face of it, been defeats for local government, like the fares issue, resistance to selling council houses in Norwich, or Lothian's attempt to resist cuts, do you think, nevertheless that something has been gained, that there are lessons to be learned?

KL Well there's no such thing as complete defeat in a struggle between labour and capital. You could look at all the advances in provision of housing as a gain for capital as well, because it relieves capital of the need to provide housing for its own workforce. However good a victory looks at the time there are always benefits in it for capital. Similarly, even in our defeats there are still benefits.

Do you think, however, that the opposition could have been more effective against cuts, against the pressure to cut fares subsidies? Individual authorities were largely isolated, they weren't able to mobilise wide support or to make links.

KL It would have been a major advantage if the leadership of the Party nationally had co-ordinated the struggle. That would, however, have required the national leadership to achieve a broad consensus, to believe in it itself, and to establish a commanding presence on the political stage. All this has been lacking. Even though a lot of councillors are terrified of surcharges, a strong lead nationally with firm commitment to reimburse people who have been bankrupted might have made a lot of difference. If we had that sort of strong leadership nationally, local councillors might be a bit more confident, the government would win the next election and be in a position to indemnify them. That's the major weakness we've had, but then that's been there ever since the war – and I don't mean the Falklands War.

The lack of leadership is one thing. But what would you be looking for from an incoming Labour government in the way of legislative changes, changes in the financial system, and increased local autonomy?

KL In the first place, I don't think an incoming Labour government would necessarily have a clue how to cope with the first difficult moments. I don't think priorities have been thought through. The work on how to proceed as and when we win just isn't being done nationally and that's part of the weakness. Therefore, the struggle to establish priorities would take place after the election, which will make for a lot problems. But we're stuck with that, there's no way out of that one. If we get a Labour government, I think there does now seem to be some sort of genuine commitment to struggle around local government. Eighteen months ago, when we first raised the demand for the repeal of legislation around the auditor and *ultra vires,* this was dismissed out of hand. Now in the space of a year this has shifted. I think we could actually persuade an incoming Labour government to do that – it would be a real struggle, because all the civil servants and the media would immediately try and win them back to a commitment to a centralised state, and try to water down any commitment to independent local government. We would just have to wait for the outcome of the struggle to see who could win the soul of the next Labour government. Whether we won would all hinge on who actually got elected and on the economic circumstances. I think we could have a radical socialist government elected which would, after a difficult period of transition, deliver the goods.

I would hope that as a result of that struggle the social services system, the health service, the police, and administration of DHSS benefits, would all pass to local government. And while national government can set minimum standards, I think administration in these areas should be at the local level. The real problem comes with the argument that you can't have an independent financial base. I think you've got to have a local income tax within about five or six years and I would certainly want to see a local income tax with commercial rating retained as the mechanism whereby you get money out of industry and commerce – the last thing you want is a local corporation tax because they won't pay that any more than they pay national tax. If you could get that commitment, you could establish the structure of the new authorities and their powers. Initially, however, it would have to be a case of a Labour government giving authorities grant for the bulk of the funding, with not much more in the way of financial independence. It'll still be a major step forward, but until you get a local income tax you aren't going to be able to prevent an incoming Tory government rolling back all the gains that have been made. Once you had established that, independent local political parties could resist any move towards recentralisation very strongly. I think it would most probably be irreversible.

Given greater local autonomy, is there a problem that you have then given greater autonomy to Tory councils around the country?

KL   Not if central government retains the power to set minimum national standards. I would see the debate at general elections being around the minimum standards the different parties were prepared to commit themselves to. Labour would be trying to push up minimum standards. You'd get the Tories at the election saying leave it all to local government, with virtually nil minimum standards. The Labour Party would be commiting itself to very high standards in particular services, and to ensuring there was an adequate form of redistribution in whatever form of funding was set up, that would allow councils to achieve them. Even if we have local income tax, the element of redistribution is going to have to be at least fifty per cent going into a national pool, in order to allow local government in Hackney, Lambeth, Liverpool etc. to survive. It may even have to be larger. Providing you have that type of fairly clear and understandable system of redistribution, which isn't subject to annual manipulation, then councils could plan over a period of some years on an expectation of future income. It really has to be a clear, understandable system tied to indices of need, not subject to the annual run-through the computer fifty times to see which system is worst for Labour councils.

Can we pick up the same kind of theme, but at the local level? There are many Labour authorities, particularly in London, wanting to build closer links with the community, to build policy from the grassroots upwards, building relations with tenants' organisations, women's groups, and unions. How do you see these sorts of relationships developing? How much central direction do you need to establish radical policies and how much can you afford to devolve to the locality?

KL   My view is that given the contraction of the industrial base in this country, the labour movement has to make a fundamental change in its own structure. A Labour Party based in the industrial trades unions was credible in the 1940s and 1950s, but the contraction of the industrial base means that the Labour Party is going to have to be based on service unions, many of them white-collar, which isn't an adequate base on its own. Our own white-collar union here in the GLC, the staff association, is deeply reactionary, whilst maintaining that it is apolitical. The same thing would be true if NALGO came into the Labour Party. There's this incredible split personality within NALGO. You go to Lambeth or Lewisham or Camden and you meet the branch executive, and it's all people who are on the Left of the Labour Party or from SWP and they've got an absolutely wonderful position on everything, you know, that you can't help but agree with. Then you get a general meeting of NALGO which everything turns on and then the crunch comes. The leadership of NALGO in London is very much in line with radical socialist policies, but it's completely out of sympathy with the bulk of its membership and therein lies its weakness.

My view is that the Labour Party has to change its own structure so that women's organisations, black organisations, community organisations have a direct input rather than via the trade unions. Black political organisations should be affiliated to the Labour Party, as should various feminist groups. What we should aim for is to build a labour movement that represents not just the trades unions, but also these other sections of society which have been neglected by the labour movement in the past and whose demands have not been articulated. We have been, if anything, deeply conservative on the issues that matter to them. This is the historical problem of being a colonial society. The craft unions grew up as much out of the benefits of colonialism as British capital did, and the craft unions are still very much the bedrock of the Right in the Labour Party. They're the ones who laugh loudest about gay rights or feminism, the ones who are most reluctant to give a strong lead on racism. It's in the unions that represent the unskilled workers that the Labour Party has made advances, NUPE and the T&G and so on. I think a lot of people in the Labour Party will no doubt find this a ridiculous proposition but this really is a heritage from our colonial past and it affects the labour movement radically. We have to break this because there isn't a natural majority in this country for a craft union-based Party anymore. This was fine a hundred years ago when fifty per cent were industrial workers. We never even in fact reached fifty per cent in this country. Now however, there is no prospect of building a governing majority on the basis of the old trades union structure. It has to be built on the trades unions allied to all those groups that have not been through or are just starting to go through collective work experience. This is the way forward for the Party in the future.

Of course local government is able to respond to that much more quickly than the trades union structure or the formal Labour Party structure. Trying to change the British labour movement is a really long slow process, whereas you can start to change the way local government operates much more rapidly. It's a question of getting perhaps no more than twenty or thirty radical socialists elected to a council and of them getting involved in a long drawn-out struggle with the central bureaucracy, but its much quicker to change that than it ever will be to change the Labour Party. I think the Labour Party will actually learn fron the lessons here and then adapt, once it sees the advantages. If you actually look at borough council election votes in the wake of the Falklands War, the Labour vote in London in unskilled working-class, black and Irish areas actually went up, sometimes by as a much as a quarter. In the old, more settled working-class areas, places like Hornchurch, Hayes and Harlington, based very much on the craft unions, the Labour vote collapsed by half. There's this tremendous difference and it is repeated all over the country. The Labour Party, whether it likes it or not, has become a party that can only win power if it actually maintains its skilled working-class role, but also attracts the votes of the really poor and of those without work experience in a way that it has not done successfully. To try and appeal to both wings is really very difficult and the Party hasn't really given it any thought. I think most people in the Labour Party aren't even aware that this is the future. You see, in responding to all your questions, I don't separate the Labour Party from local government. Everything we are doing relates to both.

But within that, one thing that is at issue, and certainly something that David Blunkett emphasised when we were talking with him, is the 'battle of ideas'. How do you pursue this?

KL   I think the fares compaign is really the best example of winning the struggle of ideas. Polls before the fares cut showed a majority of three to one against us doing it and, after six months of the experiment, a two to one majority in favour. We won the argument by showing how it would work. I think that is the way forward for the movement. We've got to make socialist policies relevant to people in their localities and in the workplace, and to show that they do work. I don't think people will buy a packaged ideology just because it's been well sold by advertising. It's really something that builds up from the base, from people's workplace or their estate, based on their own experience. Given that the Labour Left see not just the redistribution of wealth but the redistribution of power as important, you have to make sure there is real democratic control. It's no good just having the whole national wealth in the hands of the state – you have that in Eastern Europe but it's still a bloody awful system. If anything, Morrisonian nationalisation reduced the power of individuals to control their own lives. People feel even more helpless in a centralised state bureaucracy because it's so much more difficult to attack state bureaucracy than it is to attack private ownership in your industry.

Can we turn to some of the specific issues that the GLC has been developing? The GLC, along with Sheffield and the West Midlands in particular, has been pushing ahead on the economic development and employment front. A particular question that raises is how this might relate to Labour's 'Alternative Economic Strategy' at the national level?

KL   I often characterise what we are doing as a local version of the national enterprise board that Benn was talking about before he was sacked from the Department of Industry, and Wilson neutered the NEB and removed the compulsory planning agreement provisions. That's a very broad brush, but it's something people recognise when you're talking to them because they remember the row about it. I suppose it's much more truthful to say that the development of the industry and employment section really grew out of a lot of debate, from the criticisms of the NEB and the last Labour Government and its failure. In setting up the Economic Policy Group we brought in people like Mike Cooley, Hilary Wainwright and Robin Murray who *had* been critical of the failures of the last Labour Government. So our strategy is already based on criticisms and the failure of the industrial policy of that government. It's feeling its way forward very slowly. We're very conscious of the danger that we could slip into being I suppose just a socially aware merchant bank. We don't want that. What we're seeking to do, and what Hilary Wainwright in particular is doing, through what we call popular planning is to involve the community in devising projects and having control over those projects. We had a recent edition of the *Londoner* in which we devoted a whole page simply to showing how large companies were tearing London apart and saying, if you'd like to get involved in saving jobs then write in. There wasn't a flood, but in the first stage if you get fifty or sixty projects working and other people see them, next time you appeal you'll get five or six hundred. People don't necessarily have the confidence to come forward and say they think they can run their own cooperative. It won't be until we have our first few success that this will start to happen in a big way. That's the difference. The Wilson Government merely operated a slightly socially aware merchant bank, which was very centrist. Our strategy is completely localised. That's where new jobs will be created on any great scale. It won't be large, centralised job creation at all.

Can we move on to another area. You have a Women's Committee, with officer support and a budget. On the other hand most GLC members, as elsewhere, are men and although there are many women employed by County Hall they are predominantly in lower grades. What do you think can be achieved in this area specifically through women's committees?

KL I think the question of women and the GLC was the major weakness in our Manifesto. We had a very small number of women involved in drafting the Manifesto. I did make a great effort to persuade women to stand for election. Shortly before the election however, two women pulled out of safe Labour seats for different reasons, and two others who should have won just didn't quite get the swing requried. So women are very under-represented. One lesson we've drawn from this is that we've started to set up manifesto working parties for the next election now. We've written round to constituencies and instead of saying what we did last time, send us a nominee, we've said send several and women and people from ethnic minorities. So in drawing up next year's manifesto we'll have working parties that actually reflect the balance. Having said that, I think the GLC Labour Group has really given a lead to the Labour Party outside in terms of compensation for that omission. The only way we are able to strengthen a feminist perspective in the GLC is by bringing women in from outside. The Women's Committee has thus agreed co-options from a sort of open meeting of all women's groups that come along and discuss what we should be doing, and a number of working parties have been set up. This is the pattern that's been followed by other women's committees, like Camden where there is a whole set of working groups with women from outside the Council advising the Committee what it should do. Our Women's Committee is learning, as are the Borough Council Committees. Women's groups and women as individuals are for the first time beginning to think how to come along to a council and start articulating their demands. Both sides are learning how to proceed.

I reckon this is our major weakness. Whereas no one in the Labour Party will nowadays generally be openly racist, it's still quite acceptable for men to be openly sexist and it's much harder to get anything on sexism through the Labour Group than on racism. Because you are forcing men to examine so much of their own motives and their own past of which they are extremely uncertain and ashamed, it will be a much harder struggle. It really is quite an uphill effort to get policies on feminism through the Group. You start talking to the sort of men that are involved in elected politics about the problems of patriarchy and the link between patriarchy and war, and you're asking people to jump a thousand years of consciousness in one step. Initially the Women's Committee put down a couple of points for the Council that actually explored the issue and the men went berserk! The women's movement outside and the women's groups here are going to have to work on the men involved and change them, recognising this as one of the major stumbling blocks.

Can we switch to the area of race. The GLC is taking a range of initiatives relating to race, policing, and equal opportunities. You've mentioned already that you would want to see police under local authority control. Where do you think the priorities lie in this broad area?

KL   I don't really think in terms of priorities. We're proceeding in changing our own internal structures and trying to get a common career structure, because the present staff structure in this building is deeply racist and sexist. Then there's the public campaigning role, which I think is perhaps the most important because the question of changing public attitudes is really more vital than changing structures here. Then there are all the ways in which the GLC can influence outside bodies through our contracts, compliance code and so on. All of those things need to be done, and we have agreed to expand the Ethnic Minorities Unit so they have sufficient staff to do them. I wouldn't say there are priorities within that. Our major problem is that we haven't got enough people to be doing all the things we should be. This is the problem of having a small majority. In something like the Ethnic Minorities Unit however, by getting good people to run it, it has able to take over work that members might otherwise have been doing. That's how we've proceeded.

The police really represent a much bigger problem than I think most people realise. Over the last twenty or thirty years there has been a strong development of areas in society which have become the preserves of the Right. The police, the immigration service and the armed forces no longer have the degree of balance in political views they had twenty or thirty years ago. A conscript army meant there was always be a range of opinion in the armed forces. While the police force has no doubt always had a right-wing bias, we have got to the point now when any sort of radical or socialist would just not join the police force and would find it intolerable if they did. Many of the attitudes which prevail in the immigration service could have come straight out of a National Front manifesto. You have the question, then, of how to deal with those areas of society which, because they represent mechanisms for controlling the population, are unlikely to be attractive to the Left in British society, and therefore become inward-looking and isolated. I think the only way forward is through a lot of popular control, with control of the police force generally being based in the local community and the police forces drawn more strongly from the community. This then means a major change in personnel. If we got a Labour Government elected, and control of the police by the GLC and boroughs in the case of London, I think first of all we'd have to spend quite a lot of time in the States looking at how certain cities which had deeply racist police forces in the 1960s, and then came under either progressive or black mayors, set about improving their own police forces. From what I've seen, very much at second-hand, it does seem that there was a fairly massive programme of early retirement. We would have to say quite clearly that it is not acceptable to be a racist in the police force. In this way we could expand that part of the police force both drawn from and policing the local community. The problem in Brixton is that half the police force comes in from the suburbs, with no idea of the culture or nature of the people, whereas if you actually look at black and white people in Brixton they get on very well together. The problem comes in from outside each day. The police unit in the GLC is once again working on the basis of a group of people who've been brought in, who are able to construct a package of policies which we can then adopt, because we simply don't have the members with the time actually to draw up this vast range of proposed changes for the next Labour Government.

One problem for members anywhere is not having enough time, and one of the ways of countering that is to make political appointments of various kinds, as indeed has been the case for some time in the GLC. This is becoming more common in many authorities now. Do you see it continuing? Is it essential?

KL   There's no way we could survive in this building without having a support staff. We've got about forty now, our own personal office that supports and assists the members. On top of that, in those areas where we want to make general changes, like women, ethnic minorities and economic policy, we're bringing in people from outside, because within this structure we haven't got a sufficient pool of people who think in a radical and progressive way to draw from to start these units. It's one of the great problems we face, how do you change an inherently conservative bureaucracy? We're now getting to the point where the Labour Group is aware enough of what needs to be done, but its a matter of whether it's got the will to do it. It involves breaking up the central bureaucratic control system, and having the ordinary free-standing departments linked much more closely to their service committees. We're in a much worse position than the average borough council. This place has been modelled on the civil service and one of our objectives has got to be to achieve normal local government thinking, seeing departments as there to provide a service and that's that!

Turning to the role of the courts, there have been a number of conflicts – the GLC fares case, disputes over council house sales even perhaps levels of expenditure and the rates – which are increasingly conducted in the shadow of the courts. How do you handle that in the GLC? How serious a threat to local politics is this increasing presence of the courts?

KL   I have a commitment to a sort of ideal concept of the law as a genuine impartial arbitrator. That means, of course, changing most of the present laws which serve the interests of capital and changing a substantial proportion of the judiciary that professionally couldn't operate a system that was fair and impartial between capital and labour. We were completely unprepared for the range of legal challenges, as were the officers. It came as a shock to them. They've had to struggle to cope with it, and of course it makes members extremely cautious. Provided you removed the role of the District Auditor and personal surcharge, I think people would be a lot more confident in handling the law. That's one of our major problems. Then you could learn to use the legal system. We've gradually learned to use the legal system for radical purposes. The legal challenges on civil defence policies have actually been dramatically successful, forcing the government to come back with new proposals to try to tighten control. We redrafted plans for what looks like a lawful fares cut. You can use the law once you think in positive ways about doing it. But I would hope to see the Labour Party develop a policy towards the public sector with, say, a national legal service so that everyone has access to the law. It would clearly be better if, in a system of local government that had national minimum standards, the mechanism for control over that was the right of local residents and tenants and workers to take the council to court if it wasn't complying. Much better to have the pressure coming from below than above. So I'm not opposed to the intervention of the law in local government *per se,* provided you remove this dreadful link between that and personal surcharge of members when they lose on key cases. That's the crippling thing, not the actual intervention of the judiciary. You've also got to get the Labour Party thinking about what sort of legal system it wants,

whether it wants a judiciary which is professional or to carry on
with the present form, or even a judiciary which is elected. There is
actually a need to change virtually all the Law Lords and to
undertake a massive redrafting of legislation so that it is usable by
ordinary people.

*Does that mean then that defying the law as it stands at the moment
is not on any more for local councillors?*

KL   The only way you can defy the law is as we tried to do in the
Fares Fair campaign when, after the Law Lords judgement, the
Council had to decide whether to comply and instruct London
Transport to increase the fares. I argued that we shouldn't and that
we should precipitate a crisis, in which it couldn't be forseen who
was going to win or lose. We lost the vote by twenty-seven to
twenty-four. It's remarkable that we got that close – only the
stupidity of Tory tactics allowed it to happen. So the only way a
local council can defy the law is when central government say
you're got to do something and you refuse to do it. If you try to
defy the law by instructing your officers to do something that's
illegal they'll refuse to do it anyhow. The great debate about
whether to increase the rates or make cuts is totally academic,
bceause if you didn't carry a budget the officers would carry on
running the council as they felt best until a new political majority
could be formed. Our officers won't break the law, so this debate
about local government stepping outside the law only arises with
something like the fares cut or the Housing Finance Act or the sale
of council housing. I do think very often that to challenge the law
would be good providing you don't just fling councillors at the
brick wall and hope that eventually the bodies pile up sufficiently
so you can get over the top, and provided you choose the right issue
on which to challenge the law, one which will get public support.
Fares would have been that case – but we lost.

*For authorities like the GLC and others, struggling to establish
socialist policies as best they can at the local level, what are the
major problems and what are the best hopes in the forseeable
future?*

KL   You make it look like that's the final thing, that we're going to have a total victory or total defeat. The truth is probably that even with Thatcher re-elected we will continue to struggle along and even though we will face defeats on overall spending or particular projects, the lessons we learn and the links we build up between the labour movement and those groups we haven't responded to in the past will lay the basis for future major advance, once the national party leadership can be brought into line with what the Labour Party now is.

Does that need concrete success?

KL Yes, I think so, but then we do get these concrete successes. The whole women's policy and grants policy is a very concrete success. The fares reduction, second time around, is an important victory. If Labour had been elected in 1983, I think we would have had just about enough understanding and knowledge through what's been happening in local government to extend these achievements to the national level. If there really was a prospect of four years of total and sustained defeat then most likely our strategy wouldn't work, but that's totally unrealistic. We will win some and lose some. It's not the individual policies, whichever we're currently most preoccupied with. It's the actual structure being built up and the body of knowledge which is being accumulated which is the biggest long-term gain for the movement.

Coming finally to the government's most recent moves, what are the implications for local government of rate capping, removal of London Transport from GLC control, and the abolition of the GLC? What scope does that leave for radical initiatives?

KL Leaving aside for the minute outright abolition, if rate capping goes through, it effectively transfers control of the council to the Tory Party. There will be negligible opportunity to do anything along the lines the council has experimented with since May 1981. The government's target requires an expenditure cut from us of over 30 per cent. Given that a substantial part of our expenditure is on debt charges, we are talking about an effective cut of over 40 per cent in terms of services and staffing. We don't feel it's achievable. Within that there is just no way we could operate as an administration, nor would I be prepared to continue to try and run the GLC under those circumstances. There would be such a scale of industrial action – and member support for it – that there would be a real chance of the council just ceasing to function.

Do you see the removal of London Transport from GLC control as paving the way for the removal of the GLC itself or as more narrowly conceived?

KL   I think it was purely to take away London Transport so as to make eventual abolition easier. There is no justification, for example in the argument that it will lead to an integrated transport system. We are ready to have an integrated transport system. So is British Rail, but they are simply not allowed under present legislation to integrate with London Transport. We do not need a new structure. We just need the government to stop blocking BR's desire to integrate. I think it is also part of the government's aim to shift towards privatisation in a major way. In setting up London Transport under a committee of businessmen with privatisation the main goal, the aim, is the break-up of the integrated LT services to let their friends get their snouts in the trough.

How will that relate to the GLC's earlier fares campaigns?

KL   Clearly they are thinking in terms of a fare increase in the order of 30 or 40 per cent if the figures they have asked us to comply with are to be believed. Removal of London Transport from the GLC would pave the way for fares increases, service cuts and privatisation.

Would this consolidate support for the GLC?

KL   I think it would help us to mobilise support for the GLC simply because it means that the first stage of the attack is on our strongest ground where we have already won majority support. We will be having a major campaign to mobilise support for continued GLC control.

Turning to the proposed abolition of the GLC and metropolitan counties, an element of Labour Party policy has been the establishment of unitary authorities. How would you relate that to London?

KL Labour Party policy on this has always excluded London. There was no committment in the last manifesto or in Labour's Programme agreed by Conference to abolish the GLC. The position of the Party Conference is now solidly to support the metropolitan counties and the GLC. The government's attack has tended to bring the whole Party round to supporting us and has won the metropolitan counties more support than they would have got if people were looking at the thing objectively.

What would be the implications of abolition?

KL With the abolition of the metropolitan counties, the transitional councils and then the new joint boards which take over, comprised of district councillors, will be Labour-controlled. But because the joint boards will remain Labour-controlled the government is proposing to retain control of budgetary and staffing decisions for three years. It is effectively direct rule. In London the same applies but in the transitional year, with the exception of the ILEA Board which would remain Labour-controlled, you would actually have a Tory majority. The Tories here are actually achieving a change of political control without an election. The borough elections are not for another year after we cease to hold office. In that transitional year the Tories would put into power a group who were elected to run borough councils a year before. This to me is totally unacceptable. After the transitional year I should imagine you will have a Labour majority on the London boroughs. To little purpose, however, because they will be administering services under the direct control of central government. The same is true of ILEA. Effectively Keith Joseph will set the staffing and budgetary levels for education in London, and that is frightening!

It has been suggested that some London boroughs might welcome an increase in powers and finance and are worried about the impact of the GLC rate on their local areas.

KL Who has said that? They are not getting an increase in powers and finance. They are getting a further constriction of their powers because the government will have even greater control over grant via all the new boards being set up. The government will effectively determine the level of services. All that Labour councils are being offered is the opportunity to sit there and vote 'yes' to Tory cuts. I have not heard any one say a word and I doubt if they would say publicly if they have got any doubts, because the overwhelming majority of the London Labour Party is behind the GLC.

There was a comment in the White Paper that the GLC and metropolitan counties had sought a 'strategic' role which might have little basis in 'real needs', I think that was the phrase. Is there a problem in trying to defend the GLC if people see it as primarily strategic? Is it harder for people to grasp this?

KL   People don't have any trouble grasping it. Transport is the biggest strategic function, industry and employment is clearly a strategic function, that's job creation which people clearly understand. You have things like the fire service which I think can't be seriously run by anything smaller. Similarly the management of the debt. If you actually look at it, the GLC budget is just under £900 million. The government is only proposing the transfer of £200 million to boroughs. The rest is all coming under quangos and joint boards. And £60 million or so of that is pensioners' bus passes. It is not a shift in responsibility to local authorities. It is a shift in power to central government.

The joint boards are constituted by members nominated by the borough councils. Leaving out the transitional year, which I agree is a nonsense, I had certainly expected more of a mix on the joint boards, with non-elected members being appointed.

KL   But they don't need to worry about the political balance. They are setting the budget and the manpower target. It really is irrelevant to them whether the 5,000 firefighters you will have after you have been required to cut 2,000 to comply with the budget are going to wear red uniforms or blue uniforms. Their primary concern is with the numbers and the total budget, and that is what counts.

You are saying, then, that the one-year transition and the three-year control of budgets and manpower is crucial?

KL   Yes.

Do you think, finally, there is any scope for scuppering the government's plans?

KL Yes, I think there is a good 50-50 chance of defeating the legislation simply because it is so bad, such a constitutional outrage, and so clearly a major invitation to serious cutbacks for Londoners. I think there is a very good chance that public anger will galvanise a lot of Tory MPs and Lords to vote against it. And that would apply to rate capping as well. I don't think any of these struggles are forgone conclusions.

Also by Macmillan

Public Policy and Politics

Series Editors: Colin Fudge and Robin Hambleton

This series is designed to provide up-to-date, comprehensive and authoritative analyses of public policy and politics in practice.

PUBLISHED
Christopher Hood, *The Tools of Government*
Peter Malpass and Alan Murie, *Housing Policy and Practice*
Ken Young and Charlie Mason (eds), *Urban Economic Development*

FORTHCOMING
Tony Eddison and Eugene Ring, *Management and Human Behaviour*
Colin Fudge, *The Politics of Local Government*
Robin Hambleton, *An Introduction to Local Policy-Making*
Ken Newton and Terence Karran, *Local Government Finance*

Index